Printing

A guide to systems and their uses

W. R. Durrant

Heinemann Professional Publishing

To my wife, Ann, for her forebearance and understanding, and to my daughter, Fiona, for really helping out when it was needed

Heinemann Professional Publishing Ltd
Halley Court, Jordan Hill, Oxford OX2 8EJ

OXFORD LONDON MELBOURNE AUCKLAND SINGAPORE
IBADAN NAIROBI GABORONE KINGSTON

First published 1989

British Library Cataloguing in Publication Data
Durrant, W. R.
  Printing: a guide to systems and their uses
  1. Printing
  I. Title
  686.2

ISBN 0 434 90379 5

Printed in Great Britain by
Butler & Tanner Ltd, Frome & London

Printing

**FRANCIS CLOSE HALL
LEARNING CENTRE**
Swindon Road, Cheltenham
Gloucestershire GL50 4AZ
Telephone: 01242 714600

**UNIVERSITY OF
GLOUCESTERSHIRE**
at Cheltenham and Gloucester

NORMAL LOAN

420 3/2011

Heinemann Media Series

Series editor: **F. W. Hodgson**

Broadcast Journalism   Andrew Boyd
Creative Newspaper Design   Vic Giles and F. W. Hodgson
Law and the Media   Tom Crone
Magazine Journalism Today   Anthony Davis
Modern Newspaper Editing and Production   F. W. Hodgson
Modern Newspaper Practice   F. W. Hodgson
Newsman's English   Harold Evans
Pictures on a Page   Harold Evans
Writing Feature Articles   Brendan Hennessy

Contents

List of illustrations   vii

Acknowledgements   x

1   Introduction   1
General survey of the printing industry – Origins and development of the different
printing processes – Letterpress, lithography, gravure and the contribution of
photography to the printing processes – The current situation in relation to the
developments in printing technology

2   Desktop systems   13
Definition of the term desktop publishing – Basic requirements of software and
hardware – Programs – Central processing unit – Typographic and graphic display
systems – Print-out devices – software – Peripheral equipment – Limitations of
desktop systems

3   In-plant production   25
The scope of in-plant production – Photocopying – Duplicating and small-offset
Printing – Text and graphic origination for in-plant work – Printing masters and
plates – Basic finishing techniques

4   Origination   47
Graphic origination – Sources of copy – Preparation of original material – Line,
monochrome, colour and halftone processes – Cameras for graphic reproduction –
Halftone screens, graphic arts films and film processing – Colour separation, colour
correction and masking techniques – Colour scanners and terminology associated
with scanning – Text origination – Basic typography – Typographic terminology –
Typeface dimensions – Text setting systems – Text setting systems via standard
keyboards, photographic systems, video display units, cathode-ray tubes and laser
imaging systems – planning and assembly – The design brief – Production of
dummies and layouts – Film assembly – Multicolour film assembly – Pin
registering, masks, step-and-repeat work – Electronic page make-up –
Comprehensive studio systems for integration of text and graphics – Inputs and
outputs – Terminology – Processing, proofing, platemaking and cylinder production

5 Sheet-fed production   89

Lithographic plates and platemaking – Proofs and proofing techniques – Proof presses – Control of variables – Colourproofing – Control strips – Non-press proofs – Basic construction of sheet-fed litho presses – Sheet feeders, printing units and delivery systems – Inking and damping – Different types of presses – Wet-on-wet printing – Press controls – Non-printing operations – Finishing operations including cutting, folding, insetting and gathering – Paperback and hardback book make-up – Ancillary operations including hot-foil stamping, embossing, die stamping, thermography, laminating and numbering

6 Web-fed production   129

General principles of web-fed production – Reelstands, web feeding and automatic reel changing systems – Web-offset printing – Design of printing units – Special considerations for inking and damping on web offset presses – Photopolymer relief (letterpress) web printing – Production of photopolymer relief plates – Proofing – Design of printing units and presses – Multicolour printing – Flexographic printing – Basic principles of flexography – Design of printing units and presses – Plate and cylinder making – Proofing – Flexo inks and inking systems – Drying systems – Laser engraving of flexo images – Photogravure printing – Basic principles of gravure – Design of printing units and presses – Production of cylinders – Proofing – Inks – Electronic engraving of gravure cylinders – Web control – Design of folders, sheeters and rewinds – Finishing techniques

7 Non-publication printing   179

Screen process printing – The printing of flat, cylindrical, irregular, and continous web materials – Packaging and converting – Identity marking – Non-paper substrates – Bar codes – Business forms production – Fixed and variable-size presses – Security printing – Special considerations for currency, cheques, credit and charge cards

8 Quality control   202

Subjective and objective assessment of quality – The terminology of quality control for printing – Specifications – British and International Standards – Principles of densitometric inspection – Quality control patches and strips – Press control systems – Standards for papers and boards

9 Conclusion   223

The current state of the printing industry – Trends and developments – Future prospects for printing

Glossary   225

Appendix 1   Some British Standards relating to printing   232

Appendix 2   Bibliography   233

Appendix 3   Useful addresses   234

Index   236

Illustrations

1   *Johannes Gutenberg – inventor of letterpress printing*
2   *Page from Gutenberg's 42-line Bible*
3   *Sixteenth century wooden press and composing frames*
4   *Koenig's first 'cylinder' printing press*
5   *Alois Senefelder – inventor of lithography*
6   *Senefelder's lithographic press with stone bed*
7   *The Xerox 'Documenter' desktop publishing system*
8   *Example of the versatility of desktop publishing*
9   *Principle of ink-jet printing*
10 *Dot-matrix principle – the American standard code*
11 *Duplex photocopying by Kodak*
12 *Small-offset printing press – Heidelberg's TOM*
13 *'Systems' presses*
14 *Additional operations*
15 *Basic print finishing techniques*
16 *Ring binding*
17 *Basic types of camera*
18 *Camera for direct screening*
19 *Step-and-repeat camera*
20 *Percentage dot formation*
21 *Halftone dot shapes*
22 *Pulsed-xenon lamp assembly*
23 *Spectral emissions of pulsed-xenon and mercury-vapour lamps*
24 *Characteristic curve of a graphic arts film*
25 *Comparison of development times between 'lith' film and 'rapid access' film*
26 *Automatic film processor*
27 *Development of achromatic theory*
28 *Basic construction of a colour scanner*
29 *Examples of different forms of typefaces*
30 *Variations on a basic typeface*
31 *A selection of Monotype digitized exotic scripts*
32 *Image quality of different methods of text production*
33 *Principle of photosetting by (a) stroboscopic flash, and (b) cathode ray tube*
34 *Principle of the CRTronic system*
35 *Principle of the Lasercomp system*
36 *Principle of the Linotron system*
37 *The digiset page make-up system*

38   *Checking a sheet at the delivery of a multicolour litho press*
39   *Automatic platemaking*
40   *Direct platemaking*
41   *Litho proofing presses*
42   *Sheet transport*
43   *Litho blankets*
44   *Damping system on a litho press*
45   *Sheet feeding*
46   *Continuous pile changing*
47   *Convertible press design*
48   *Basic construction of a guillotine*
49   *Basic folding principles*
50   *Automated print finishing line*
51   *Casemaking*
52   *High-speed reel changing*
53   *Festoon splicing*
54   *Web-offset printing units*
55   *Web-offset publication press*
56   *Variations in colour capacity on web presses*
57   *Liquid polymer plate system*
58   *Plate distortion problems*
59   *Principles of flexography*
60   *Laser engraving of flexo plates*
61   *Sleeve mounting systems*
62   *Stack-type flexographic press*
63   *Electronic engraving of gravure cylinders*
64   *Gravure printing unit*
65   *Circulating ink system on a gravure press*
66   *Electrostatic assist in gravure printing*
67   *Multicolour gravure press*
68   *Principle of hot air drying*
69   *Integrated drying system*
70   *Basic web folding principles*
71   *Sequence of folding for pocket book production*
72   *Slitter-rewinder diagram*
73   *Principles of screen process printing*
74   *Slitting and rewinding*
75   *Bar coding*
76   *Business forms press*
77   *Guilloche patterns*
78   *Magnetic ink character recognition (MICR)*
79   *Examining a proof sheet*
80   *Detail from a standard specification*
81   *Proof correction marks*
82   *Example of marked-up proof and corrected proof*
83   *Principles of reflection and transmission densitometers*
84   *Pin registering system*

85 *GATF slur gauge*
86 *Quality control by signal strips*
87 *System Brunner – micro patches*
88 *International paper sizes*

Colour plates

1 *(a) Spectral reflectance of process inks and (b) principle of colour separation and masking*
2 *Typographical terminology*
3 *Basic construction of an offset lithographic press*
4 *Inking system on a litho press*
5 *Remote control of inking*
6 *Koenig and Bauer's 'densitronic' system*
7 *Enlarged detail of System Brunner quality control strip*
8 *Examples of quality control strips*
9 *Plate reading*
10 *Press information systems*

Acknowledgements

Sincere thanks are due to the many friends, colleagues and business acquaintances throughout the printing industry who have contributed towards the information contained in this book. A number of people are indirectly acknowledged in the text and in the illustrations by reference to the organizations with which they are associated. I hope that they will forgive me for not mentioning them all by name.

A special mention is due to Freddie Hodgson, who gave continued and constructive advice on the content, presentation and detail of the book during its formation period.

1 Introduction

Printing, with its associated activities of publishing, papermaking and packaging, is a multibillion pound international industry. Defining its boundaries is a difficult exercise in itself. The manufacturing of printing equipment, materials and supplies together with their sales, servicing and maintenance is another sub-industry as is the distribution of publications and other printed matter, together with their advertising, communications systems and transport to retail or individual outlets. In these instances printing pervades, supports and reinforces many other industries.

Most adults with a good general education background could give a reasonable account of the basic techniques of, say, farming, fishing, mining or building. Printing, however, is the great unknown industry. It is rarely included in the curricula of schools, colleges or universities, except in a few limited and highly specialized instances and yet there are hundreds of thousands of printing and print-related firms around the world employing millions of people. In the UK alone it is estimated that there are around ten thousand such firms employing more than a quarter of a million souls.

This book sets out to explain the basic principles of the various printing systems currently in use by describing the equipment, techniques and processes used in specific sectors of the industry. This introductory chapter briefly traces the development of printing from its origins in the fifteenth century to the current situation, and subsequent chapters deal with defined areas of work in progressive order.

In the beginning

Writing a book in the fifteenth century was a tedious business. First, one had to kill a calf or sheep and strip it of its skin. The pelt had then to be scraped clean of hairs and fat and soaked in a bath of salts to make it suitable for writing upon. It was then dried and cut to a suitable size. If a book were to be of any significant length these procedures would need to be repeated many times. There were, of course, alternative materials such as bark, cloth or paper for writing upon, but these were not considered to be as substantial or durable as the genuine vellums and parchments made from animal skins.

Next, a fully grown goose was required to contribute a good sized feather or 'quill', which would be cut skilfully at its pointed end so that when it was dipped in a thin paint or ink its hollow centre would take up a quantity of the coloured fluid and then allow it to flow out on to the skin at the will of the writer. Each letter had to be carefully drawn as errors were difficult to expunge or correct. At the completion of a page the skin was left, preferably in a warm, dry room with good air circulation, to allow the ink to permeate thoroughly into the substrate.

A competent author could easily compose a thousand or more words between sunrise and sunset, while important personages could dictate their words to a secretary who would write down the very words as they were spoken.

When all the pages of the manuscript were completed and dried they would then be pressed flat and cut to the final shape and size. Additional coloured decoration or 'rubrication' might be added to embellish the work and the complete volume passed to the binder for encasing in a leather, cloth or wooden cover.

Copying a book once it was written was comparatively easy. Provided the original script was legible it could be copied letter by letter, one page at a time by skilled scribes, usually employed in the monasteries. A team of, say, fifty scribes working together in a large monastery could produce an accurate copy of a major work such as the Holy Bible in a matter of days.

For someone to *read* a book in those days was a comparatively rare event; readings of the Bible, for example, were often public occasions. To *own* a book was even rarer, as only the rich could afford to acquire such a valuable possession, and to actually write a book or any other original document was a privilege afforded to only a very few gifted persons.

The population of Western Europe at that time was probably less than ten million and fewer than one in ten could read or write. The number of living authors of books at any given time was probably rarely more than a few dozen.

There were, of course, other means of reproducing images. Carving patterns or pictures in wood or other material, applying ink and impressing them on to an appropriate material had been practised for centuries; as had the art of stencil making in which images were cut out of a thin sheet of wood, cloth or metal and paint dabbed through the apertures. None of these methods, however, were suitable for the reproduction of the written word, and in this field the scribes reigned supreme.

Gutenberg

All of this was to change as the impetus of the Renaissance in fifteenth century Europe gained momentum. The new thirst for knowledge was expressed in a demand for copies of books and other manuscripts and the need to communicate via the permanency of the written word. A German businessman, Johann Gutenberg, was very much aware of this need, and around the middle of the century developed the technique of producing a number of individual letters or 'types' which could be assembled to form a page of 'writing'. A page of letters could be inked and impressed upon

Figure 1 *Johannes Gutenberg, the inventor of letterpress printing*

skin or paper in less than a minute and a team of two or three men could ink and impress a hundred or more papers in an hour.

Although the production of books was speeded up dramatically using this method, the manufacture of the type letters was a tedious, time-consuming and highly skilled business. Gutenberg had contacts in the local mint and probably drew on some of the techniques and skills which were necessary to produce coins. First, a master had to be cut from hard

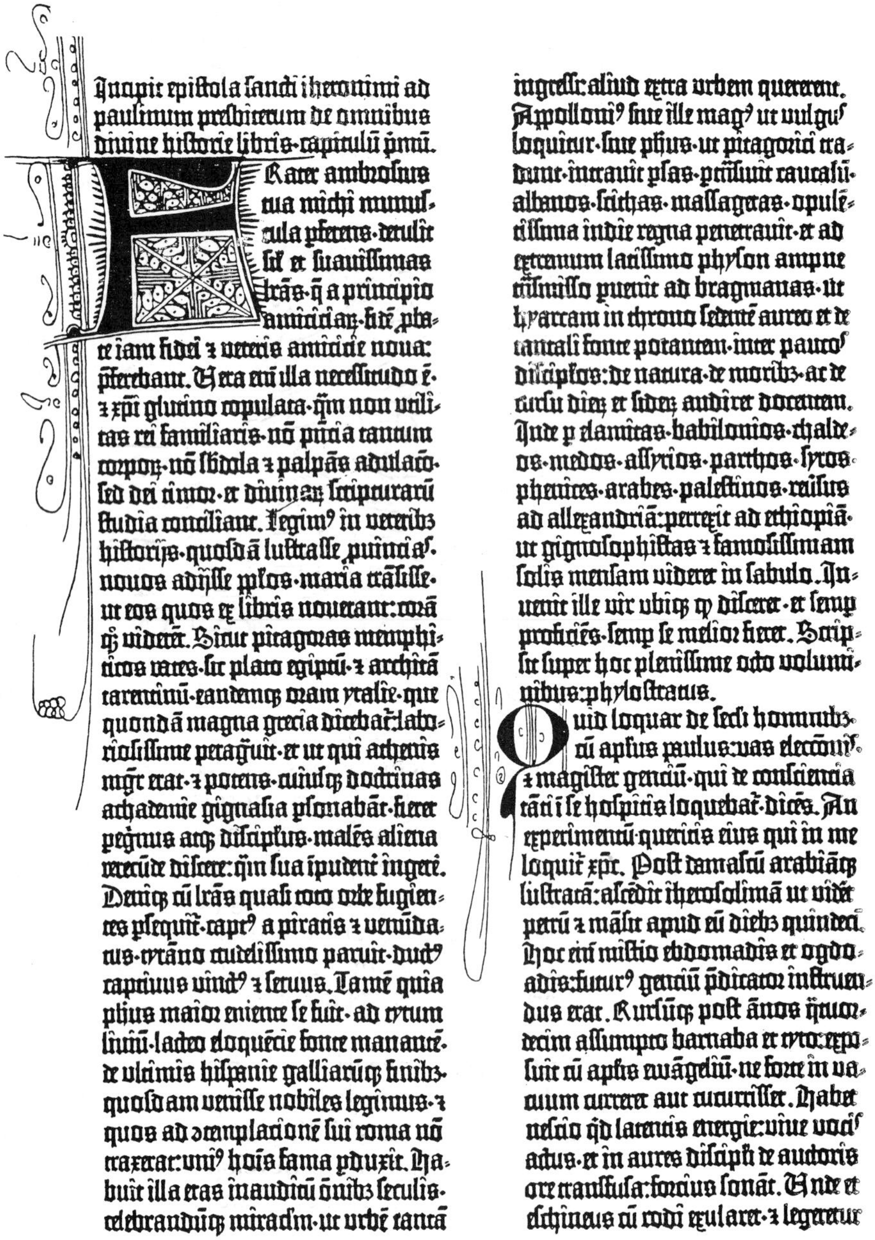

Figure 2   *A page from Gutenberg's forty-two line Bible*

metal and this was used to punch its image into a softer metal, making a matrix from which the types could be cast in a molten, lead-based alloy. The matrix could be used for making an infinite number of lead types, which could be assembled and disassembled as required, and eventually re-melted to make fresh type.

Figure 3 Detail from a wood engraving showing the operation of a wooden hand press in the early sixteenth century, with compositors setting type in the background

The new invention was not received enthusiastically in all quarters, and certainly not in the scriptoriums. Printed books were condemned by some as imitations or forgeries of the real thing, and were even considered to be the work of the devil. Gutenberg did not become rich as a result of his invention, falling prey to even shrewder businessmen who exploited the discovery and sold its 'secrets' to others. By the end of the century, however, the church and mammon were largely reconciled and the art of printing had spread to the major industrial and commercial centres in Europe.

Gutenberg's invention was modified, refined, adapted and improved steadily. The original wine or apple press became, in an adapted form, the mould of the printing press; improved punch-cutting and type casting techniques were developed; paper quickly replaced skin, thus establishing a whole new industry to meet the demand for printed matter.

Despite all this, the basic technique of *letterpress* printing did not change fundamentally for the next 400 years. It was not until the nineteenth century, for instance, that the first iron press was built, and it was often noted that Gutenberg himself could have walked into a nineteenth-century printshop and carried on exactly where he had left off four centuries earlier.

What did occur during the four centuries of hand press dominance was that typefaces were gradually evolved to suit the needs of the process and to aid legibility, while at the same time creating a pleasing image for the reader to enjoy. Printing was no longer considered to be imitation writing but was seen as a craft in its own right. The day of the typographer and his art had arrived, and persons of extraordinary talent and skill were designing and creating typefaces with extreme sensitivity and insight.

Many of these typefaces are still, hundreds of years on, recognized as works of genius, often forming the basis of the standard texts which we read every day. Most modern typographers and designers of typefaces will readily acknowledge the debt they owe to earlier exponents of the art, many of whose names live on in typefaces still in common use such as *Aldus, Baskerville, Caslon, Garamond, Jenson, Plantin*, etc.

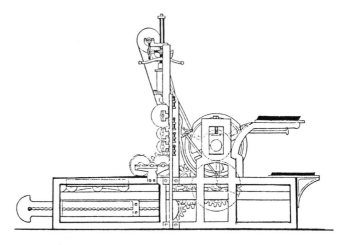

Figure 4   *Koenig's first 'cylinder' printing press*

A time of change – the nineteenth century

The invention of the iron press at the beginning of the nineteenth century did not in itself change the basic process of letterpress printing, but it was a sign of things to come. The application of steam power, and later electricity, to machinery, enabled ingenious engineers to devise entirely new types of equipment which did not depend solely on hand skills and muscle power. 'Cylinder' presses developed in which the paper was held on a cylinder which rolled across the bed of type at speeds of several hundred impressions an hour.

By the middle of the century the 'rotary' press had been invented, with the type or printing plates being held on one cylinder, which printed on to paper held on an opposing impression cylinder. Paper was now being made in reel form and the next obvious step was the reel-fed rotary. The paper web could be taken from one unit to another and a complete newspaper, for example, produced at the rate of thousands of copies an hour.

Automatic typesetting machines were developed towards the end of the century, enabling lines or columns of type to be produced either directly from a specially-designed keyboard or indirectly from punched papertape. Woodcuts were gradually replaced by etched or engraved 'blocks', but colour prints were a rarity. 'Duplicate' plates in the form of curved stereotypes made from papier-mâché moulds enabled high-speed production of multiple plates for the expanding market of newspaper printing as circulations rose from tens of thousands to hundreds of thousands.

There were, by this time, other printing processes becoming established:

Intaglio, or *recessed printing*, was typified by 'copperplate' engraving in which the image was cut into a metal plate by hand. The incised image was then filled with ink, the surface wiped clean, and an impression made by laying a sheet of paper over the plate and passing it through a roller press under high pressure to draw the ink from the recesses.

'Etching' techniques were also in vogue, in which the printing plate was covered with an acid resistant wax coating, the image scribed into the resist, and an acid applied to etch into the metal, forming an intaglio

Figure 5 *Alois Senefelder, the inventor of lithography*

image which could then be processed in a similar manner to a cut engraving.

Lithography had been developed by Alois Senefelder towards the end of the eighteenth century, Senefelder had discovered that a certain type of limestone, when levelled and polished, could be drawn upon with a wax crayon and if then soaked in water could be rolled with a greasy ink which would be repelled by the water and accepted only in the crayoned areas. The lithographic process could produce delicate shades and tints unobtainable by any other medium and was steadily refined and developed for the production of artwork, book illustrations and posters.

Towards the end of the century the 'offset' press was developed initially for printing on tin, in which the litho image was transferred from the stone to a rubber blanket and from thence to the metal substrate.

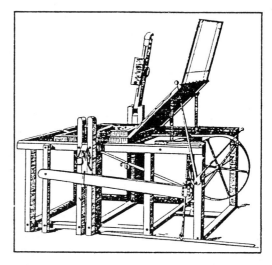

Figure 6   *The first lithographic press as designed by Alois Senefelder. Paper was laid on the stone and covered by a metal plate. The stone, paper and plate were then passed under a scraper blade under pressure to ensure thorough transfer of ink to paper*

Photography

The development of photography around the middle of the nineteenth century was recognized by entrepreneurs as being significant to the printing process and many attempts were made to apply photographic principles to the printing image. Early efforts to produce relief plates via photography for letterpress printing were largely unsuccessful until the 'halftone' principle was established. In this technique the continuous, graduated tones of a photographic image were translated into patterns of dots of varying sizes which the eye perceived as corresponding to various shades.

The breakthrough in halftone printing was the invention of the Levy screen – a grid of finely drawn cross lines on a glass base. This was placed between the original photograph or artwork and the light-sensitive material, at a critical distance, which would cause the image to be broken up into a pattern of dots corresponding to the amount of light reflected from the copy. Thus the technique of photo engraving was born.

The recessed intaglio method of printing, or *gravure* as it became known, was quick (by nineteenth century standards) to adapt to the photographic process. The first attempts used a 'grained' surface treatment to carry the inked image, simulating the manner in which silver halide images were developed on film or paper. Later developments, mainly by the Viennese, Karl Klic, used a variation of the crossline screen to reproduce the total effect by enabling minute cells to be etched to different depths according to the 'tone' required.

Lithographic researchers were also experimenting with photographic applications, mainly aimed at reproducing the subtle continuous-tone effects for which lithography was noted. The halftone dot technique of letterpress printing was tried, but not generally accepted as true lithography, and it was not until well into the twentieth century that halftone lithography was developed to a commercially acceptable standard.

Period of consolidation

The first half of the twentieth century was largely preoccupied with the two world wars and their aftermaths of economic and technological depression. Letterpress in one form or another continued to prevail in the commercial printing market as presses became faster, automatic sheet-feeding devices were developed and automatic reel changing for web presses. Multicolour printing became more common as the colour halftone process was developed and refined, and multicolour presses became more common as a result.

In the publication world web-fed 'rotogravure' presses were developed to cater for the demand for mass production of magazines, but the great majority of newspapers were still produced on letterpress rotary presses from curved stereotype plates in much the same way as they had been printed at the end of the nineteenth century.

Lithography continued to improve its quality for printing on metal and coloured illustration work, but was still dependent on metal type for most of its original text. Meanwhile it was making slow progress in the field of colour halftone printing.

'*Aniline*' printing had been invented towards the end of the nineteenth century by Bibby and Baron of Liverpool, who cut simple shapes in rubber which were attached to a wooden cylinder and inked with coloured transparent liquid containing the newly discovered aniline dyes. The quality of printing was poor by conventional standards and restricted mainly to the printing of cheap bags and wrappers. By the middle of the twentieth century the process had improved considerably and the term 'flexography' had been adopted to distinguish the improved method from the original aniline process.

The age of technology

By the second half of the twentieth century printing had passed through the adolescent stages of being an art metamorphosing into a craft, and was maturing as a technologically-based industry. Automated devices were perfected to set type, operate cameras, make plates or cylinders, run presses and control equipment for finishing the product:

Photocomposition of type freed the printing processes from the need to produce individual letters of lead, and two-dimensional page make-up was being developed as a replacement for physical three-dimensional assembly.

Scanning devices could look at graphic copy to be reproduced and separate a coloured image into the various elements required for printing, as well as altering the sizes, shapes and tonal qualities at the operator's will.

Planning, make-up and platemaking all became automated to a degree, within an integrated pattern of production, and it was possible to design a system in which information flowed at will from one station to the next with the minimum of physical intervention.

Printing presses improved to the stage where it was possible to print more than 200 full-size multicolour sheets per minute – 100,000 or more copies in a day. Web-fed presses became capable of even greater volume via multiweb, multiunit installations which could produce millions of copies of a newspaper or magazine in a matter of hours.

Offset lithography established itself as the major printing process, with the adoption of photocomposition for text production, while at the same time developing the colour halftone technique to new standards of excellence. Resolutions of 100 dots per centimetre could be achieved and plates could print a hundred thousand or more impressions instead of the few tens of thousands previously obtained.

Letterpress in the 'lead type' sense virtually ceased to exist, except in a few specialized instances, The 'relief' process, on the other hand, was far from dead. Rubber and plastic 'duplicate' plates were being increasingly used for a growing variety of printed matter, and 'photopolymer' relief plates could be made quickly, cheaply and with greater durability than the average litho plate. This, coupled with the fact that there was no need to maintain an ink/water balance, gave the relief process a competitive edge in many ways.

Gravure cylinders were produced by electronic engraving, without the need for complicated film planning or chemical etching within time schedules hitherto considered to be impossible. The inherent durability of the chromium-plated gravure image ensured its place in the fields of long-run publication and packaging work.

Flexography developed into a major process in its own right. The simplicity of the two-roller 'anilox' inking system, together with refinements in technique had enabled the process to move into practically every aspect of package printing and most areas of publication work, including newspapers and magazines in full process colour.

Finishing processes had to keep pace with the increasing rate of production, and therefore automated finishing, gathering, collating and binding lines were developed to ensure the efficient flow of work from press to despatch.

The electronic era

During the last twenty-five years the ability of electromechanical machinery to mass produce printed information appeared to reach its peak potential. The techniques of typesetting, camera operating, planning, platemaking, machine printing and finishing had reached the practical limits of the mechanical and electrical equipment available.

Even so, the need for collection, classification, storage, retrieval, reproduction and dissemination of information to an ever widening and more demanding society, required ever more sophisticated technologies to be employed. Devices were developed to store increasingly greater quantities of information in decreasingly smaller spaces. Data compression via microcircuitry, microelectronics, fibre optics and bubble technology enabled millions of bits of information to be stored in a tightly confined space. A machine the size of a brief case could hold all the information known to the civilized world a century or so earlier.

The digitization of images for both text and graphic input, as a result of computerization, has allowed flexible patterns of access and reproduction of images so that text and graphics can be managed and manipulated with greater freedom, coupled with faithful reproduction of the most minute and subtle detail. Data can now be transmitted and disseminated to practically any part of the world at the speed of light. Communications satellites can send unlimited information as fast as it can be presented. Facsimile printers can reproduce the most complicated images at a distant location, and with great fidelity, in the time it would once have taken to make a photocopy.

All this allowed decentralization of printing to steadily proceed throughout the 1980s. In the 1970s, for instance, the great majority of the national newspapers in England were printed in an area less than one kilometre square, commonly referred to as 'Fleet Street'. The method of production had not changed significantly for best part of the century. During the hours of darkness tens of millions of newspapers were produced from a multitude of printing presses, each capable of producing more than a thousand completed, multi-page newspapers per minute. From this site in the middle of London the great distribution trek started. Hundreds of vans, cars, trucks and lorries would collect the papers as they spewed from the presses and take them to railway stations, airports, seaports and distribution centres, whence they would be further distributed until each individual paper arrived at its final destination.

Today, there are few, if any, newspapers actually printed in Fleet Street. The physical production of national newspapers takes place outside the city centre and often in several places simultaneously, thanks to the ability to send information quickly and accurately via satellite, cable and facsimile transmission. Similarly with other forms of publications such as books and magazines it is quite common to produce original copy in one country, have it typeset in another, and printed in a third or even in several countries at the same time in different languages, without the editorial staff moving from their desks.

Publications are obvious examples of printed matter to spring to mind, but they are by no means typical of the broad range of products which are produced by this industry. Printing is intimately concerned with practically every aspect of our daily lives from the clothes we wear to the decoration and furnishings of our homes and workplaces. Our personal communications, financial and business arrangements, holidays, hobbies and pastimes, transport and travel arrangements, all centre around printed artefacts. We could not find our way from one place to another without atlases, charts, maps and direction signs. Most of the food we eat and the liquids we drink are held in printed containers which inform us of the nature of their contents.

The following chapters explain the many techniques involved in the production of printed matter and the choices which may be made depending on the nature of the item and its requirements in terms of quality, quantity, function and end purpose.

2 Desktop systems

The term desktop publishing, often contracted to DTP or even dtp, is a comparatively new development in printing and publishing and owes its origins to earlier work in the fields of word processing and microcomputing.

The *purpose* of a desktop system is to originate, create, manipulate and publish complete documents. Its *intention*, as the name implies, is to produce the work in a desktop, or minimum-space environment, as compared with the multistation methods used in 'conventional' printing and publishing.

The terms 'document' and 'publishing' need to be defined within the overall context. *Documents* are usually pages or collections of pages in single leaves which make up the final document such as a report, manual, journal or book. *Publishing* is intended in the limited sense of 'to make generally known' or 'to issue for public information', rather than the large-scale dissemination and distribution of printed publications which may otherwise be understood. It must be emphasized that the production of one document does not automatically assume the publication and distribution of several million identical documents.

The *scope* of desktop publishing is quite broad and may range from internal 'house' memoranda to complete journals or books. Illustrations may be included with the text and colour reproduction is possible.

Basic requirements of hardware and software

The requirements in terms of equipment (hardware) and programs (software) can vary considerably, depending on the nature of the final type of document to be published. Factors to be taken in to account will include:

- Total volume of work anticipated in, say, pages per day.
- Page sizes, numbers of pages and quantities to be published.
- Time scale available from conception to publication.
- Typographic style and quality requirements.
- Graphics input: line or halftone; monochrome or colour.
- Cost factors such as initial capital costs and eventual cost per page.

The basic items of *hardware* in a desktop system are:

- A microcomputer with a disc drive.
- A 'monitor' in the form of a video display unit (VDU).

- A keyboard, with appropriate instructions, for operator control of the system.
- A print-out device, usually in the form of a laser printer.

In addition to these initial items, there are a number of ancillary or 'peripheral' devices which may expand and amplify the basic system.

The system may be installed as a 'stand-alone' work station in which the basic items are purchased as an integrated package, probably from one supplier or manufacturer. Alternatively, a 'modular' system may be built up from compatible units to suit the specific needs of the individual user.

Figure 7 *The Xerox documenter, a desktop system for office publishing*

Programs for desktop publishing

Programs for desktop work fulfil the same functions as for any other computer-orientated system. These are stored sets of instructions which govern the operation of the computer and its related components. For simplicity, programs can be classified as primary and secondary software.

Primary software

Primary software controls the general routine functions of the computer. This may be held in the computer's 'memory' as a permanent or semipermanent program which may not be altered by the operator. This is referred to as a 'read-only memory' (ROM), often contained in a compact disc (CD) in which case it may be referred to as a CD/ROM.

Secondary software

Secondary software is employed for special purposes related to the nature and level of the work to be undertaken. This may include special programs for word processing, pagination, typographic instructions, editing and correction, graphics, image manipulation and so on.

There are a number of programs available from various suppliers under each heading and it is important to ensure first, that the program will undertake the functions required from it, and second, that it is compatible with other, related software and, of course, the hardware with which it will be employed.

The central processing unit

The *microcomputer* used for desktop work will need to be significantly more powerful than its word processing predecessor. A far greater memory will be required to handle the more complicated programs for typography, graphics and other enhanced features.

'Memory' relates to the quantity of information which the computer can store and is measured initially in electrical signals referred to as binary digits or 'bits'. A group of bits, which may form a character, for instance, is referred to as a 'byte' and a group of bytes may form a 'block'. The memory may be integral with the computer in the form of a read-only memory (ROM), as referred to earlier, or it may be an 'accessible' memory in the form of a 'random access memory' (RAM) which can both read and write. *Storage capacity* is measured in kilobytes (KB) and/or megabytes (MB).

Greater memory will also be required for the high-resolution monitors which are used with these systems. For this purpose the image to be produced is translated electronically into a grid of minute picture elements or 'pixels'. The finer the resolution required of the image, the greater the number of pixels and the greater the storage capacity of the computer.

Typographic and graphic display systems

The *monitor* or screen should ideally be capable of showing the whole of the full page in the same detail as that of the final print. A term commonly used in connection with desktop monitors is 'What you see is

Text and Images together

PAINTING grew to be an extremely important way of expression in both China and Japan. It was natural that this should be so, for the written characters of both languages demanded extreme skill with the brush. It took years of training to learn to be a calligrapher, and the quality of brush strokes and the beauty of the characters themselves became as important as the content of the story or poem.

The earliest Chinese painter of whom there is a record lived in the fourth century, and painting flourished from that time on. Except for a few murals, the paintings which have survived are of two types—hanging scrolls and horizontal, or hand, scrolls. These were kept rolled up except when being shown; then they were unrolled a little at a time, allowing the viewer to travel through the painting as if he were moving from scene to scene. Since painting and poetry were considered to be of equal importance, most painters also were poets. Scholars, emperors, and princesses were also accomplished artists. As a result, elegant scenes of life in the court were popular subject matter for Chinese scrolls. But at the same time, the search for unity with nature which drove the Taoist hermits to retire to the mountains, was expressed by the court painters in poetic landscapes of mountains, trees, and waterfalls, often with tiny meditating figures (Figure 5-3). To be one with nature was important to the contemplative Chinese, and the Zen sect of Buddhism which developed in China in the sixth century A.D., encouraged this love of the natural world. Because of these influences, Chinese painting was not so much concerned with the landscape itself, but with showing its inner essence in order to arouse a poetic response in the viewer. "The branch drooping in the fog, the butterfly on a blossom, the beggar in the filth of the courtyard—they are all Buddha," said the painter Hsia Kuei. This appreciation of landscape, common to both Chinese and Japanese painting and poetry, surpasses even the love of nature found in Western Romantic landscape painters from the nineteenth century.

Just as Japanese architecture and sculpture developed certain typical elements, traditional painting in Japan reflects the differences and similarities in outlook between the peoples of the two countries. In Japan, the calm philosophical discipline of China is replaced by an animation and vitality. Until the tenth century A.D., Japanese painting was close to Chinese in style, but after that a typically Japanese style of painting religious subjects developed, in which the Buddha was surrounded by lovely Boddhisattvas playing musical instruments and dancing in a delightful but quite wordly paradise. The secular scrolls painted from the twelfth century on were filled with humor, satire, drama, and the mundane events of life—quite different from the meditative Chinese paintings. Later, Zen Buddhism influenced Japanese painting, and the colorful style of the storytelling scrolls was replaced by paintings in which insignificant humans were shown contemplating the grandeur of nature. But even here, the Japanese brush technique had a different quality from that of the Chinese and was full of vitality. The Zen painters used a few quickly splashed lines and washes of ink to express their responses to the natural world, reflecting the flashes of sudden enlightenment after meditation, characteristic of Zen experience.

After years of close association with China, Japan, in the early 1600s, finally cut herself off from China as well as from the rest of the world. No foreigners were allowed to enter the Japanese islands, and no Japanese could leave until 1868. During that period Chinese influence waned because of the lack of contact, and Japan was able to develop a national style of her own.,

Architecture in the Orient Most of the early Far Eastern buildings were constructed of wood, so not many ancient ones are still standing. The oldest, at Nara in Japan, dates from the seventh and eighth centuries A.D. and shows how complex the wooden construction became. The traditional structural forms of these temples came originally from China, where we know they had remained unchanged for centuries, because clay models found in tombs dating from 200 B.C. show similar construction. Building probably was the most conservative of the arts in the conservative Far East, and the basic building methods have remained essentially the same throughout the history of both China and Japan.

Certainly, Japanese craftsmen developed the art of making wooden buildings to its most refined expression. The elaborate temples and palaces were built on a stone base with wooden posts and rafters which were fitted together in beautifully crafted joints. The pagoda form, with its wide curved roof, became popular and may have derived from the umbrella like forms which often capped the stupas in India. There were gates leading into temple enclosures just as there were around the stupas, and the wooden Oriental gates are similar in design to the stone gates of the stupas.

In Japan, the traditional form of domestic architecture was a wooden house or palace with sliding screens. Scroll paints from the twelfth century show wooden buildings whose style still looks familiar to us today. This style of building has had a strong influence on modern home architecture in the West. In particular, Frank Lloyd Wright, who went to Tokyo in the early 1920s to build the Imperial Hotel, was so impressed with Japa-

*Output on a Linotronic 200P(B) at 1693dpi
Composed using Adobe Illustrator '88 &
Aldus PageMaker on the Macintosh
Sample 1203*

Figure 8   *An example of the versatility of desktop publishing*

what you get', often abbreviated to WYSIWYG. This may be true in a general sense, but because of the limitations of the cathode-ray tube, this description does not always stand up to close examination.

The face of the monitor should ideally show a full A4 page (210 mm × 297 mm) plus any marginal information. It is worth noting here that not all documents are upright or 'portrait' and that the 'landscape' format is quite commonly used.

The definition or fineness of detail which can be resolved on a monitor will be largely dependent on the number of lines of dots which can be 'scanned' across the tube. This in turn will be related to the *resolution* of picture elements (pixels) which make up the projected image. Resolution may be measured in pixels per inch or centimetre. Few monitors have a resolution better than 30 pixels per centimetre, which is significantly inferior to the resolution of laser print-out devices which are rarely rated at less than 120 dots per centimetre.

The size of the screen may also influence the apparent sharpness of definition. If two screens of different sizes both have the same number of dot lines, then the smaller screen will have more dots per centimetre and the reduced image will appear to be sharper.

Colour reproduction on the screen may also not be what you get on paper, as the pattern of light dots on the tube will rarely match the toners or inks on the final document.

Print-out devices

Impact and non-impact devices

'Impact' devices such as typewriter, golf ball, daisy wheel and dot matrix printers, often used for word processing, are not suitable for desktop publication work owing to their limitations in terms of typographic variety and style, as well as their inability to produce graphics. '*Non-impact*' devices are therefore used because of their versatility and their ability to be digitally controlled. These fall in to three main categories: ink jet; laser; and raster image processors (RIPs) or photosetters.

Ink jet printers

Ink jet printers form the image from minute droplets of liquid ink, formed by forcing the ink through a fine orifice. The stream of droplets becomes electrically charged and can then be directed to impinge on the substrate by oppositely charged 'deflection' plates. Unwanted droplets may be diverted from the substrate and returned to the main supply, and the equipment is virtually silent in operation.

Most ink jet printers are microprocessor controlled and banks of jets may be arranged to work in synchronization for higher output and more efficient production. Coloured inks may be used, matched to printing ink shades, and definitions of up to 100 drops per centimetre per colour can be achieved. Even so it may take two or three minutes to print out a full A4 sheet in colour. This quality may be quite acceptable for proofing and inspection purposes, but not necessarily acceptable as definitive prints or as suitable copy for production purposes. For these reasons ink jet printers still tend to be used more in the word processing and personal computer field than for desktop publishing.

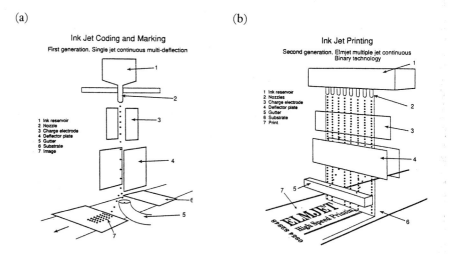

Figure 9 *Principle of ink-jet printing. (a) Ink is forced under pressure through a small nozzle which causes the jet to break up into drops which can be charged by an electrode. Charged drops are deflected into a gutter for recirculation and uncharged drops continue to form the printed image. (b) Multiple-jet systems can contain several jets per linear millimetre. The illustration shows a 25 mm wide printing head containing 100 nozzles capable of producing 7,500,000 drops per second*

Courtesy Elmjet Limited

Laser printers

Laser printers form their image from a minute, digitally-controlled beam of laser light, which is directed via an optical system towards a rotating drum. The drum is coated with a photoconductive material and the pulses of light make the photoconductive layer selectively attractive to tiny particles of powder, supplied from a toner cartridge. As the drum turns, the powder image is electrostatically transferred to the paper stock and then fused to the paper by heat. The combined mechanisms of the printer are commonly referred to as the 'engine'.

This type of printer has become more or less standard for desktop systems, being compact, fairly quiet, more versatile and faster than most alternatives. They are expensive and can account for more than half the cost of the system in some instances. Laser printers have their own central processing unit, are software driven and require a substantial memory (often several megabytes) in order to cope with the extensive demands of the various graphic and typographic images which are to be reproduced in meticulous detail. They may be supplied with a software package including a page description language, a selection of typefaces and styles, and a graphics program. These can usually be supplemented by additional typeface 'cards' and/or additional graphics packages.

Resolution is nominally at least 120 dots per centimetre, which is quite satisfactory for most desktop work. Some models can more than double this, although finer definition may be at the expense of speed of print-out. An A4 sheet may take from a few seconds to a few minutes to produce, depending on the amount of information on the sheet and the detail required.

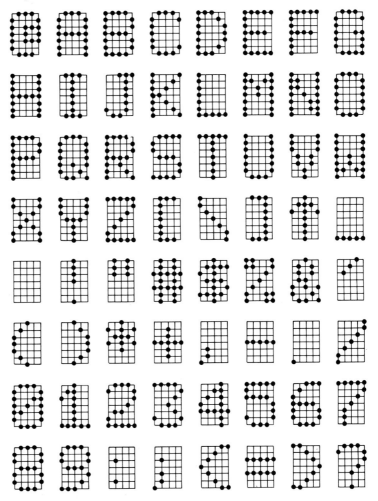

Figure 10   *The dot-matrix principle based on the American standard code – ASCII*

Photosetters

Photosetters are commercial text setting devices which may be employed where even the definition of a laser printer is not considered good enough to reproduce the typeface in sufficient detail. Resolutions of up to 1000 dots per centimetre are possible and a great variety of typefaces and styles are obtainable. These are not true 'desktop' devices as they are usually free-standing floor space models and the cost may be many times that of a complete desktop system. However, it is possible to use the output from a desktop system to drive a major photosetter, and several models have been designed with this particular purpose in mind.

Commercial photosetting systems are covered in more detail in Chapter 4.

Software

The developments in hardware during the 1980s were more than matched by the radical improvements in software, which enabled more powerful and detailed programmes to be developed specifically for the needs of the desktop market.

The first impetus came via improvements to existing personal computers (PCs) via specialized microprocessor software (MS) for disk-operated systems (DOS). MS-DOS software developed by the Micro Soft Corporation especially for IBM PCs, laid the foundation for upgrading the personal computer to what is now recognized as desktop publishing standard. MS-DOS systems follow on logically from PC software as they are based initially on:

- Keyed-in commands.
- The selection of 'menus'.
- The maintenance of detailed information in 'files' on the various disk drives, which may be accessed by coded file names.

The true 'revolution', however, came in the mid-1980s with the advent of Apple Corporation's Macintosh system, using the ingenious 'WIMP' technique: WIMP standing for windows, ikons, mouse and pull-down menus.

- *Windows* are localized sections within the screen that can be accessed at will and used independently within the main image. Multiple windows are possible.
- *Ikons* are pictograms or symbols depicted on the screen, indicating possible courses of action. An appropriate ikon can be selected by means of a key, cursor or 'mouse' to initiate an action.
- A *mouse* is a rolling indicator which can be moved freely around the desktop to control a pointer on the screen. This may be used to select ikons or menus, and to perform other tasks without using the keyboard.
- *Pull-down menus* (sometimes called 'pop-up' menus) are located around the screen and can be pulled in to the picture, and opened up by the action of a mouse. The mouse can also be used to select one of the options offered in the menu, which can then be returned to file.

The two basic approaches – MS-DOS and WIMP – are usually, but not invariably, hardware specific. Therefore, care must be taken to ensure that software programs are compatible not only with each other, but also with the hardware which they are to drive. A degree of 'cross pollination' has taken place to enable the best features of the various systems to be more generally available, but it should not be assumed that any program can be run with any given item of equipment.

Whichever approach is taken and whatever hardware is employed, software for desktop work will need to be chosen to fit the needs of the end product. A variety of options are available and they fall in to the following broad categories.

Word processing software

Word processing (text entry) software is concerned with the organizing of letters into words, words into sentences, paragraphs, etc. together with means of altering, amending, correcting, editing and re-arranging the text matter. The text may be 'styled' into **bold** (thick letters), *italic* (sloping letters), underlined or proportionally spaced. Other functions may include: centring of text, ranging to the left- or right-hand margin and tabulating. Rules may be included for hyphenation, justification (equalizing right- and left-hand margins) and even spelling. Entry may be by direct keyboarding, or by calling up previously stored information, or input from another source. The monitoring screen enables corrections and other modifications to be made before releasing the text for storage, further processing or printing out.

Layout programs

Page layout programs relate to the arrangement of text matter on a page, including:

- Number and widths of columns of type.
- Number of lines per column or page.
- Interline spacing.
- Allowance for head, foot, back and fore-edge margins.
- Headlines and running heads.
- Pagination and the location of page numbers or folios.

Typographic software

Typographic software relates to the typefaces, sizes, styles and quality which will be required in the eventual publication. There are many hundreds of typefaces available to publishers, and quite often dozens of variations on each face (see Chapter 4). Standard typographic software is usually based on a selection of the more popular faces and styles which can be handled by the print-out device. For greater variety and/or finer definition then can be obtained by the standard desktop laser printer, the information will need to be output to a commercial photosetter which has access to a wider range of typefaces and styles as well as being capable of greater print quality definition.

Graphics

Graphics software falls into a number of categories including:

- *Structured* (geometric) images based on standardized shapes and patterns, which may be initiated by cursors, plotted figurations or stored reference diagrams.
- *Business graphics* which are concerned with graphs, bar charts, flow diagrams, pie sections, etc.
- *Freehand graphics* which allow the user to construct diagrams and illustrations ad lib. These can be either 'drawn', i.e. outlined by means of a light pen, mouse or other drawing implement, or 'painted' by use of graphic devices such as electronic paint brushes, tints, stipples or airbrush patterns, which simulate commercial artwork techniques. These can be either used immediately, stored or used later.

Page description languages

Page description languages (PDLs) have been developed to translate some or all of the previous software images into a common 'language' for outputting. Every element of the image, be it text, line diagrams, or halftone illustrations, is recorded digitally in the most minute detail. This information may then be used to instruct the print-out device, which may range from a desktop laser printer outputting at 120 dots per centimetre to a photosetter outputting at 1000 dots per centimetre or more. In the absence of a high level page description language the final print out may fall far short of the ideal expectation.

Peripheral equipment

In addition to the basic items of hardware referred to earlier, the desktop publisher may take advantage of a range of additional equipment to supplement the basic system.

Screens

Large screens can be obtained, often from specialist suppliers, to supplement the monitors provided with the basic system. Some standard monitors have been criticized as the image size is smaller than that of the eventual print-out. Larger screens allow closer inspection of detail, especially where diagrams or other illustrations are concerned, and therefore come nearer to the WYSIWYG philosophy.

Optical character readers

Optical character readers (OCRs) are devices which can 'read' pre-printed text matter and convert the information in to signals which can be recognized by the DTP microprocessor. The obvious advantage of OCR is the avoidance of re-keying information which has already been keyset.

Best results are obtained when the text has been set in a specially-designed 'machine readable' typeface; however, increasingly sophisticated readers are being developed which can read a wider range of typefaces and styles.

The 'scanned' text is usually converted into signals conforming to the American Standard Code for Information Interchange (ASCII) or an equivalent language. This information can then be used for viewing and editing on the monitor and either stored or output to the print device.

Image scanners

Image scanners (digitizers) take OCR one stage further in that they can 'read' illustrations as well as text. These are ideal for monochrome line work, which can be defined with a reasonable degree of accuracy. Halftone illustrations and continuous tone photographs are not always accurately reproduced due to the limitations of the digital information which can be held, particularly within the range of a 120 dots per centimetre laser printer.

Graphics tablets

Graphics tablets are flat plates comprising a fine network of contact points which can be drawn upon by a stylus. The tablet is connected to the monitor so that images traced or drawn on the tablet are projected on to the screen. The projected images may then be manipulated in the same manner as other information for integration into the final page.

Facsimile transmission

Facsimile transmission (Fax) devices are designed to transmit copy up to any distance via a telephone line. This is a comparatively cheap method of sending and receiving information as the equipment is basically quite modest, comprising a transmitter and a receiver (which may be combined into one station) and a telephone handset. The telephone link-up usually takes just a minute or so and a complete A4 page of monochrome text and illustrations can be transmitted in a matter of a few seconds to a few minutes, depending on the particular installation.

Limitations of desktop systems

Desktop publishing can be a fast, efficient, flexible and economical way of initiating the copy for a document. There are, however, a number of limitations:

- The *size* of the sheet that can be made up and printed out true to size, is usually based on an A4 maximum page, although there are some A3 systems available.
- *Substrates* are limited to standard print-out paper stock, unless the image is to be output on to a commercial RIP image setter or the like.
- *Colour* is available only to a limited degree.
- *Halftone* illustrations require secondary outputting via a commercial system.
- *Multiple* copies are not practicable from a desktop system, therefore the output must go for copying or commercial printing where mass production publications are required.

3 In-plant production

The 'paperless' office as promised in the 1970s never materialized in the 1980s and is now seen as a false trail. Most business establishments of any size at all will have some means of originating and reproducing documents of various kinds, partly for internal use and partly for sending out to customers and other business connections.

Documents produced may range from simple office forms including record sheets, circulars, invoices and pay slips, or internal stationery items like letterheads, envelopes, labels and cards, through to more ambitious work such as leaflets, manuals, catalogues and brochures.

The equipment employed will vary according to the sizes, types and ranges of products to be produced, as well as the quality and volume of work to be undertaken. For the smallest office a typewriter or word processor, with access to photocopying facilities, may be sufficient, whereas a large multinational organization may require a plant resembling a commercial printing department with the ability to cope with a whole range of work from business forms and mailing shots to mail order catalogues and packaging.

This chapter covers the range of techniques and equipment which may be used in typical in-plant situations.

Photocopying

The standard A4 electrostatic copier is a basic item in most small offices, where the main need is to reproduce a limited number of pages of information quickly and at a reasonable cost. The information to be copied is usually typewritten documents and/or some straightforward monochrome illustration work.

The simplest machines still work on the principles developed by Xerox in the 1940s. A revolving drum coated with a photoconductive material such as Selenium is electrostatically charged and then exposed to light reflected from the copy. The light reflected from the white areas of the copy dissipates the charge on the drum, leaving only the image areas electrically sensitive. The drum is then cascaded with a fine 'toner' powder of the opposite charge to that on the drum, which results in the powder adhering to the image. The powder is then transferred to the paper stock, again by electrostatic charging, and the image 'fixed' by heat to fuse the powder and key it to the substrate.

Basic models are simple to operate, with the document to be copied being placed on the scanning table by hand and the paper fed in from a 'cartridge'. The whole operation takes but a few seconds and further copies may take one or two seconds each to complete.

Systems copiers

Systems copiers are designed for multiple-sheet documents and faster production can be achieved than with the basic model. The pages are automatically fed to the copier, in sequence, and the appropriate number of copies run off from each original. Two-sided (duplex) copying is provided for in most systems to reduce the quantity of paper required and minimize the bulk of the final document. The copies may then be delivered in to separate racks or 'bins' which allow multiple-sheet documents to be collated in correct order and assembled for final make-up.

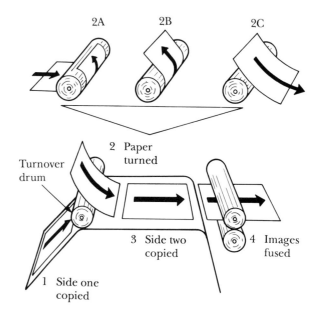

Figure 11   *Duplex photocopying by Kodak*

Editing copiers

Editing copiers may take an A3 sheet and will have provision for enlarging and reducing the original image, within limits, usually by means of a zoom lens system. On some models 'anamorphic' distortion is possible, in which the image is enlarged or reduced in one dimension more than the other. This facility can be useful for making a neat fit to slightly out-of-size originals or for graphic emphasis purposes. Other editing techniques allow for selected areas of the original to be masked out and material included from other sources. Another useful facility is the ability to edit out unsightly file holes and paper edges of documents smaller than the copy size.

Colour copiers

Colour copiers are available, with a range of options. The simplest models employ a changeable toner 'cartridge' which can be selected when a coloured copy is required. Multiple coloured copies can be produced if desired, by passing the sheets several times through the copier and printing selected image areas with different coloured toners.

In other models the colour toners are a standard feature of the machine, and either the whole copy or selected areas may be coloured by using the appropriate controls to achieve the desired effect.

The most advanced colour copiers employ laser printing technology and will include a full range of facilities from editing and enlarging to distortion and image manipulation, as well as producing passable photographic colour reproductions. Some will even accept input from external sources, including 35 mm transparencies, for inclusion in the final copy.

Duplicating

The term 'duplicating' usually refers to certain origination and reproduction processes which do not fall neatly into the category of either copying or printing. It is interesting to note that until fairly recently even some small-offset litho press manufacturers referred to their machines as duplicators. However, it is now generally accepted that there are two main duplicating processes: spirit duplicating; and stencil duplicating.

Spirit duplicating

Spirit duplicating is probably the simplest and cheapest of all reprographic systems in that no particular skills or training are required and capital outlay is minimal. The information to be reproduced may be typed, written, traced or drawn on to a 'master' sheet of paper via an intermediate carbon sheet, the coating of which is based on a sensitive 'hectograph' emulsion.

The master sheet, with its hectograph image is then clipped on to the drum of the duplicator, which is turned by hand or automatically, according to the model. As the drum turns, the image is 'wetted' by a roller containing the spirit, which softens the carbon image, allowing it to transfer to the paper stock as it passes between the drum and an impression roller.

Various colours of hectograph carbon are available and a unique feature of spirit duplicating is the ability to draw in several colours on one master sheet and produce multicolour copies at one pass through the machine.

The main limitations of spirit duplicating are:

- The limited number of copies which can be obtained – 50 to 100 at most.
- Impermanence of the image, which will fade under strong light, etc.
- Sheet size, normally A4 or thereabouts.
- Printing stock, which needs to be a smooth, absorbent, dye-receptive paper.
- Image quality, which is somewhat inferior to conventional printing systems.

Stencil duplicating

The 'stencil' in this instance is a sheet of thin, porous paper coated with a wax-like film. The sheet may be typed, or drawn upon with a special stylus, which has the effect of removing the coating, thus allowing the thin ink to pass through the stencil.

Previously-typed copy and line illustrations can be reproduced by means of an electronic stencil cutter, in which the original is wrapped around a drum and scanned by photocells which control the stylus cutting mechanism located above the stencil at a different part of the drum. An A4 stencil would take two or three minutes to produce, at a cutting pitch of around 150 lines per centimetre.

Stencil duplicators usually comprise a perforated ink drum covered with an absorbent cloth material, which becomes saturated with ink from within the drum. The stencil is placed in position over the ink pad, and as the drum turns, paper is fed between the stencil and an impression roller, forcing ink through the stencil and on to the sheets. Automatic machines are quite common, often with preset sheet counters and automated stencil mounting and demounting.

Up to a thousand copies can be expected from a good quality stencil, and they may be saved for repeat runs. Corrections can be made by 'rewaxing' with a fast-drying liquid 'correction fluid' and then recutting.

The printing stock is limited to a special, absorbent, duplicator paper, which is available in a wide range of colours; but the quality achieved is acceptable for most internal and general-purpose work. Colour printing is not really practicable for stencil duplicating, although some models do have provision for interchangeable drums which can contain different colours of ink.

Offset lithography

Copying, duplicating and desktop systems have their various limitations in respect of such factors as sheet size, substrate, volume production, colour and image quality. Where these limitations are of significance the in-plant printer will look to a more orthodox printing process, which in the majority of instances will mean reproduction via offset lithography.

The lithographic process requires the production of a plate or 'master' in which the image areas are receptive to ink but the non-image areas are not. This can be achieved in a number of ways, but the essential principle in any lithographic system is the preparation of the surface to provide ink attracting and ink repelling areas.

In the simplest instance a water-receptive ('hydrophilic') plasticized sheet of paper can be typed upon, using a special, greasy litho ribbon in place of the normal carbonized ribbon. The master can also be drawn upon with special pens, pencils and materials, and the master mounted on the cylinder of the press. Moisture is then applied to the master via a 'damping' solution, which is accepted by the hydrophilic non-image areas, and ink is applied which adheres to the grease-receptive image areas, but is rejected by the non-image areas. The inked image is then transferred to a rubber blanket on a second cylinder (the offset cylinder), which in turn transfers the image to the printing stock as sheets are fed automatically between the offset cylinder and the impression cylinder.

The elementary system described above will result in a printed image which is noticeably better than a duplicated copy and, according to the type of master used, will give runs ranging from a few hundred to a few thousand. However, for the best results it is necessary to look at each aspect of production more closely, particularly in respect of copy origination, planning, platemaking, printing and finishing.

Text origination

The in-plant house may have access to a variety of type or text input systems from typewriters, word processors and desktop output to 'rub-down' or transfer lettering and phototypesetting.

Typewriters

Typewriter composition is usually limited in respect of typefaces, styles, sizes and other typographical features, including not least the quality of the image. This is particularly true of traditional 'standard' typewriters which impress their characters on to paper through an ink-saturated fabric ribbon. These are often limited to one typeface only, without the ability to 'justify' the type (i.e., make even margins left and right) or to space the letters proportionately according to their widths (i.e., the letter I requires less space than a letter W).

Dot-matrix typewriters

Dot-matrix typewriters produce character forms as patterns of dots formed by a set of pins or 'needles' which are selectively 'fired' through a matrix printing head as it passes along the sheet. The patterns are determined by a logic control centre, and may conform most commonly to the ASCII standards, or certain alternatives. A common matrix is based on a pattern of seven dots per character in the vertical direction and five horizontally, and many systems will provide a limited variety of type styles as well as proportional spacing and automatic justification.

The image is usually formed via a carbon-coated 'total transfer' ribbon in which the impact of the needles causes the carbon to transfer from the plastic ribbon to the paper. Even so the image quality is rarely acceptable for any but the simplest of printing applications.

Letter disk and typesphere typewriters

Letter disk (daisy wheel) and typesphere (golf ball) typewriters offer better image quality and greater variety of typefaces and styles. Both systems employ relief type characters which impact through a total-transfer ribbon on to the paper to give a solid, black image of good quality. Interchangeable heads give a good choice of popular typographic faces and most machines will justify, proportionally-space, and carry out a range of other typographic instructions.

Transfer lettering systems

For larger typefaces and a wider selection, as needed for headlines, display work, advertisements, posters, etc. it is necessary to look beyond the typewriter keyboard. The simplest and cheapest method of achieving these is by pressure-sensitive, dry-transfer lettering. The characters for this purpose are printed on to sheets of paper or plastic material and can be transferred to another substrate by the application of pressure. As well as letters and numbers, a wide selection of special characters, symbols, rules, borders, tints and stipple patterns can be obtained. Some suppliers will also make special characters to order, such as company logos or motifs.

A little skill and a great deal of care is needed to obtain the best results with dry-transfer materials, and to make the most of this versatile and flexible process. However the technique is only suitable for one-off or small-scale projects as it can be time-consuming. Another problem with transfer sheets is that it is impossible to predict the exact numbers of any given characters that may be needed, therefore the sheets tend to be used at random, with the less frequently required characters being left unused on the sheets.

Ribbon lettering systems

Ribbon lettering systems offer a faster and more efficient means of obtaining lines of display type, without the problem of unused or unwanted characters. In the simplest of these devices a ribbon of the image transfer material is fed into the lettering device together with a film carrier ribbon and impressions are made via relief characters held in the perimeter of a type disc. The characters are thus transferred to the carrier film which can be cut and stripped in to the art work, etc. as required.

A wide variety of type styles and faces are available and only the characters required for the particular purpose are transferred to the carrier ribbon. Transparent, opaque or coloured tapes can be obtained and type sizes up to 5 cm high are available.

Basic ribbon lettering machines are operated by hand, but for more efficient production the type discs may be keyboard operated and linked to a display device so that the image can be checked, and if necessary amended before committing the characters to tape.

Photolettering

Photographic methods of setting headlines, captions, etc. offer the widest possible range of typefaces, styles and sizes, plus flexibility in operation for design, layout and display purposes. The equipment available ranges from basic 'strip' printers through to enlarging headliners and keyboard controlled planning and make-up typesetters.

Strip printers

Strip printers carry their characters, usually in negative form, on master strips or discs ('type masters'). The required characters are positioned to the light-sensitive material and exposed one at a time. Most strip printers can be operated in 'daylight' conditions and may print on to film or paper, although developing may be a separate process. The simplest devices are 'contact' printers in which the final characters are the same size as the original typemaster. In these instances separate discs or strips need to be purchased for each change in size. More elaborate printers will have provision for a limited range of enlargement or reduction, thus saving on the number of typemasters required, and some will have arrangements for pre-viewing, editing and proofing the result before finalization and exposure.

Enlarging headliners

Enlarging headliners offer a wider range of type sizes and styles than most strip printers, together with greater flexibility in layout and arrangement of the type. As well as enlargement and reduction, many of these headliners will include optical devices to slant, overlap, expand and condense the characters, etc. to give a greater variety of options from the basic typemasters. Additional flexibility may also be provided in that the characters need not be formed in a strip, but may be positioned as required on the paper or film in accordance with a predetermined layout.

Keyboard controlled systems

Keyboard controlled systems are designed to speed up the selection, positioning and exposure of the characters. There may be some loss of flexibility when compared with the more versatile enlarging headliners, but where a significant volume of work is entailed and speed is essential, and particularly if the requirements fall into a fairly standard pattern, a keyboard controlled headline system could be a worthwhile investment.

Photocomposing

In-plant printers who are required to produce quantities of body text on a regular basis will need to look at photocomposing systems which combine total flexibility with speed of production and a true typographic quality. These will, of course, be more expensive than any of the systems mentioned earlier and will require some degree of operator training to acquire the skills necessary to produce really professional results.

A high proportion of in-plant houses find it more convenient to buy in their text from commercial 'trade' typesetters where the volume of work does not warrant the purchase of a complete system. This is quite common where desktop origination is employed and the output disc may be sent to a specialist house for typesetting.

However there are a number of 'minor' systems which are suitable to the needs of the in-plant printer, and these generally come under the heading of 'direct entry' photosetters where the inputting keyboard has a direct link to the photosetter and a monitoring screen. The operator may key in the text, observe it on the screen edit as necessary and, when satisfied, send it for either storage, proofing or photosetting. These systems often include a whole range of editing and correction facilities, plus typographic options and additional functions found in 'major' systems, which are covered more fully in Chapter 4.

Graphics origination

The in-plant printer may receive graphics input from various sources including; desktop origination in the form of laser print-outs, line diagrams and other hand-drawn artwork, either monochrome or coloured; photographic prints or transparencies in monochrome or colour.

As with text input, where the material is of the correct size and quality for printing purposes without needing any modifications or additional work, a print master or plate may be made directly from the copy.

The majority of work, however, will need some preliminary work to be done such as enlargement, reduction, image reversal, converting positives to negatives or continuous tones to halftones; separation of colours and planning up various component parts into a whole to conform with the design brief. The final document may range from a single-sided, A4 monochrome information sheet to a multipage handbook or brochure including process colour work.

Simple, same-size work may be transferred, overlaid or contacted to paper or film for final processing and platemaking. Where the size needs to be changed and/or colours need to be to separated out, it will be necessary to use a process camera to photographically enlarge or reduce the original and if necessary separate out the various colours by means of filters placed in front of the lens. Continuous tone photographs and transparencies will need to be converted to dot formations by the use of a halftone screen, either by contact printing or at the process camera stage.

As with text origination; for the occasional process job the in-house printer may send out to a trade house for colour separations and the more complicated halftone work. The volume and frequency of colour halftone work will determine whether the in-plant printer is justified in investing in a complete process studio on the lines of a commercial installation as described in Chapter 4.

Planning

Although the 'customer' for most in-plant work is also the printer, this should be no excuse for substandard work. Every establishment should have at least one person on the staff capable of initiating, planning and approving all printed matter, whether produced internally or externally. This should ensure a consistent house style and the maintenance of aesthetic, typographic and print quality standards.

Every job, even the most elementary, needs to be planned in advance. The amount of copy must be made to fit the space available, or vice versa. Page layout, margins, headlines, the general arrangement of the text and the integration of illustrations must be predetermined if shoddy and amateurish results are to be avoided.

The degree of planning may vary from the preparation of a 'rough' outline of the work, indicating the general style and arrangement of the job, to a carefully-drawn 'mock-up' of the finished piece, showing the precise layout of the items on each page. Booklets and brochures, etc. will require a complete 'dummy' of the publication specifying the page-by-page locations of each component and wherever possible, true-to-size proofs of each item.

The printers should be left in no doubt as to how the end-product is to look, and pre-planning should ensure that the result is realistically and economically attainable. Calls for a series of proofs, followed by numerous alterations is a sure sign of inadequate planning.

Make-up and assembly

Where text, headline and graphics information come from different sources, it will be necessary to assemble the various items on to one base sheet of paper or film prior to platemaking.

Paper make-up

Paper make-up is the simplest technique, particularly where the components may have been originated on a paper base as with desktop print-outs, photocopy material and transfer lettering. Skill and care are needed to position the items cleanly and accurately on the base, and to avoid untidy edges and unwanted marks on the copy. It is helpful to use an illuminated table or bench, where the base sheet can be superimposed on a grid sheet or a ruled-up layout for quick and precise location of the components. A photocopy proof may then be taken and any final corrections made before going to platemaking.

If the 'paste-up' copy is to be used directly for platemaking, it is important to check at this stage that there are no hard edges, scratches, finger marks or other unwanted matter on the copy. Where the copy is to be translated into a positive or negative film, minor corrections may be left until the film is examined prior to platemaking.

Film make-up

Film make-up is used for more demanding work, particularly where photographic origination is involved as with halftone and multicolour work. It will be necessary to convert any paper-based origination, such as bromide prints and flat artwork to film negatives or positives, depending on the platemaking system to be employed.

The basic approach is to tape the layout sheet to a light table and position the base 'carrier' film over this. The individual items can then be located in place on the base film by means of transparent tape or adhesive.

The composite film 'flat' may be used directly for platemaking or photographically contacted to another sheet of film to provide a definitive one-piece base for printing down. Multicolour work is particularly suitable for film make-up as the different colour images can be superimposed over a common layout and registered accurately and automatically by means of holes punched or drilled in each foil.

There are a number of variations on the basic technique of film make-up and these are covered in more detail in Chapter 4.

Litho masters and plates

The term 'master' is usually applied to litho printing images carried on paper or plastic bases. These are used mainly in the shorter run field and on the smaller and simpler presses used for in-plant work, which are still sometimes referred to as litho duplicators. Where longer runs, larger presses and more demanding work is required, a metal base will be preferred and these are more commonly referred to as 'plates'.

Direct-image masters

Direct-image masters, as referred to earlier, are paper or plastic laminates which can be typed or drawn upon directly in order to form the image. These are certainly the cheapest and simplest of lithographic image carriers, but have limitations in terms of:

1 The number of copies which can be printed – usually only a few hundred.
2 The orgination sources available – typing and hand drawing.
3 The quality of the final printed image, which although better than most 'duplicating' systems, is not as good as with other litho printing surfaces.

Chemical-transfer masters

Chemical-transfer masters – also referred to as diffusion-transfer – normally require a positive original copy as the first instance. The copy is held in close contact with a sheet of light-sensitive, negative-working paper in a vacuum frame and exposed to a light source which causes a photographic change in the negative paper. The exposed negative paper is then fed into a developing unit, together with a blank printing master and the image developed and transferred to the master in one continuous operation. The master then needs to be 'fixed' with a desensitising solution, and it is ready for the press.

Chemical-transfer masters may also be made via photographic enlargers, which will allow original copy to be enlarged or reduced, and will also cater for the use of transparent originals such as film positives or negatives.

Direct photographic masters

Direct photographic masters (photo-direct) are made straight from the artwork by means of specially-designed platemaking cameras. These are high throughput installations which can make an A3 plate in a matter of minutes.

Copy is usually in the form of black and white artwork including text and line illustrations. Halftones are possible by means of pre-screened photographic illustrations, but there may be limitations on the degree of enlargement or reduction which is practicable. Filters may be used to separate out colours, but it is usually preferable to prepare separated copy for photo-direct work, particularly where the requirements are for simple line illustrations or text.

The master material is usually a plastic laminate, often held in roll form for easy dispensing and quicker production. Developing and processing of the material is carried out automatically as an in-line process, with completed masters, capable of several thousand impressions, being delivered cut to size and ready for the press.

Electrostatic masters

Electrostatic masters can be made on paper or plastic bases which are coated with a photoconductive material such as zinc oxide. The image is formed in a similar manner to photocopying. The material is first 'charged' by passing through an electrostatic field and then exposed to the copy, which should be a good quality black and white original with positive definition. An oppositely-charged 'toner', in powder or liquid form, is then applied and will adhere to the image areas only. Fusing by heat will consolidate and fix the image to the base, and a final 'etching' solution is applied to reinforce the moisture-receptive properties of the non-image areas.

Pre-sensitized aluminium plates

Pre-sensitized aluminium plates are used for longer runs, larger machine sizes and where the highest quality of printing is required. The processing techniques and the equipment required for the production of these plates can be somewhat more complicated than with the printing surfaces earlier described, but there are often occasions where the use of metal plates is justified for in-plant work.

A wide range of plates is available to accommodate different qualities and classes of work and to provide for print runs from a few thousand to several hundreds of thousands. The methods and procedures involved will be similar to those employed in commercial platemaking and printing situations, and are therefore covered more fully in Chapter 4.

Printing presses

Offset litho presses used for in-plant printing are designed on the same principles as commercial presses and may be similar in many respects. The significance of presses intended for in-plant use is that they are of smaller size, usually A4 or A3; designed for simple operation and appropriate for the shorter runs and quick changeovers usually required for in-plant work.

At the smallest and simplest end of the market are the table-top machines, often referred to as offset duplicators, while larger presses will be free-standing machines and are usually referred to as small-offset presses. All presses comprise a plate cylinder, offset cylinder, impression cylinder, inking, damping and paper feed.

Plate cylinder

The plate cylinder will have a means of quickly accepting the plate or master and locating it in position. It may also be possible to adjust the cylinder circumferentially or laterally in order to correctly register the printed image to the sheet.

Offset cylinder

The offset cylinder will hold the rubber blanket which receives the inked image from the plate and transfers it to the paper. The advantages of offsetting the image rather than printing directly as with other processes are that there is less wear on the plate from a rubber blanket than there would be from the hard surface of most printing stocks, and the rubber blanket will lay ink more accurately on rough surfaced papers than would a metal plate. It is also an advantage to see the image the correct way round on the plate rather than laterally reversed as with direct printing.

Impression cylinder

The impression cylinder is provided with a set of grippers to receive and hold the sheets as they are fed to the printing unit, and will take the sheets through the impression 'nip'. The distance between the impression cylinder and the plate cylinder may be varied to allow for different thicknesses of stock, from bank paper to card, and to vary the impressional strength according to the surface characteristics of the stock from smooth 'glazed' paper to rough-surfaced cartridge.

Inking

Inking is by means of a train of rollers which receive the initial supply of ink from a 'duct' which meters a continuous supply to the roller train and can be adjusted according to the needs of the image. Litho inks are based on a greasy or oily medium containing dyes and pigments for colouring and other additives to aid drying, adhesion, etc.

Damping

Damping is by means of an aqueous solution, specially formulated to adhere to the non-image areas of the plate, but not to the inked image areas. The formula usually includes a proportion of alcohol, which reduces the surface tension of the liquid allowing it to spread evenly and thinly over the plate, thus 'wetting' the non-image areas with the thinnest practicable film of moisture.

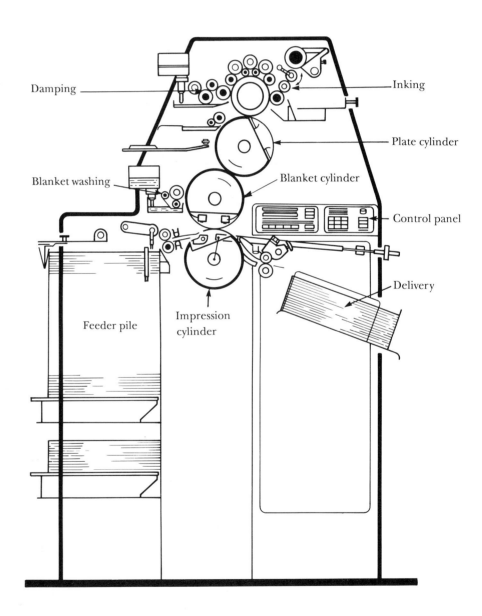

Figure 12   *Small offset litho press by Heidelberg Model TOM*

The solution is supplied to a train of rollers from a separate 'fountain' and the flow controlled according to the needs of the image. In the simplest systems the solution will be fed to the lower rollers in the inking system to arrive simultaneously with the ink, allowing the selective areas of the plate to pick up ink and moisture respectively.

For more precise control the damping system may be designed to contact the plate directly before inking. This is a more expensive and complicated arrangement but it does allow the printer to have full control over both the inking and damping applications.

Paper feed

Paper feed is automatic on all litho duplicators and small offset presses. On the simpler machines the top sheets are pushed forward one at a time by rubber or plastic friction wheels. Pneumatic separation and forwarding provides more efficient feeding for larger and faster presses, and automatic provision will be built in to check for missed sheets, doubles and other possible faults.

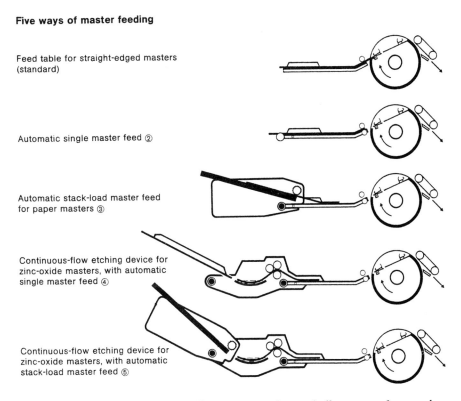

Five ways of master feeding

Feed table for straight-edged masters (standard)

Automatic single master feed ②

Automatic stack-load master feed for paper masters ③

Continuous-flow etching device for zinc-oxide masters, with automatic single master feed ④

Continuous-flow etching device for zinc-oxide masters, with automatic stack-load master feed ⑤

Figure 13 *'Systems' presses. (a) T-offset presses can take practically any type of master plate, either single-fed or batch-fed. (b) (overleaf) A T-offset press linked to an EMF super sorter for automatic collation of multiple copies*

Figure 13 – *continued*

Automatic sequencing

Automatic sequencing is a feature of all but the simplest of presses, whereby the feeding of sheets to the printing unit automatically initiates the damping, inking and impression mechanisms. Similarly, as sheets cease to be fed to the press the sequence is reversed and the impression released together with stoppage of ink and damp feed.

Systems presses

Systems presses are designed for the high throughput of multipage documents. The printing plates or masters for each page are stacked in a hopper in sequential order and the press programmed for the number of copies required in each instance. The plates are fed to the press, located on the plate cylinder, the required number of copies printed and delivered to a multi-station delivery rack and the whole cycle controlled by automatic programme.

Colour printing

Where a second colour is to be printed on a small offset press, this normally entails cleaning the ink from the rollers ('washing up'), locating the colour plate on the press, adjusting the colour balance, position, etc. and feeding the previously printed sheets through the press again to complete the work. This will naturally add cost in terms of paper, ink, plates and other materials as well as the additional time for the second print run.

Imprinting units

Imprinting units can be provided on many presses as additional printing cylinders with their own inking units located between the main printing unit and the delivery. These are usually designed to take small, relief printing plates which print directly on to the paper. This method is suitable where small patches of colour are required, such as a company logo or a colour headline and are ideal where frequent changes are made to a standard copy, such as price, date and address changes.

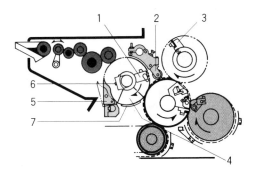

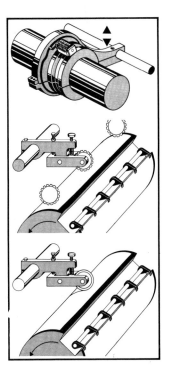

Figure 14 *Additional operations. Numbering, perforating, slitting and imprinting can all be carried out in-line on-press as optional extras by most press manufacturers. (a) A Ryobi unit*

1 Straight or convex type numbering box
2 Slitter and/or vertical perforator
3 Cross perforator
4 Nylon plate holder
5 Numbering cam
6 Mounting ring
7 Nylon or rubber plate

(b) A Miller system

Colour units

Bolt-on or swing-away colour units can be added to most standard single-colour presses to provide full-size sheet coverage. These usually comprise an auxillary plate cylinder with its own inking and damping system which prints on to the main blanket cylinder. This is a compact and comparatively inexpensive means of adding the extra colour and is particularly suitable where the colours do not overlap; although with a degree of skill and specialized technique, overlapping colours can also be printed.

Multi-unit presses

Multi-unit presses give total flexibility for colour printing as they comprise a number of separate printing units, with the sheets being passed automatically from one unit to the next to produce completed copies in one pass through the press. These are available from two to six units, depending on the manufacturer and some also have provision for 'perfecting' the sheet, i.e. printing both sides in one pass.

The field of wet-on-wet multicolour halftone printing is rarely tackled by the average in-plant printer and is therefore dealt with in more detail in Chapter 5.

Ancillary operations

In addition to printing, it may be possible to carry out a number of ancillary operations such as slitting, perforating and numbering at the same time as printing. This can be a particularly useful facility as a considerable amount of time will be saved, which would otherwise have been spent on finishing the work after printing.

For instance, an A4 document may be printed two-up on an A3 press and slit in half before it reaches the delivery, thus taking half the time to produce. Tear-off slips can also be perforated in-line to save another finishing operation, and the sheets can be numbered sequentially and checked as they arrive at the press delivery station.

Basic finishing techniques

Except in the instance of single-leaf documents, most work emanating from the printing presses will need further work before it is complete. Making up in to folders, booklets, leaflets, manuals and brochures, etc, will involve a number of additional operations and associated machinery, including cutting, folding, gathering and binding equipment.

Cutting

Single sheets or small quantities may be slit on a hand trimmer or cut with a hand guillotine, but bulk quantities will need to be cut by a power guillotine.

There are a number of small power guillotines, suitable for the in-plant market, which will accept sheets up to A2 and above, and which can cut piles of paper up to several centimetres in thickness. Sturdy construction is essential and strict safety precautions must be observed to avoid accidents. Operation may be either manual, semi-automatic, fully automatic or 'programmed'; the choice depending on the nature and volume of work to be cut, and the funds available.

Folding

Few items of in-plant work need more than one or two folds, and small quantities may be satisfactorily folded by hand. However where hundreds or thousands of sheets regularly need to be folded, it will be necessary to employ a high-speed, mechanized folding machine. For simple 'fly' sheets, i.e., one sheet folded in half to make four pages, the one fold alone may be sufficient to complete the document. If the sheet is then to be folded in half again, to make eight pages, etc. there will be a closed edge, which will need to be slit or trimmed in order to open the leaves. The backs of these sheets will then need to be glued or stapled in order to keep them together.

Gathering

Gathering or 'collating' of multiple sheets or folded sections is a necessary step before combining them in to the final document. Short

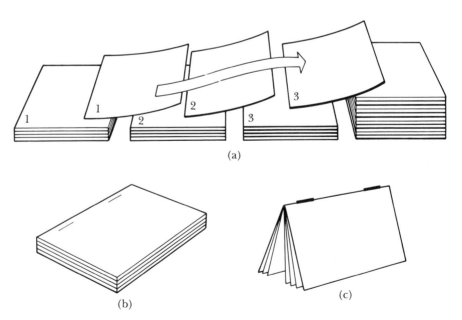

(a)

(b)

(c)

Figure 15 *Basic print finishing techniques. (a) Collating can be either manual or automatic process for assembling single sheets into the correct sequence for binding. (b) Twin stapling for pads. (c) Saddle stapling for booklets*

runs may be assembled by hand on a bench, with the sheets laid out in order. Specially designed collating tables are available to speed up this operation and for longer runs or more regular multipage work, purpose-built collating and assembling machines can be purchased.

Securing

Securing the sheets or sections together can be accomplished either by stapling through the back edges of the collected pages, or by gluing the backs together with specially formulated adhesives. Stapling is a simple, inexpensive and positive means of securing sheets up to a few millimetres in thickness, but may be considered unsightly in certain instances. Adhesive binding avoids the need for metal staples and will cope with a few centimetres of paper thickness, but special care is required to ensure that all leaves in the document are securely held.

Covering

Self covers

Self covers are the simplest means of finishing the document, as the printed sheets themselves form the outer leaves and no other work is required.

Covering materials

Covering materials, such as papers, cards, cloths or boards of superior quality to the body paper, can be used to improve the presentation of the product. These will be separately printed and may be stapled, glued or folded around the main document as a finishing operation.

Binding bars

Slide binding bars are a cheap method of finishing the document as they merely need to be slipped over the spines of the assembled sheets to secure them together. A wide range of slides are obtainable to cater for various lengths and calipers of documents and the enclosed sheets may be either stapled together for security, or left loose for changing and up-dating.

Folders

Spring or clip folders can be obtained ready made to hold varying numbers of sheets. The assembled pages are simply placed in position and the spring clip will lock them into place. Individual sheets may be added, withdrawn or replaced at will.

Binders

Ring and prong binders are also ready-made and can hold large numbers of sheets in a loose-leaf mode. Sheets need to be hole-punched for location in the binders and this must be allowed for in the planning and printing operations. Withdrawal, replacement and additions to the documents are easily undertaken with most ring and prong binding systems.

The mechanism

The O-ring is normally rivetted to the spine of the binder and its shape facilitates easy turning of pages. O-rings are available in ring sizes 11mm to 60mm. Actual paper capacity is approximately 80% of the ring size.

Capacity is approximately 80% of the ring size

D-rings are rivetted to the back cover and this shape combines two useful features — sheets stack squarely to the right and pages also turn easily. Very popular for manuals where presentation and ease of operation are important.

D-rings are available in capacities 15mm to 50mm.

Ring size and capacity are the same

Arch rings are also rivetted to the back cover and allow sheets to stack squarely to the left and right.

Available in capacities 20mm to 65mm.

Ring size and capacity are the same

A **2-ring** fitting is sufficient for general use and paper can be punched with your standard office punch.

A **3-ring** fitting suits American punching at 4¼" centres (108mm).

A **4-ring** fitting will hold sheets more securely along their full length.

A **Multi-ring** completely secures sheets along their full length.

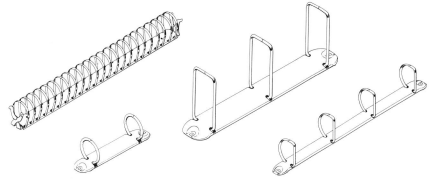

Figure 16 *Ring binding*
Courtesy Presentation Plastics

Combs

Plastic comb binding is a positive method of holding sheets together and at the same time allowing the pages to be opened flat. Combs are basically curved tubes of semi-rigid plastic with fingers or prongs designed to lock in to holes punched in the sheets. The combs can be obtained in an assortment of shapes, sizes and colours. Sheets must first be punched with slots in the spine to accommodate the plastic comb, and a special device is used to assemble sheets, covers and comb in to a complete document.

Spiral binding

Spiral binding requires a series of holes to be drilled in the back margins of the sheets, through which a spiral wire loop is threaded via a purpose-made tool. As with plastic comb binding, this is a positive method of combining sheets together and allows the document to be opened completely flat.

4 Origination

GRAPHIC ORIGINATION

The graphic input to a printed product relates to practically every non-text element. Sources may range from amateur or professional artwork, photographs, transparencies or even transmitted electronic copy. Print purchasers normally employ the services of a qualified graphic designer or an agency for work of any degree of complication in order to avoid the many pitfalls which can occur at this early stage.

Copy for reproduction

There are three initial types of copy for graphic reproduction:

1 *Line work*, which includes all hand-drawn work, either single or multicolour, plus tints, transfers and overlays.
2 *Monochrome (single-colour) halftone work* from black-and-white photographic origination.
3 *Multicolour (process) halftone work* from colour photographic origination.

Line work

Line work should be submitted on a good quality, pure white, non-reflective art board. The image, in ink or other media, should be clear, dense and non-reflective. The image may not necessarily be to the exact finished size, but it should be to the correct scale in order to avoid either distortion or cropping. If the image is to be reduced in the printing process, it should be borne in mind that the finer details will be 'sharpened' and too fine detail could be blurred or lost. If the image is to be enlarged minor faults will also be enlarged, therefore attention to detail is essential.

Colour-line work

Colour-line work is best produced via an 'overlay' method in which the base or 'key' illustration is drawn on the art board and subsequent colours drawn on to transparent overlay foils in precise register with the key. This type of work may also include tints, stipples and other 'shading' devices which the artist may indicate on the overlay. A 'library' of coded tints to which the artist refers may be available for the graphic reproduction technician to apply at the appropriate stage of production.

Monochrome halftone work

Monochrome halftone copy must be submitted on the understanding that the shades of black, grey and white in the bromide print will be converted to dots of varying sizes. This may affect, first, some of the finer detail, and second, some of the more subtle tones, particularly if the image is to be enlarged. For that reason it is helpful if the submitted bromide (or negative) has clearly-defined image areas which show good contrast between one gradation of tone and the next. It is, of course, possible to 'correct' unsatisfactory bromides or negatives, and even carry out correction procedures at later stages, but these are time-consuming and therefore expensive.

Multicolour halftone work

Multi-colour halftone (process) copy may be submitted as either 'flat' artwork colour prints, or as transparencies. In either case it is helpful if the copy is within a reasonable enlargement or reduction size for the final printed copy in order to minimize quality variations. It is not unreasonable, for instance, to submit a 35 mm transparency for full page reproduction, provided that it has been seen to be capable of satisfactory enlargement to this scale. If the 'blow up' is not satisfactory then the chances are that the final print will not be satisfactory either. Again it must be emphasized that the hues, tints and tones in the bromides or transparencies will be translated into dot patterns, and that where clear definition of detail is required in the end print it must be specifically clear in the original.

Another factor to be borne in mind when submitting colour copy for reproduction is the 'balance' of colour where multiple photographic illustrations are involved. If some transparencies appear to be 'too blue', 'too green' or 'too pink' in tone, then they will also appear that way in the final printed product, unless expensive correction procedures are employed. Careful selection of original copy for reproduction, will help to reduce the time and cost of production.

Cameras for graphic reproduction

Although it is possible to use some straightforward, same-size artwork for direct platemaking by 'contacting' etc, as described in Chapter 3, most artwork for lithography needs to be processed via camera. These cameras are designed to fulfil three main functions:

1 To enlarge or reduce the original copy.
2 To convert continuous-tone images to halftone dot images.
3 To separate out multicolour copy into individual 'process' colours.

Cameras for graphic reproduction purposes fall into five main categories:

1 *Vertical cameras* as briefly described in Chapter 3, are used for small offset and limited size work. These have the advantages of compactness, space saving and simplicity of operation. These normally need to be housed in a darkroom.

2 *Horizontal cameras*, in which the copy is outside the darkroom and the film, etc. contained within the darkroom. These are more versatile than vertical cameras particularly for larger sizes. Naturally these will be a little more complicated to operate than vertical cameras and will take up more floor space. These are variously referred to as 'darkroom' cameras or 'two-room' cameras.

3 *Vertical/darkroom cameras*, combine the advantages of the two previous types in that the external part of the camera works on a vertical basis, i.e., the lens being above the copy, while the back of the camera is contained in a darkroom. This will require the image to be turned at a right angle via a mirror system.

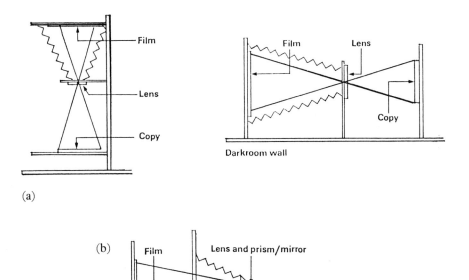

Figure 17 *Basic types of camera. (a) Vertical. (b) Horizontal. (c) Vertical/darkroom*

4 *Projection cameras* are used mainly for colour separation, particularly where the copy source is 35 mm or other transparencies. Although it is possible to use the other types of camera for transparency work, it is more practicable to employ a specialized camera where there is a constant need for this type of work.

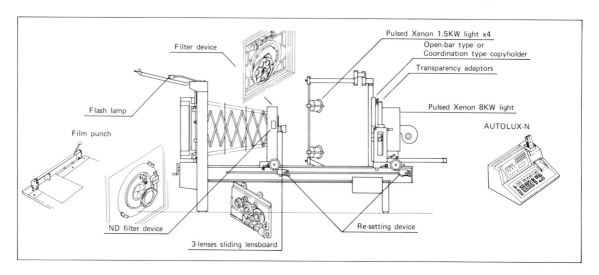

Figure 18 *Camera arrangement for direct screening*
Courtesy Dianippon Screen MFG Co. Ltd

5 *Multiple-image cameras* (step-and-repeat) are used for work such as stamps, labels, stickers and other types of work which are produced many times up on the sheet. The basic idea is to take an approved negative or positive, place it in a movable holder at the first position where it is automatically exposed and then moved laterally to the next position in the next row and the procedure is repeated. Step-and-repeat cameras may put their images either on to film or directly on to the printing plate.

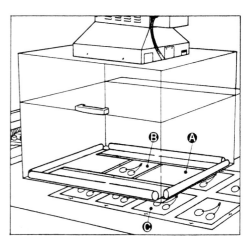

Figure 19 *Principle of step-and-repeat camera*

A Masking device
B Master film for multiple reproduction
C Presensitized litho plate

Courtesy Dianippon Screen MFG Co. Ltd

Camera construction

There are three main parts to a graphic reproduction camera: the copy holder, the lens; and the film holder. Provision must be made to vary the distances between these components in order to determine the degree of enlargement or reduction while keeping the image in sharp focus. Precision engineering is an essential requirement as the slightest fault may be magnified many times; the planes of the copyboard, lens and film holder must be in perfect relation to avoid distortion and the whole camera installation needs to be sited in a dust-free and vibration-free environment.

The copyholder

It is essential that the copy be held firmly and perfectly flat in a precise position on the copyholder. This is usually arranged by sandwiching the copy between the base board and a sheet of non-reflective glass. Air is withdrawn by means of a vacuum pump to ensure absolute flatness and absence of air-induced optical aberrations. For transparent copy the base board is replaced by a second sheet of non-reflective glass and the illumination is swung behind the copy instead of in front of it.

Illumination

Illumination of the copy will vary according to the needs of the particular type of work. The first requirement of any lighting system is that the copy is evenly illuminated over the whole of the area to be exposed; the second requirement is that the illuminant should match the spectral requirements of the film, particularly with regard to process work.

Tungsten lamps

Tungsten lamps are sometimes used for simpler, monochrome work where colour sensitivity is not too important. Special tungsten lamps with halogen additives can be obtained for this purpose, and these have the advantages of low cost and simple replacement.

Metal halide lamps

Metal halide lamps are based on the principle of the original mercury vapour lamps in which the mercury is contained in a quartz 'envelope' and the passing of an electrical current through the envelope causes the mercury to vaporize. This produces a light source rich in blue/violet and ultra-violet light. The addition of metal halides improves the spectral emissions to make them more compatible with the film materials in general use. It is also possible to select different additives to suit specific purposes.

Pulsed xenon lamps

Pulsed xenon lamps are based on tubes fitted with xenon gas. By applying an electrical current to discharge across a capacitor in the tube, a series of rapid, repetitive flashes are produced. The 'pulses' appear as continuous light to the observer, but are controllable to a fine degree, which makes these lamps particularly suitable where length of exposure is critical. The spectral emission range for xenon gas also makes this type of lamp appropriate for colour separation work.

Lenses

The lens is a combination of glass elements which have been designed and assembled for the purpose of transmitting light received from the copy to form an image on film. Lens design for graphic reproduction cameras is a precise art and modern lenses should avoid such problems as spherical aberration or astigmatism, where the detail from different parts of the image area may be distorted; also chromatic aberration, where the prismatic effect of bending light may cause distortion of colour values. These problems are avoided by careful choice of lens components of the appropriate diameter, angle, thickness and curvature. Another fault to be aware of is that of 'flare', where unwanted light intrudes on the lens to cause exposure problems. This problem can be reduced by coating lens surfaces with a transparent film – a process often referred to as 'blooming'.

The lens area will also include an iris diaphragm, which will open or close to allow more or less light in to the camera back, plus a shutter device which will determine the length of time which the lens remains open.

In many instances a selection of lenses may be provided for varying purposes such as greater enlargement or reduction. 'Anamorphic' lenses may be used for horizontal or vertical compression or expansion of the image, either to make the copy fit the space available, or to compensate for distortion which may occur at other stages.

It is also at the lens area that colour filters will be employed for colour separation purposes.

Filters

Filters are placed in front of the lens in order to split the multicolour photographic original into the separate components which will eventually reproduce the image as a series of superimposed films of coloured ink (cyan, magenta and yellow), plus black, on a white substrate.

Initially the copy is divided into thirds of the six-colour light spectrum (red, orange, yellow, green, blue and violet). A red/orange filter will separate out those parts of the copy to be printed by cyan ink; a yellow/green filter will separate out those parts to be printed by magenta ink and a blue/violet filter will separate out those parts to be printed by yellow ink.

It must be added that this simplistic view of colour separation needs to be modified in view of the fact that the spectral characteristics of filters, photographic film, printing inks and substrates are often far from perfect. The greatest imperfections are with the printing inks, which do not absorb and reflect colour wavelengths as precisely as theory would dictate.

Colour correction techniques

Colour correction techniques must therefore be employed, in which the final exposure to film is modified by reference to known imperfections of the ink, etc. At the most elementary level corrections can be undertaken by manual 'retouching' where the separations are visually examined and values adjusted by hand techniques in order to correct the colour balance; a procedure requiring a great deal of time, skill and experience.

Colour masking

Colour masking is an alternative technique whereby the spectral deficiencies of one separation are used to correct the deficiencies of another. For instance, it is known that magenta inks reflect some wavelengths of light that should only be reflected by the cyan printer; therefore, by making a low-density positive of the magenta printer and locating it in register with the cyan negative, a second, combined exposure will 'mask' the deficiency. The same technique can then be repeated with the other separations.

Darkroom

The darkroom part of the camera studio needs special consideration. A 'light trap' entrance must be provided to prevent external light intruding; ventilation must be good, a constant temperature – 18°C to 20°C should be maintained to ensure consistent results. Where film processing is carried out, the water supply must be checked for hardness, softness and impurities, and where necessary filters, purifiers and softeners installed. Liquid waste disposal should be carefully controlled to ensure that the effluent does not give rise to pollution or other environmental problems.

Room lighting must be carefully considered in studio areas. Standard 'white' fluorescent light may be used where and when there are no light-sensitive materials in view. Yellow or brown lighting may be used for 'slow' types of film as used in planning areas and red 'safe' lights may be used in darkrooms for processing films which are sensitive only to the blue/violet end of the spectrum. For films with broader spectral sensitivities it is advisable to undertake processing in total darkness, although there are some dense, dark green lights which may be used if inspection of the film during processing is seen to be necessary. Polished surfaces and reflected light should be avoided as this may cause unnecessary light to enter the lens, copyboard, film holder, etc. For this reason walls are commonly painted in a matt black.

Film holder

The film holder is contained behind the lens in the darkroom part of the camera. The film itself is held in place by vacuum suction and located in position by reference to a grid pattern on the film holding board. Pin register devices may also be located at this stage for accurate positioning and repositioning of film particularly where multicolour work is undertaken. Provision for viewing the copy, prior to exposure, is usually made by means of a ground glass screen which can be swung in to position for this purpose. Where appropriate, the halftone screen may be introduced at this stage by placing it in contact with the film base.

Halftone screens

The halftone screen is used to convert the continuous tone image as seen in a bromide print or a colour transparency into a dot pattern, which simulates the continuous tone image. This is most commonly carried out by means of a 'contact' screen, which is a sheet of film comprising a pattern of transparent dots which are dense in their centres and 'vignette' or shade out towards their outer edges.

Contact screens may be used in three main ways:

1 In contact with a continuous tone positive or negative.
2 In the camera back of a darkroom camera.
3 On the baseboard of a projection camera.

Screens can be tailored to meet a variety of requirements depending on which of the main areas of use they are intended for and whether they are to be used for producing positive or negative images.

Screen ruling

Screen ruling affects 'definition' of the image i.e., the sharpness or degree of detail which can be defined in the halftone image. This is largely related to the number of dots per linear centimetre and may vary according to the class of work. 'Coarse' screens intended for, say, newspaper work on cheap substrates, may be spaced at 26 dots per linear centimetre. For good definition on coated stock 60 lines per centimetre would be more appropriate, and for the very finest detailed work it may be necessary to employ screens up to 150 dots per centimetre.

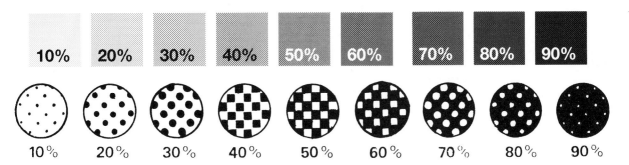

Figure 20 *Percentage dot formation*

Screen angles

Screen angles may vary according to the nature of the work. For monochrome (black) printing the screen dot pattern is angled at 45° as this is known to be least obtrusive to the human eye. For multicolour work the angle is changed for each colour; magenta may be angled at 15°, cyan at 75° and yellow – which is the least obtrusive colour – at 90°. Failure to keep the different colours well separated from each other could result in the problem of 'screen clash' or the Moiré effect.

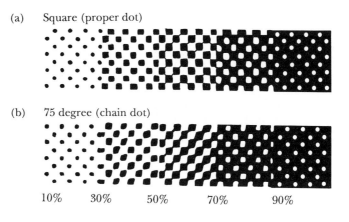

Figure 21 *Dot shapes. (a) The conventional dot pattern starts as small, circular dots, developing to a rectangular pattern at mid-tones, then progressing to round 'negative' dots at the solid end. (b) Chain or elliptical dots are angled at 75° to 80° to give a smoother gradation of tones in the middle range*

Exposure

Exposure of the film to the light reflected from or transmitted through the copy needs to be precisely controlled. Variables to be taken into consideration include: the distances between the copy, the lens and the film; the type and intensity of the illuminant and, the nature and sensitivity of the film. Devices which are used to measure and control these variables include:

- Photometers, which measure the intensity of illumination at the film plane.
- Light integrators which measure the amount of light falling on the copy and may therefore be used to adjust exposure times and accommodate variations due to fluctuations in light output resulting from voltage changes, etc.

The ideal exposure time for a given set of conditions may be established by making a set of test exposures and selecting the optimum result for the definitive exposure. This alone may be sufficient for monochrome line images, but for halftone and process work it may be beneficial to make additional exposures such as:

- An initial 'flash' exposure with the screen in contact with the film prior to the main exposure. This brief exposure is for the purpose of overcoming the initial 'threshhold' sensitivity of the film emulsion so that it becomes immediately responsive to the main exposure. This will ensure that even the deepest 'shadow' areas are faithfully recorded with their full density ranges.

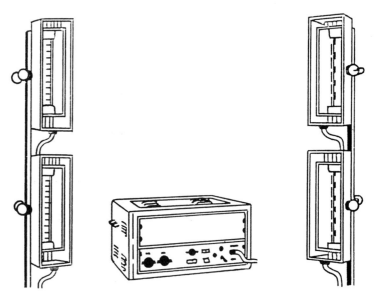

Figure 22 *Pulsed xenon lamp assembly*
Courtesy Berkey, UK

- An 'unscreened' exposure, in which the image is briefly exposed to the film, without the screen being present, thus sensitizing the whole of the emulsion surface and making it particularly sensitive to 'highlight' areas so that the minutest detail is recorded.

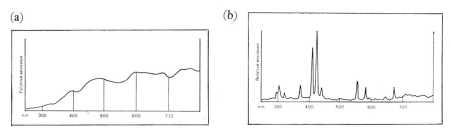

Figure 23 *Spectral emissions of (a) pulsed xenon lamps and (b) mercury vapour lamps Courtesy* Berkey UK

Film processing

The exposed film now has a 'latent' (undeveloped) image which needs to be chemically processed. This is most commonly undertaken in an automatic film processor in which the film is transported through the four basic stages of: developing; fixing; washing; and drying. The electromechanical and chemical arrangements of the processor may depend on the type of film to be processed and the class of work. In any case it is essential that the processor is systematically maintained, particularly with regard to the purity and replenishment of the chemicals. Factors that can affect the properties of the chemicals include: carryover of liquid from one section to the next, run down of chemicals as they are used up in the processing cycle, changes in temperature, and limitations on the natural 'life' of the solutions. Constant testing of the solutions is essential, including frequent processing of test strips to examine the quality of the various baths.

Films for graphic reproduction purposes need the following six properties:

1 *Stability*. During processing the film may be subjected to a number of physical, chemical and environmental stresses, but at the end of all of these the film must retain its dimensions within the register tolerances for the class of work. This is particularly important for close register and multicolour halftone work. The film should also be resistant to scuffing and scratching.
2 *Sensitivity*. This refers to the amount of time required to effect a chemical change in the light-sensitive emulsion when exposed to an appropriate source of illumination. The time cannot be too long as this will slow down the process; on the other hand, if the material is too sensitive this may lead to difficulties in determining the precise period of time to allow for exposure.
3 *Optical fidelity*. This refers to the ability of the film to contain light to the areas under exposure and not to 'scatter' within the film and thus sensitize other areas. To this purpose films need to

be as thin as practicable, and a dye-based 'anti-halation' backing is included to prevent internal reflections.

4 *Chemical fidelity*. This refers to the film's ability to confine its chemical activity to the specific exposed/non-exposed areas, and not to 'creep' into the opposite areas.

5 *Definition*. Most graphic arts film coatings are based on light-sensitive silver halide particles suspended in an emulsion. The size of the 'grains' of silver in the coating influence the detail which can be recorded. This is particularly important when the developed images are to be subsequently enlarged, and fine-grain emulsions are essential if 'graininess' is to be avoided.

6 *Contrast*. For accurate reproduction of continuous tone images, such as bromide prints or colour transparencies, the film must be sensitive to the full range of tones and colours present in the original, and this will require a 'panchromatic' film coating which has a sensitivity to match the range of the copy. For line and halftone work, however, it is essential to use a film which sharply records the image and non-image areas quite distinctly. A 'high-contrast' emulsion is therefore required to ensure that there is no ambiguity between what is the image and what is not.

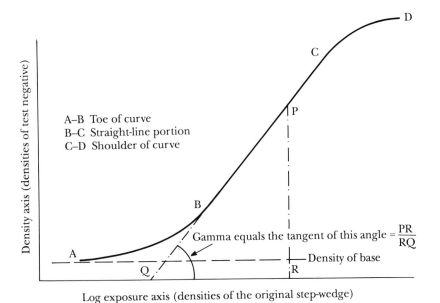

Figure 24   *Characterized curve of a film emulsion. The steeper the curve, the greater the contrast*

Film types

Types of film for graphic reproduction may be simply classified into three groups:

1 *Panchromatic film*, for recording the subtle gradations of the

images in continuous tone and coloured photographic separation work, prior to converting to halftone separations.

2 *High contrast film*, to ensure sharp separation between image and non-image areas of the film, such as line work and halftone work. 'Orthochromatic' film falls in to this category, but most suppliers will provide 'lith' type films which are particularly suited for the purpose of halftone dot reproduction. Apart from the precise initial definition of these films, it may also be possible to further treat them by 'dot etching' in order to attain a more accurate result.

3 *Negative or positive working films* may be used according to the end requirements.

In addition to these basic types of films there may be others such as: 'rapid access' films, which together with their associated chemistry are intended to improve the throughput of film in the processor. This is achieved by attacking the 'threshold' time taken to overcome the emulsions initial resistance to chemical activity, thus obtaining earlier and faster development. There may be some minute quality loss when compared with standard 'lith' film, but rapid access is entirely suitable for a whole range of graphic reproduction work.

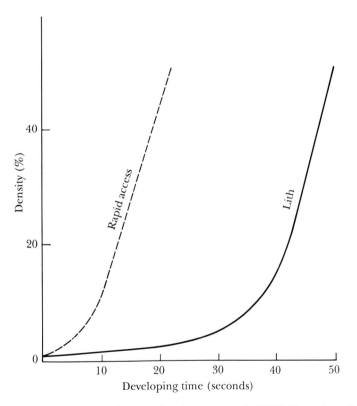

Figure 25 *Comparison of development times between a typical 'lith' film and a typical 'rapid access' film*

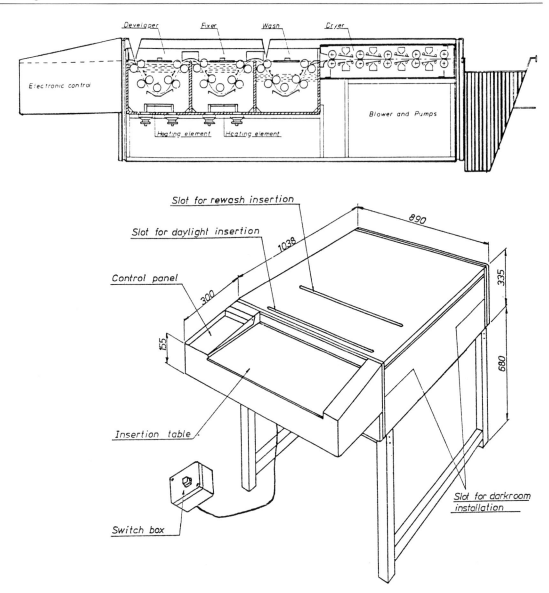

Figure 26   *Principle of an automatic film processor*
Courtesy Luth International

Colour scanners

Although graphic arts cameras can and do undertake colour separation of both transparency and reflection copy, where any reasonable volume of this type of work is required it is common practice to use a colour scanner. Scanners are computerized electronic devices intended initially for the purpose of separating continuous tone colour copy in to the three primary printing colours and in addition to compute the value of the black printer.

The basic construction of a typical scanner will comprise:

- The *copy drum* will usually be arranged to take either transparent or reflection copy and will rotate as it is scanned by the 'analysing' light source.
- The *analysing light source* is usually a tiny, pulsed spot of light which examines the copy in minute detail as the copy drum revolves beneath it.
- The *optical system* will comprise an arrangement of lenses and mirrors which receive light from the copy and convert the information to electrical impulses which are forwarded to the computer console.
- The *computer* will receive the light-generated electrical signals and by reference to its programmed instructions will use them to control the exposure of the film.
- The *exposing light source* must be capable of extremely rapid but finely controlled pulsation as the exposure drum revolves below it. The light must also be appropriate for activating the sensitive photographic film. Modulated argon lasers are most commonly used to produce the image by electronic dot generation (EDG) although other sources, such as pulsed xenon can be used where appropriate.
- The *exposure drum* will hold the photographic film upon which the final digitized images will be contained. This drum is linked electromechanically to the copy drum to ensure precision recording of the information received from the original.
- A *control panel* will be provided to enable the operator to set up the equipment and instruct the scanner in the details of the variables to be examined and controlled.

Flatbed scanners

Flatbed scanners are used mainly for monochrome work, often as an output or ancillary to electronic page make-up systems. They have a number of advantages over 'drum' scanners in terms of cost, simplicity and versatility. Flat scanners are economical for smaller formats and where the artwork cannot easily be curved around a drum. They may be designed to accept transparent, opaque or digitized copy.

As the term implies, the copy is held flat and scanned as it passes beneath the reading head, which in most cases is based on charged coupled device technology. Charged coupled devices (CCDs) are wafer-thin, metal oxide semiconductors used in microelectronics for storing information at very high densities – up to several thousand elements per square centimetre. They can only be accessed serially, which makes them appropriate to the linear scanning techniques used in flatbed scanners. VDU monitoring is usually provided, together with provision for correcting, enlarging, reducing or otherwise manipulating the image. The digitized information can then be used to drive a laser output device for producing either proofs or final film positives or negatives.

The simplicity and versatility of the flatbed CCD scanning method has encouraged manufacturers to produce versions which can also read colour copy and produce separations in the same manner as drum scanners. These adaptable devices are usually compatible with other computer-based microprocessor equipment and are becoming more widely used as their potential is realized.

The advantages of using a scanner rather than a camera include:

- *Speed*. A four-colour set of separations may be obtained in a matter of minutes; positives or negatives, right reading or reversed, enlargements or reductions can be produced automatically.
- *Simultaneous multiple separations*. All four separations can be progressed at the same time, rather than the one-at-a-time technique usually employed by cameras.
- *Direct screening*. Most scanners can be programmed for continuous tone separations if required, but the main emphasis is on producing screened separations in one step. Screen rulings (dots per centimetre) and dot shapes may be varied at will to suit the needs of the particular type of work.
- *Automatic colour correction*. Data relating to the printing variables such as ink, paper, films, etc. can be built in to the computer program or input by the operator, thus avoiding the tedious and time-consuming procedures of colour masking and hand re-touching.
- *Image manipulation*. Digitized computer control makes it possible to manipulate such factors as; contrast, highlight and shadow definition, colour balance, and sharpness of image, etc. in accordance with predetermined parameters. It may also be possible to store information on disk or tape for future reference or repeats.

Scanning terminology

Much of the terminology associated with camera techniques will also apply to electronic scanning. The following factors are of particular importance.

Density range

Density range refers to the difference between the most dark and the most light areas of the image.

Tonal graduation

Tonal graduation refers to the degree of differentiation between tones of the image from darkest to lightest, and is related to the 'contrast' of the image. This factor can be shown by means of a 'characteristic curve' in which a steep curve would indicate a high-contrast and a shallow curve would indicate a low-contrast. Tones are often broadly divided in to 'highlights', midtones and 'shadows'.

Contrast compression

Contrast compression refers to the fact that the density range and contrast in most transparency origination is far greater than required in the final print. The density range and tonal graduation therefore need to be adjusted, often quite considerably, in order to compensate for this.

Grey balance

Grey balance is the term used to define the adjustments that the scanner will need to make in order to reproduce a neutral grey in the copy as a pattern of dots on the four separations. It should be pointed out that this will not necessarily mean that all four dot patterns will be of equal size and shape. This factor is helpful in standardizing the final appearance of the print when compared with the original, particularly when it is necessary to balance up originals from various sources.

Undercolour removal

Undercolour removal (UCR) refers initially to the removal of the coloured image in areas where a black solid or shadow is to be printed. In the early days of process colour printing there were attempts to print with the three colours only. Blacks and shadow areas were rarely satisfactory, therefore it is now common to employ a black printer to obtain solid blacks and a full range of tones.

Evidently there is little point in printing a solid yellow, solid cyan, solid magenta and then superimposing a solid black image. It makes sense to remove colour in black areas. Determining the degree of UCR by camera separation requires a high degree of expertise, but by computer controlled separation the removal of colour in shadow areas can be precisely calculated.

In practice it is not always desirable to remove all colour in shadow areas, as some additional colour helps to strengthen the depth of the image and improve more subtle shades. This basic principle does not always apply equally to the mid-tone and highlight areas.

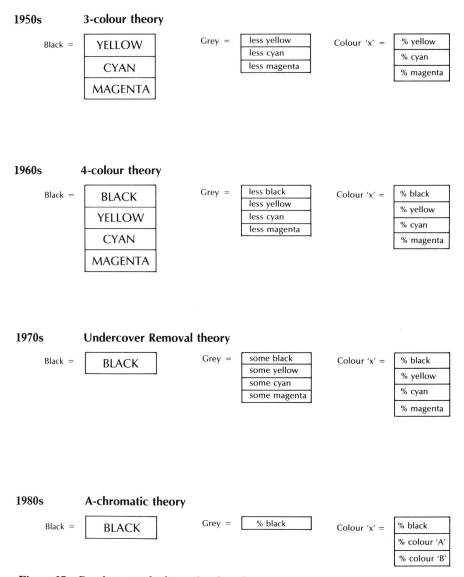

Figure 27   *Development of achromatic colour theory*

The primary advantages of UCR are: savings in ink, fewer problems on the printing press and a sharpening of the image.

Achromatic colour separation

Achromatic colour separation (ACS) takes the UCR theory one stage further, beyond the black and shadow areas, by saying that, in theory:

- It should never be necessary to have all three colours plus black in any area. The combination of three colours will produce a grey element, which could be produced by the black printer only. Therefore the proportions of the colours can be reduced in favour of the black printer.

● Further to this, it should never be necessary to have all three colours present, owing to the fact that the colours tend to 'degrade' each other and subtract colour from their opposites. Therefore the colour of least importance (say, the one with the smallest dot size), which is merely degrading the other two colours can be removed and replaced if necessary with an equivalent black dot.

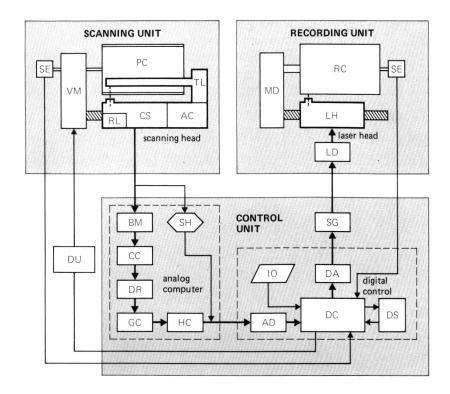

Figure 28 *System block diagram of DS SG-701*

PC	Copy cylinder	DU	Motor drive unit
TL	Transmission light	BM	Basic masking
AC	Autocalibration	CC	Colour correction
CS	Colour separation optic electronic	DR	Density range
RL	Reflection light	GC	Gradation
VM	Motor drive mechanism	SH	Sharpness
SE	Shaft encoder	HC	Highlight control
MD	Motor drive mechanism	IO	Power input
RC	Recording cylinder (vacuum)	AD	Analogue/digital convertor
LH	Laser light source	DA	Digital/analogue convertor
LD	Laser drive unit	DC	Digital control computer
		DS	Digital storage

Courtesy Dianippon Screen MFG Co. Ltd

● In summary *any shade* can be represented by *not more than two colours plus black*.

In practice ACS, as with UCR, may be subject to modification depending on the individual circumstances. Versions of the basic technique are variously referred to as extended UCR, integrated colour removal (ICR), programmed colour removal (PCR), etc. depending on the individual supplier or manufacturer.

The types of scanners currently available range from comparatively simple bench top devices for straightforward colour separation through to sophisticated scanners capable of a great variety of image manipulation functions in addition to colour separation.

More advanced 'studio' systems will include the ability to receive, store and retrieve information from other sources; undertake montage, page and sheet make-up; manipulate colours and re-proportion images, plus incorporating text and other input sources.

TEXT ORIGINATION

Although most of the text matter for printing is now originated photographically or electronically, much of the terminology associated with this aspect of production stems from the original metal type system in which individual, three-dimensional characters and even the spacing materials, were placed in position, one at a time, by hand. Five hundred years of metal typesetting do not die easily!

Basic typographic terminology

Some of the basic typographic terms relating to text origination are dealt with first of all.

● *Typeface*, or just 'face', refers to the style or individual character of the text image. There is no universally accepted method of classifying typefaces, but there are a number of broad divisions which are generally accepted, such as:

● *Roman*, which is the traditional style used for body text, etc. In this style of face the main character strokes are finished off with a curved final stroke or 'serif' which aids legibility.

● *Italic* is a sloping style, originally based on early Italian typefaces, but now mainly used to give emphasis within the 'roman' text. Originally italics were individual typefaces but are now often slanted versions of the Roman.

● *Moderns* are faces in which the serif is little more than a thin line drawn at right angles to the main strokes. The first 'moderns' date from the eighteenth century.

● *Sans serif* faces, as their name implies, have no finial strokes or serifs. The character strokes are often of even width, and early versions were termed 'grotesque' or 'grots' in view of what then appeared to be their unnatural appearance.

Caslon

abcdefghijklmnopqrstuvwxyz
ABCDEFGHIJKLMNOPQRSTUVWXYZ
1234567890 .,;:"«»&!?

Cartier italic

abcdefghijklmnopqrstuvwxyz
ABCDEFGHIJKLMNOPQRSTUVWXYZ
1234567890 .,;:"«»&!?

Bodoni

abcdefghijklmnopqrstuvwxyz
ABCDEFGHIJKLMNOPQRSTUVWXYZ
1234567890 .,;:"'«»&!?

Gill Sans

abcdefghijklmnopqrstuvwxyz
ABCDEFGHIJKLMNOPQRSTUVWXYZ
1234567890 .,;:"«»&!?

Egyptienne

abcdefghijklmnopqrstuvwxyz
ABCDEFGHIJKLMNOPQRSTUVWXYZ
1234567890 .,;:''«»&!?

Coronet

abcdefghijklmnopqrstuvwxyz
ABCDEFGHIJKLMNOPQRSTUVWXYZ
1234567890 .,;: `«»&!?

Choc

abcdefghijklmnopqrstuvwxyz
ABCDEFGHIJKLMNOPQRSTUVWXYZ
1234567890 .,;:''«»&!?

Figure 29   *Examples of different forms of typefaces. From top to bottom:*

Roman. Caslon Old Face
Italic. Cartier Italic
Modern. Bodoni
Sans Serif. Gill Sans
Slab Serif. Egyptienne
Script. Coronet
Display. Choc

Courtesy Mergenthaler Type Library

- *Slab serifs* on the other extreme have greatly exaggerated finials. The heavier slabbed versions, with no curve at the join of the serif are often refered to as 'Egyptians'.
- *Scripts*, as their name implies, are faces which imitate a style of handwriting.
- *Display and decorative types* are not designed to be used for main 'body' text, but for particular situations such as advertising, posters, headlines or other eye-catching situations.

Within each broad division there are specific typefaces which were historically named after their originators such as *Caslon*, a traditional roman face, *Bodoni*, a classic 'modern' face, and *Gill*, a famous sans serif.

Helvetica®
abcdefghijklmnopqrstuvwxyz
ABCDEFGHIJKLMNOPQRSTUVWXYZ
1234567890 .,;:''«»&!?

Helvetica® condensed
abcdefghijklmnopqrstuvwxyz
ABCDEFGHIJKLMNOPQRSTUVWXYZ
1234567890 .,;:''«»&!?

Helvetica® italic
abcdefghijklmnopqrstuvwxyz
ABCDEFGHIJKLMNOPQRSTUVWXYZ
1234567890 .,;:''«»&!?

Helvetica® bold
abcdefghijklmnopqrstuvwxyz
ABCDEFGHIJKLMNOPQRSTUVWXYZ
1234567890 .,;:''«»&!?

Helvetica® light
abcdefghijklmnopqrstuvwxyz
ABCDEFGHIJKLMNOPQRSTUVWXYZ
1234567890 .,;:''«»&!?

Helvetica® black
abcdefghijklmnopqrstuvwxyz
ABCDEFGHIJKLMNOPQRSTUVW
XYZ 1234567890 .,;:''«»&!?

Helvetica® light italic
abcdefghijklmnopqrstuvwxyz
ABCDEFGHIJKLMNOPQRSTUVWXYZ
1234567890 .,;:''«»&!?

Helvetica® black extended
abcdefghijklmnopqrstuvw
xyz ABCDEFGHIJKLMNOP
QRSTUVWXYZ1234567890

Helvetica® ultra light
abcdefghijklmnopqrstuvwxyz
ABCDEFGHIJKLMNOPQRSTUVWXYZ
1234567890 .,;:''«»&!?

Helvetica® ultra compressed
abcdefghijklmnopqrstuvwxyz
ABCDEFGHIJKLMNOPQRSTUVWXYZ
1234567890 .,;:''«»&!?

Helvetica® Ultra light italic
abcdefghijklmnopqrstuvwxyz
ABCDEFGHIJKLMNOPQRSTUVWXYZ
1234567890 .,;:''«»&!?

Helvetica® bold outline
abcdefghijklmnopqrstuvwxyz
ABCDEFGHIJKLMNOPQRSTUVWXYZ
1234567890 .,;:''«»&!?

Figure 30   *Variations on a basic typeface. Just a few examples of the many versions of a standard typeface. In this instance Max Miedinger's classic Helvetica*
Courtesy Mergenthaler Type Library

The current trend is to give descriptive names such as Univers, Futura and Eurostyle to convey the ethos of the face.

Having established the individual typeface, the designer may offer variations on the basic theme.

- *Bold* face has the main strokes of the character strengthened to give a blacker and more emphatic stress.
- *Extra bold* is an exaggeration of the bold image.
- *Light* face is the opposite of bold, in that the main strokes are thinner, thus reducing the emphasis.
- *Extra light* is an exaggeration of the light face.
- *Condensed* faces are those in which the characters are compressed laterally and therefore appear to be taller vertically.
- *Expanded* faces have their characters extended laterally and therefore appear optically to be shorter vertically.

Combinations of these variations may also be available such as Futura light condensed or Univers bold extended.

A collection of variations on a basic typeface is referred to as a 'family'.

A *fount* (or font, as the Americans will have it) refers to the total number of characters and other symbols including upper case (capital letters), lower case (small letters), numerals, punctuation marks and any special 'sorts' or 'pi' characters which may be necessary in order to meet the needs of the publication. Traditionally a fount refers to a set of characters of one size only.

Typeface dimensions

Type dimensions are traditionally referred to in 'points' (0.35 mm). 12 points make a 'pica' (4.2 mm) and 72 points or 6 picas make approximately a standard inch (25.4 mm). Continental type measurements are often based on the 'Didot' point which is slightly larger than the Anglo/American point, at 0.38 mm.

Vertical dimensions

The vertical dimensions of type characters are usually measured in points. The smallest faces in common use are only 4 points high. Although it is technically possible to produce much smaller faces, these could not normally be read by the unaided human eye. There is no upper limit in size apart from the limitations of the composing system. This vertical measurement includes strokes which rise above the main body of the lower case characters, such as h, l and b ('ascenders'), and strokes which fall below the main body, such as g, y and q ('descenders'). An important common denominator is therefore the height of characters without either ascenders or descenders, and this measure is referred to as the 'x-height'. This factor is significant in many ways, as it may influence the choice of typeface, its legibility and readability and the overall appearance of a body of text.

خسن *Arabic*
'Monotype' Arabic Naskh 784

خسن *Arabic*
'Monotype' Arabic Naskh 804 bold

خسن *Arabic*
'Monotype' Arabic Naskh Abridged 816

خسن *Arabic*
'Monotype' Arabic Naskh Abridged 826 bold

ԻՈՇՈՐԳԻՐ *Armenian*
'Monotype' Armenian 638 upright

ল্যান্সটেন *Bengali*
'Monotype' Bengali 700

ল্যান্সটেন *Bengali*
'Monotype' Bengali 701 bold

မြွဥဒကာ: *Burmese*
'Monotype' Burmese 558

កាសាំង្ស *Cambodian*
'Monotype' Cambodian 1241

漢字系 *Chinese*
'Monotype' Chinese 830

ΚΥΠΤΑΙΟC *Coptic*
'Monotype' Coptic L370

देवनागरी *Devanagari*
'Monotype' Devanagari 855

देवनागरी *Devanagari*
'Monotype' Devanagari 856 bold

Colm-Cille *Gaelic*
'Monotype' Colm-Cille 121 upright

ქბჯლჩრ̃ჯჯლ *Georgian*
'Monotype' Georgian 587

Ἑλληνικῆα *Greek*
'Monotype' Times New Roman 565 upright TM

Ἑλληνικῆα *Greek*
'Monotype' Times New Roman 566 inclined TM

Ἑλληνικῆα *Greek*
'Monotype' Times New Roman 567 bold upright TM

Ἑλληνικῆα *Greek*
'Monotype' Times New Roman 667 bold inclined TM

Ἑλληνικῆα *Greek*
'Monotype' Gill Sans 572 upright TM

Ἑλληνικῆα *Greek*
'Monotype' Gill Sans 571 inclined TM

Ἑλληνικῆα *Greek*
'Monotype' Gill Sans 672 light upright TM

Ἑλληνικῆα *Greek*
'Monotype' Gill Sans 675 bold inclined TM

Ἑλληνικῆα *Greek*
Haas/Stempel
'Monotype' Univers 889 medium upright TM

ગુજરાતી *Gujerathi*
'Monotype' Gujerathi 460

ગુજરાતી *Gujerathi*
'Monotype' Gujerathi 518 bold

ਪਰਮੇਸਰ *Gurmukhi*
'Monotype' Gurmukhi 604

ਪਰਮੇਸਰ *Gurmukhi*
'Monotype' Gurmukhi 601 bold

אותפנינ *Hebrew*
'Monotype' Peninim 489 pointed

ꦤꦏꦸ *Javanese*
'Monotype' Javanese 1138

ವಿಷಯಗಳನ್ನು *Kannada*
'Monotype' Kannada 588

ವಿಷಯಗಳನ್ನು *Kannada*
'Monotype' Kannada 788 bold

ປະເທດລາວ *Laotian*
'Monotype' Laotian 1238 upright

ປະເທດລາວ *Laotian*
'Monotype' Laotian 1239 inclined

Figure 31   *Selection of Monotype digitized exotic scripts*

Linear measurement

The linear measurement is usually in picas and the significant factors are the line length or 'measure' and the number of characters per line. Evidently the shorter the line length and the fewer the characters per line, the more often word breaks are likely to occur, resulting in either an unacceptable number of line-end hyphenations, or unsightly gaps between words. This can be a particular problem in narrow-column work which is to be 'justified', i.e., the interword spacing adjusted so that the text conforms to a regular margin on both right- and left-hand sides of the column.

All of these factors are of importance for 'copy fitting', i.e., determining the amount of space which a given quantity of text is to occupy. In one instance it may be necessary to make the copy fit the space allocated to it; in another it may be necessary to adjust the space to fit the needs of the copy.

Other factors will include the widths of the margins and the amount of space, if any, between the lines of text. If no space is allowed between lines, the type may appear visually cramped and its readability impaired. For these reasons it is good typographic practice to allow some space between lines. This is commonly referred to as leading (pronounced ledding) owing to the metal type practice of putting thin strips of type metal between the lines. The ideal degree of interline spacing can only be determined in the first instance by visual assessment.

Text setting systems

Previous chapters have referred to what may be called 'minor' text setting systems such as 'strike-on' methods based on typewriter origination, transfer lettering, strip printers and desktop production.

For volume production of text, especially where speed is essential and a high typographical standard is also expected, it will be necessary to move up to a 'major' system which can cope with this type of demand. These systems usually comprise a number of modules which form steps along the route, from the initial input, through the various methods of image formation to the final output.

Input

Keyboards

Keyboards are the initial form of input, as somewhere in the system keys must be struck in order to originate the information. A text setting keyboard will necessarily be more detailed than a typewriter or word processor keyboard as it will need to have special function keys to give typographical instructions such as: typeface, typesize, line length, interword spacing, interline spacing and tabulation, as well as formatting instructions such as; justified or non-justified setting, centring lines or ranging them to either the left- or right-hand margins, indentation, etc.

On simpler systems the keyboard may be 'on-line', i.e., directly connected to the text setter. This has the benefit of immediacy, but the disadvantage that the speed of setting is limited by the skill of the

```
Many people who have tried a spa
dreamed about having one all to
own home, because once you have
in warm, massaging water, an ord
again.  The dream remained a fan
was generally thought that spas
for those with money to burn.
```

Many people who have tried a spa
having one all to themselves in th
have experienced the sheer bliss c
bath is never quite the same agair
because it was generally thought t
those with money to burn.

```
Many people who have tried a spa
probably dreamed about having on
privacy of their own home, becau
sheer bliss of relaxing in warm,
bath is never quite the same aga
with most people because it was
simply a luxurious indulgence fo
```

**Many people who have tried a spa
club have probably dreamed abou
themselves in the privacy of their
once you have experienced the she
warm, massaging water, an ordina
quite the same again. The dream
with most people because it was g
spas were simply a luxurious indu
money to burn.**

Many people who have tried a spa
club have probably dreamed abou
themselves in the privacy of their
once you have experienced the she
warm, massaging water, an ordina
quite the same again. The dream
with most people because it was g
spas were simply a luxurious indu
money to burn.

Figure 32   *Image quality of different methods of text reproduction. From top to bottom: daisy wheel typewriter using total-transfer ribbon; electronic dot-matrix typewriter using total-transfer ribbon; word processor using simple dot matrix printer and continuous ink ribbon; laser printing on an Apple Laserwriter Plus at 120 dots per centimetre; electronic text setting on the Linotronic at 1000 dots per centimetre*

keyboard operator. Modern text setting systems are capable of setting at a rate of several hundred characters per second, and for this reason among others, keyboards for major systems are generally used 'off-line'. These keyboards are therefore designed to record their instructions on a tape or disc, which will then be used as the input to the text setter, thus enabling it to work at its full potential.

Video display units

Between inputting and before outputting it is desirable to be able to view the work in progress before it is committed to film or paper. This is usually provided by a VDU at an appropriate station in the system. The VDU screen should be capable of displaying at least one full page of text with good quality typographic definition. Facilities for editing and correcting the displayed information should also be included to ensure that only approved and corrected copy is forwarded to the next station. Some VDU editing and correcting stations also have provision for paper print-out for reading and proofing and purposes.

Image formation

There are three basic methods of forming the text image:

1 *Photographically,* by means of film negatives or 'photographic matrices' stored in grids, discs or drums. An electronic flash through the 'photo-mat' will expose the sensitized material via a lens system.

(a)

(b)

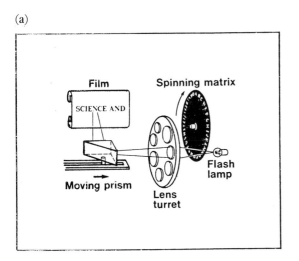
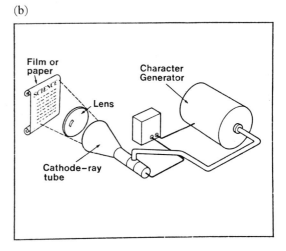

Figure 33   *(a) Principle of photosetting via spinning photomat disk and stroboscopic flash. (b) CRT text setting. Digitized character generation via cathode ray tube*
Courtesy Kodak

2 *Cathode ray tubes* (CRT). In these systems the information necessary to produce the text is stored within the central processor in digital form. The tape or disc input generates images on the CRT which is then used to expose the sensitized material.

3 *Laser scanning and exposure.* As with CRT systems the initial information is stored digitally in the central processor. However, in this instance the sensitized material is exposed directly by the laser which projects a minute, but extremely precise pattern of dots to form the characters.

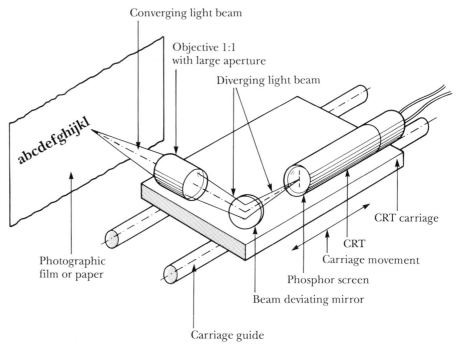

Figure 34 *CRT text setting. Principle of the CRTronic system. Courtesy* Linotype Ltd

Photographic systems

Revolving disc photomatrices were the first real breakthrough in to high-speed photosetting. The spinning disc contains several hundred characters in concentric rings (the 'character store') and as it revolves an electronic flash device, triggered by the input system, will catch each particular character as required and expose it via a lens system on to the sensitized receiving material. Each exposure will obviously take milliseconds and requires the highest degree of expertise and precision in engineering and electronics. Discs may be easily changed to allow for a variety of typefaces, founts and typesizes.

Grids are alternative character storage devices in which the images are arranged in vertical and lateral rows. In this instance the character store is stationary and character selection is by electronically coordinated lens systems.

Drum photomatrices provide greater storage capacity than discs or grids as the drum configuration has a greater surface area than a flat disc or grid. Flash tubes are located within the drum and triggered by the input device to expose the characters as the drum revolves.

Discs, grids and drums may all be used in conjunction with CRT text setters.

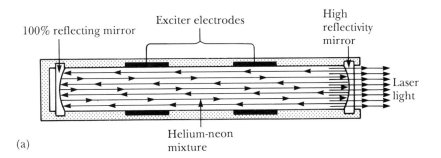

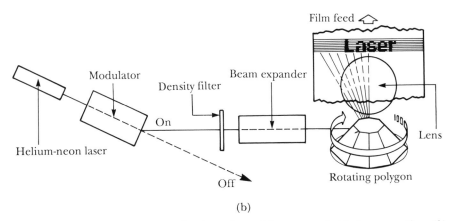

Figure 35 *(a) Principle of a helium/neon laser light source suitable for text setting. (b) Principle of the lasercomp system*
Courtesy Monotype Corporation

Enlargement and reduction on photographic systems

One of the advantages of photographic text setting is that the same fount of photomatrices may be used for larger or smaller sizes, whereas with metal type each size required its own individual fount of type.

Magnification and reduction are undertaken via the lens system, which may vary from one manufacturer to another. For instance a 'zoom' lens may be used which has the advantage of requiring only one lens for enlargement and reduction. An alternative is to have a 'turret' of lenses, which may be moved into place according to the degree of modification required.

This technique, however, must be used within limitations. It is a fact that the visual appearance of a typeface will vary upon enlargement or reduction. Type designers will therefore adjust the various elements in the face such as: widths of strokes, 'counters' (openings in a's and g's, etc.) serifs, ascenders and descenders, x-height, etc. to allow for this in each size required. For ideal results perfectionists would still insist on the 'one-size, one-fount' principle. However it is generally agreed that a degree of enlargement or reduction from a standard fount is acceptable.

For instance it is suggested that a given 'master' fount should never be more than doubled or less than halved in size. Therefore, a 10-point fount may be reduced as far as 5 points and enlarged up to 20 points without too much aesthetic visual damage. This will cover the majority of body text sizes in common use. For higher typographical standards a narrower range may be specified.

It may also be possible to play photographic 'tricks' with specialized lenses to produce 'expanded' or 'condensed' versions of the face, and even sloped or 'italic' versions.

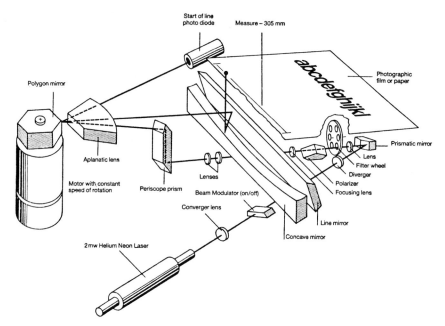

Figure 36 *Laser text setting. Principle of the linotron system*
Courtesy Linotype Ltd

Cathode ray tube (CRT) systems

Photographic matrices are not the only way of storing information relating to text production. Computers can store information in digitized form and a single computer disk can contain data relating to many thousands of type characters. This information can be used to input image on to a CRT at very high speed, and the CRT output used to expose the sensitized material.

CRTs work on the same principle as a television tube in that a 'flying spot' of light traverses the screen at high speed in order to create the image. The 'quality' of the image may be defined by the number of lines of dots per centimetre (l.p.c.), which in the case of a television tube is about 250 l.p.c. For text production the number of lines per centimetre will vary according to the quality of the product. 500 l.p.c. or more may be expected for the finest image quality. However, finer resolution, i.e., greater number of lines per centimetre, may slow down the imaging process, therefore a given quantity of text will take longer to set. For this reason a coarser definition may be used for rough proofing or where image quality is not of high importance.

Enlargement and reduction on CRT systems

At first sight it might seem that the limitations on enlargement and reduction which apply to photographic systems might not apply to CRT text setters. However, the information stored in the computer or on disc is still based on an original pattern as determined by the type designer for a given point size.

For CRT reproduction the designer will superimpose each character on a 'grid' which replicates the pattern of light spots on the CRT screen. The grid divides the image into a number of 'picture elements' (abbreviated to pixels or pels). The character is then scanned to record a pattern of binary signals as either 'image' or 'non-image' spots. This information is then stored in digitized form for future use.

Enlargement or reduction of the image will therefore be subject to the same constraints as with photographic systems. Excessive increases or reductions in size will require reference to an appropriate base fount.

Laser systems

Initially laser imaging starts off, as with CRT systems in that the original type designs are based on grid systems which reduce the image to picture elements, which are then scanned and stored for future retrieval. The difference with laser imaging is that the stored information can be retrieved directly and used to form the image on the sensitized material via an exposing laser beam, rather than indirectly as with CRT systems.

The exposing device may be a helium/neon laser which can generate tiny points of sharply focused light, at extremely high speeds, under minutely controlled conditions on the sensitized material. The light spot may be less than 0.01 mm in diameter, enabling as many as a million pixels to be generated on a square centimetre. This is equal to a resolution of 1000 lines per centimetre, which should give a definition fine enough to satisfy the most precise typographical standards.

Direct imaging via a central computer also allows for the introduction of graphics, from simple geometric forms to digitized versions of more complicated images. Depending on the power of the computer, a 'library' of digitized images can be stored, ranging from special 'pi' characters such as logos, symbols, accents and 'house' characters through to customized graphic images.

Output

Where the final copy is to be text only, it may be possible to output directly on to the printing plate. At the other extreme, more complicated systems may require the output to be stored for further use in a total imaging system, which will incorporate both graphics and text. However in most instances the final image from most text setters is put on to either sensitized paper or film.

It is worth noting here that whichever base is used the sensitized emulsion must be many times faster than for any other graphic arts material owing to the microscopic period of time available for the exposure of each individual character.

Paper

Paper is generally considered to be cheaper and simpler than film in terms of cost, time and materials. It can be used immediately for simple proofing, reading and correcting procedures. Paper text output can also be used as reflection copy in conjunction with other art work for graphic reproduction and planning. In many ways it is easier to work with than film due to its convenience for 'paste-up', blanking out or photocopying.

It should go without saying that no ordinary paper can be used. An important characteristic is that the material must be 'stable', i.e., not change its dimensions throughout the printing cycle. A fraction of a millimetre stretch or shrink could exceed the printing tolerance.

Film

Most text setters will accept film or paper. Film is usually accepted to be more stable than paper, which is critical when working to fine tolerances. Some experts argue that the quality, i.e., the 'definition' of the image on film is better than that on paper, but this is a difficult point to prove, particularly as the image may be transferred or copied two or three times during the planning and platemaking process.

More important is the method of planning. If the final planning is to be by positive or negative film make-up, then it is an advantage to have the output from the text setter in the same form. Proofs from film can be quickly and cheaply made by means of diazo processors which enable the work to be quickly checked and sent for reading and/or correcting.

In these simple devices the film is fed to a nip in contact with the base paper, which is coated with a diazonium (diazo) compound. A light source will sensitize the base paper, which is then developed by exposure to ammonia fumes within the processor.

PLANNING AND ASSEMBLY

Where the graphic elements of the work and the text elements are produced separately and in individual pictures, pages, columns, separations, etc. it will be necessary to assemble these together prior to making the printing plates.

As mentioned in earlier chapters, for simpler types of work such as text-only, single-colour or colour-line work it may be possible to assemble the various elements by VDU screen manipulation, or by 'cut and paste' techniques on to a paper-base.

For more complicated work, however, especially where close register and multiple halftone work is undertaken, it is more common to use film origination and plan on to a transparent film base. There are two basic steps in this operation:

1 *Planning*: to determine in advance where each element is to be placed.
2 *Assembly*: in which the various elements are physically located in position according to the plan.

The design brief

Before any other operation can commence, a plan or 'layout' must be produced. This is a technical drawing showing the location of all image elements as they will finally appear on the printing plate. The planner will need to be able to interpret the design brief and 'see through' the printing process in order to produce a working layout for production purposes.

Dummy production

The design brief may be in the form of a 'dummy' or mock-up of the final job. This should give the planner the following information:

- Number of pages.
- Final, trimmed page size.
- Widths of margins at head, foot, back and foredge of each page.
- Location of graphic and text elements on each page.

The planner will then confer with the printing department to determine the following information:

- *Sheet size* upon which the work is to be printed.
  This will enable the planner to work out:
  1 The number of pages which can be printed on a sheet.
  2 The number of sheets and therefore the number of layouts required.
- *The press* which will print the work.
  This will be necessary as the planner must know:
  1 The dimensions of the plate for the press.
  2 Allowance for 'grip', i.e., that part of the sheet which is held by the press grippers as it passes through the printing nip, and is therefore not available for printing.
  3 Other areas of the plate outside the paper area which may be necessary for fastening to the plate cylinder etc.
  4 Whether the job is to be printed one colour at a time on single-colour press, or in one pass on a multicolour press.
  5 Will the sheets be turned over and backed up (perfected) on a second run through the press, or will they be 'perfected' in one pass on a 'perfector' press, etc.

The planner may also consult the print finishing department to determine:

- The best method of folding the sheets into individual sections or 'signatures'.
- Where and how sheets and folded sections should be cut and trimmed, and the allowance to be made for this.
- Coding systems for indicating the individual sections for gathering, collating and making up in to the final publication.

Other factors which the planner may take in to consideration include:

- *'Bled' illustrations*, i.e., illustrations which run off the edge of the printed page. This will require extra allowance in the trimmed edges, as it is not practicable to print beyond the edges of a sheet of paper.
- *Register marks* may be added at the planning stage if not included earlier. These are usually in the form of finely drawn crosses, reproduced on each working of a colour job. The superimposed crosses are normally located in the trim areas and will be useful guides to the accuracy of register at later stages.
- *Quality control strips* may also be included at the planning stage. These are assemblages of film elements which can be used to check various quality factors as the work progresses. These are dealt with more fully in Chapter 8.

Having obtained all the information necessary to progress the job, the planner can now work out the 'imposition' scheme for each layout. The imposition will show the location of each page in the scheme and its relation to other pages, allowing for margins trims and other factors.

Layout production

Production of the layout will require conventional drawing instruments and a suitable drawing table. At its simplest level the whole operation may be completely manual, but for efficiency it is advisable to use a purpose-made 'rule-up' table with built-in calibrations, cursors and other drawing aids. Automatic 'plotters' can be used, in which the information is fed to a control unit which will initiate the drawing via an automatic ruling table. These are particularly useful where standard or recurring imposition schemes are used and for high-volume work such as publications and forms.

Substrates

Substrates upon which the layouts are drawn need to be stable to environmental changes and either transparent or translucent, as they may be used as a base upon which the various film elements will be laid.

Paper bases

Paper bases may be used, such as Golden Rod which is translucent and tinted to prevent the passage of actinic light (i.e., light which affects photosensitive materials). This is useful as it is comparatively cheap and may be used not only as a rule-up, but as the physical base for film assembly.

Generally speaking, however, paper bases do not have sufficient stability for best quality work.

Plastic bases

Plastic bases are more stable than paper and are transparent. Special versions are produced for planning and assembly purposes in which the surface is treated to give a matt finish, which prevents reflections from the otherwise shiny surface and reduces internal refraction of light.

Acetate films

Acetate films are sometimes used as these are comparatively cheap and can be drawn upon with appropriate pens and pencils. However, they are not as stable as other films.

PVC films

PVC (polyvinyl chloride) is not so sensitive to humidity changes and therefore offers a more stable base. This film can be dyed or drawn upon comparatively easily, but it is temperature sensitive and may crack or split under the wrong storage conditions.

Polyester films

Polyester is the most stable of base material films but in its 'raw' state may be difficult to draw upon and is liable to surface 'static' charges which may attract dust, etc. and cause sheets to stick together. It is important, therefore, to ensure that polyester films have been surface treated to make them suitable for this purpose.

Grid sheets

Grid sheets are sheets of plastic film material with a prepared grid of crossed lines, which may be used either in conjunction with the base sheet or directly as base sheets themselves.

Film assembly

In its simplest form the assembly of film elements requires that a transparent sheet of, say, polyester film is taped over the layout, which in turn is taped to a light table. The various film elements can then be placed in position either by an appropriate adhesive or with transparent tape. The greatest care must be taken to ensure that elements are positioned precisely within the register tolerances for the work in hand, and the utmost cleanliness must be observed to avoid unwanted marks on the film. This completed assembly is then known as a 'flat'.

Multicolour film assembly

For multicolour work, the first set of elements laid down should be those which are most useful as a guide to subsequent sets, i.e., those which contain the most useful information. A second transparent sheet will be laid over the first set and used as a base for the second set of film elements. Care must be taken to ensure precise alignment for process work and parallax error should be avoided by examining the overlaid images through a magnifying tube spy glass. When satisfied with the second set, the assembler will remove this flat and proceed with subsequent sets.

Pin registering

An aid to precision is to punch or drill holes in the film, which can then be located on to pins at a subsequent stage. For instance, the layout sheet and all sheets of base film can be punched or drilled with precision holes before assembly. They can then be quickly located in place on the planning and make-up table without time-consuming visual inspection.

The principle can be taken further. It is practicable to punch or drill film at the camera or scanner stage to ensure easier registration later. Pins may also be used at the platemaking stage to ensure accurate location of the image to plate, and the printing press can be fitted with pins to accept the pre-punched plates, thus saving time in visual location.

'Key' assembly

Assembling directly on to the layout sheet is not always ideal, as the individual elements for any one colour may not provide sufficient information for subsequent colours. For instance the cyan printer may be considered as ideal for superimposing the other colours, but may not be suitable for the text. For these reasons it may be preferable to assemble in the first instance the 'key' information for each page on a clear plastic sheet superimposed on the layout, and use this assembly to produce a photographic key sheet. This is achieved by passing the assembled flat, in contact with the sensitized key material through an appropriate processor which will form an image of the composite layout on the key film. The key can then be used in place of the layout sheet.

There are two basic variations of this technique:

1 The blue key where the image is produced in a shade of blue which 'actinic' light will pass through as easily as plain film. The blue key can therefore be used *either* in place of the layout sheet *or* directly as a base assembly sheet.
2 The red key where the image is produced in a shade of red. This type of key is more commonly used *beneath* the base planning sheet in place of the layout.

Masks

Although the assembled 'flat' is seen initially as being two-dimensional, it is in fact comprised of a number of layers of material such as the base film, image elements and adhesive tapes, each of which has its own thickness. Exposure of such an assembly to the printing plate may result in film or tape edges, etc. showing up as false marks on the plate due to internal refraction of light.

This may be avoided by cutting a mask to separate out the printing and non-printing areas. Exposing the plate separately to the mask will ensure that the non-printing areas (in which the tape and film-edge lines normally occur) are 'burned out'. The separate exposure to the image will then be safe from film edge marks, pinholes, etc.

Primitive masks may be made from tape and paper, but it is preferable to use special-purpose masking films. These are usually two-layer 'peelable' films in which a translucent red or amber film is laid upon a transparent film. The masking film is placed over the layout and careful work with a scalpel will remove the unwanted tinted film from the transparent base. It is also possible to produce masks mechanically at the planning stage via automatic 'plotting' devices as used for preparing layouts.

Multiple images (step-and-repeat)

Where multiples of the same image are required to be printed on one sheet of paper, as for stamps, labels, coupons, etc. it would be tedious, time-consuming and expensive to produce many negatives or positives and assemble them in the manner previously described. For this type of work a step-and-repeat camera is necessary, in which a single negative or positive is placed in a film holder, exposed to the first position then moved automatically to the next position in the row and so on. At the end of the row the film holder will move down to the first position in the next row and start again.

These machines will work to a programme, obtained initially from the layout data and input to the equipment by tape or disc information based on simple x–y coordinates. Step-and-repeat machines may output on to film or directly on to the printing plate.

ELECTRONIC PAGE MAKE-UP

Where mass production with fast turn-round times are required as with, say, the production of a large-circulation, multicolour daily newspaper, it will be necessary to instal a comprehensive 'studio' system which will coordinate and integrate both the text and the graphics. The system should be capable of accepting input from the composing source and from the various graphic origination sources, then converting the input into digital information which may then be assembled, edited and manipulated electronically to form, first whole pages and eventually the completed product.

These can be complex, modular arrangements, often requiring a number of components and items of peripheral equipment which may be 'tailored' to the needs of the user. Some of the basic elements comprising an electronic page composition (EPC) system are as follows:

At the centre of a typical electronic page composition system will be the composition console comprising a full-size, high-resolution monitor capable of showing a full newspaper page or a pair of magazine pages. In front of this will be a digitized planning table with keyboard, cursor, mouse and other control devices, where the operator will plan the work by reference to a master plan.

Supplementary monitors may be provided for preplanning, editing or calling up additional information. This type of system will need immense storage capacity, of multimegabyte order, which may be provided by hard Winchester fixed discs, backed up by supplementary floppy discs or tapes.

Input to the system may be from electronic composition systems, colour scanners, hard copy, transparencies or stored library or 'archive' material. In some EPC systems it is even possible to input video recorded material including 'frozen' frames at an appropriate point in the recording.

With access to all this information the operator will have complete freedom to plan up the pages on the monitor with a genuine WYSIWYG (what you see is what you get) facility, so that they are not released for proofing, storage or printing until they precisely conform to the terms of the page, layout and the requirements of the final printed product.

Control features

In addition to the standard editing and image manipulation features referred to earlier, the studio control operator of an electronic page composition system has even greater and more flexible ability to plan, edit and manipulate the image. The degree of control and the variety of features will vary depending on the particular make and model of EPC system, but could include some or all of the following features:

- *Grid planning*, is standard to most EPC systems. The operator works to a prepared grid sheet placed on the planning table showing the intended locations of the main features to be included in the page. The various items of text and graphics can be called up from the input sources and located on the monitor for inspection and modification as required.
- *Framing and ruling* around the perimeters of features can be included by means of cursors, mouse control or light pens.
- *Irregular shapes* can be generated and the copy, either text or graphics, fitted into or around the shapes.
- *Text 'run-arounds'* can be arranged by allowing the text to 'flow' around either features indicated on the page grid or special shapes generated by the operator.
- *Overmatter*, i.e., text which cannot be fitted into the page can be highlighted for operator decision. The page plan may be modified to include the overmatter or the excess text can be referred to the next page.

- *Image 'sharpening' or 'softening'* is a useful feature. A particular graphic image may have its outline and components sharply defined in order to make it stand out from the background. Alternatively, the image may be softened to enable it to blend in to the composition as a whole.

- *Cut-outs* of selected images can be made by electronic 'masking' techniques, and the cut-out image used as required to make up the final page.

- *Re-sizing, distortion and rotation* of a given image are common features of EPC systems which allow full flexibility for imaginative page make up. The re-orientated image may then be used directly or stored and retrieved as required.

- *Montage* facilities will enable a number of separate images to be brought to the screen, manipulated and re-arranged to form a new original.

- *Image merging* will allow two or more separate images to blend in to each other under the operator's control until a satisfactory result is obtained.

- *Retouching* of the image electronically, either locally or overall enables the operator to alter details of the image to suit either the copy or the final print requirements.

- *Colour editing* allows the operator total freedom to modify the colour of any given area within the overall image. A delineated 'red' area may be changed to pink, blue or green as required.

- *Magnification* of selected areas of the image enables close inspection of detail for the purposes of examination and correction. In some instances a magnification of several 100 $\times$ is possible.

- *Pixel-by-pixel retouching* enables the most minute amount of information to be altered on the monitor. This combination of magnification, colour editing and retouching allows minor blemishes such as spots, scratches and other unwanted minutae to be meticulously corrected. Minor changes to the copy can also be carried out by this technique.

- *Electronic 'airbrushing'* allows a gradual build up of translucent or opaque colour over chosen areas of the subject to give special shading, tinting or haloing effects.

- *Seamless montages* can be created in some systems, where a repetitive design can be merged in to a continuous pattern on a one-piece cylinder without the 'seam' which would be evident where individual printing plates are butted against each other.

Outputting

Having composed the page the operator then has a number of options for further action including:

Storage

Storage of the composed information for future retrieval and use may be via disc or tape, depending on the convenience and economics of the system. Whole or part pages may be stored, retrieved and progressed as required nearer the time of printing and publication. Items such as repeat advertisements or 'standing' information may be committed to an 'archive' file for future use.

Proofing

In network systems the image may be sent to another monitor for approval, editing or correction, prior to processing. Where a print-out peripheral device is incorporated, such as an ink-jet or digital laser printer, a page proof may be obtained and sent for approval, editing or correction, before processing in the case of publications for example.

Processing

Processing here usually means the passing on of approved image information to an outputting device which will initiate the production of film negatives or positives for platemaking. In the instance of colour halftone work, this will include an outputting scanner to produce full-size, screened colour separations.

Platemaking

In some EPC systems the output may be used directly to make printing plates. These 'filmless' systems have the merit of economy of materials and speed of production. They are useful where the publication is mainly black and white with maybe some 'spot' colour, but full colour provision is possible if needed.

Complete cylinders

Complete cylinders may be produced for some printing processes such as gravure and flexography. The output from the EPC system may be used, in the case of a gravure publication for instance, to engrave a number of pages on a complete cylinder by means of multiple cutting heads. In other instances complete seamless cylinders may be produced for textiles, wall coverings or decorative laminates.

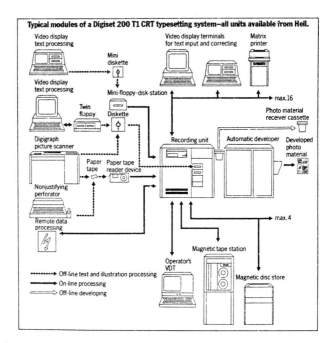

Figure 37   *Complete text setting system for page make-up. The Digiset CRT system Courtesy* D. Ing Rudolf Hell GmbH

5 Sheet-fed commercial printing

Desktop publishing has its limitations in sheet size, colour printing, image quality and mass production facilities; while in-plant production, as a captive service department of a parent organization, also has limitations in terms of the nature, quality and quantity of work which it may be produce.

Print purchasers who do not have their own means of originating copy or producing work internally will seek the services of a commercial printer, of which there are several thousand in the UK alone and several hundred thousand around the world.

The most common printing process in commercial use today is offset lithography, which is capable of producing high quality work at a reasonable cost for a wide range of printed products from posters to postage stamps and catalogues to cartons. It is estimated that there are more than a million offset litho presses around the world today, catering for printed work on sheet sizes from a few centimetres in width to more than one and a half metres.

This chapter explains the procedures employed to progress work through the various stages of sheet-fed offset litho production from the preparation and making of the litho plate to proofing, printing and finishing the work.

Plates and platemaking

The lithographic image may be produced in a number of ways and on a variety of base plate substrates. Paper and plastic bases can be used for small offset production, as referred to in the previous chapter. Thin-gauge aluminium may also be used for smaller presses; but for larger presses and longer runs a more substantial and stable base is required.

Originally zinc was used for litho plates, but these are now obsolete commercially. Aluminium is now the most common base for most litho plates due to its relative cheapness, stability and surface properties. Manufacturers will supply their plates already grained, anodized and coated.

Graining

Graining is the practice of roughening up the otherwise smooth surface of the plate so that it forms minute recesses which help to retain water in

Figure 38   *Checking a sheet at the delivery of a multicolour litho press*
Courtesy MAN/Roland

the non-image areas and acts as a key to the image itself. Traditionally carried out by placing plates on a vibrating table and covering them with a layer of metal balls and abrasive substances, this process is now most commonly carried out in-line on continuous rolls of aluminium by mechanical scrubbing and abrading (brush graining), electrochemical treatment, or a combination of both.

A fine balance needs to be established between the 'roughness' of the grain, which aids water retention and image keying, and the 'smoothness' which influences the degree of detail which can be held.

Anodizing

A 'raw' aluminium plate exposed to the atmosphere will automatically react with the oxygen in the air to form a film of aluminium oxide on its surface, which helps to protect it from other atmospheric or chemical attack. This natural effect is exploited by electrochemically treating the sheets or reels of aluminium so that a reinforced layer of aluminium oxide is deposited on the surface. This is referred to as the 'anodic' layer, which may be only a few hundredths of a millimetre (20–30 microns) in thickness. Anodizing therefore strengthens the surface of the plate and gives it added resistance to atmospheric and chemical attack and, as it is porous, enhances its water retaining properties.

Coating

Early lithographers made their own light sensitive coatings and applied them to the plate by hand or by means of a mechanical 'whirler' which spread the coating evenly over the surface. Today the great majority of plates are supplied pre-coated by the manufacturer as pre-sensitized plates (PSP). The first PSPs introduced around the middle of this century were based on light sensitive diazonium (diazo) compounds which were found to have greater uniformity due to batch production, longer 'shelf life' and consistent quality, including the ability to hold a good halftone dot.

Diazo coatings have continued to improve and still account for a high proportion of PSP production, but a number of other light sensitive coatings are now available including those based on tough photopolymer resins and others which combine the properties of both types of coating.

Positive or negative working plates

Plates may be exposed either to a negative film image or a positive film image, depending on the preferred method of working.

Negatives

Negatives are the normal, first-stage product from original copy via a camera, and it would seem obvious to use these to produce the plate. It is also easier to see minor spots, scratches and other blemishes in the non-image areas on a negative, and to correct these by 'spotting out' with an opaque medium.

Positives

Positives on the other hand are preferred by most planners as they are easier to see, particularly for superimposition of colour halftone images, but they may require a secondary exposure from the negatives and more detailed attention to the non-image areas to correct minor blemishes.

The nature of the coating and the method of working will depend largely on whether the plate is to be exposed to negatives or positives.

Printing down

Contacting

The plate, with its sensitized coating must next be brought into contact with the negative or positive. It is essential to ensure that total contact is made between the coated plate and the image on the surface (emulsion side) of the film. This takes place in a vacuum frame which holds the plate firmly on a rubber blanket with the 'flat' in close and precise contact, covered by a sheet of clear glass. Air is pumped out of the frame to ensure complete contact, before the exposure is made.

Exposing

Exposing through the film to the plate is by means of an ultra-violet-rich light source, such as xenon, mercury or metal halide lamps. These may be integral with the printing down frame or separate units depending on the preferred method of working. A second exposure may be necessary with positive working plates to ensure the elimination of film and tape edges, etc. via 'burn out' masks as described earlier.

The effect of exposure is to bring about a chemical change in the surface coating which enables the image and non-image areas to be established by further chemical treatment.

The nature of the coating will depend on whether the plate is to be exposed to a negative or positive image. In the case of negative working plates, light falls upon the image area and the effect of light is to harden the emulsion and key it to the plate. Subsequent 'development' by appropriate chemicals will reinforce the image and allow the unexposed, non-image emulsion areas to be washed away.

In positive working plates light falls upon the non-image areas and softens the coating. Subsequent development will reinforce the unexposed, image areas and allow the non-image emulsion areas to be washed away.

On most pre-sensitized plates a light sensitive dye will be included in the emulsion formula so that a latent image can be seen after exposure, but before development. This is helpful as the image can be checked for quality and any small blemishes corrected before the final image is developed.

Developing

Development is essentially a chemical process in which the coating in the image areas is reinforced and keyed to the plate surface, allowing the emulsion in the non-image areas to be washed away. Manual application of the developer is possible for comparatively small scale production, but care must be taken to ensure safety and health requirements. Chemicals used in some plate developers may give off toxic fumes therefore good ventilation should be provided and fume extraction included in the developing sink or table. Water-based developing systems are now available which improve the environment not only from the atmospheric point of view but also in respect of effluent disposal.

Washing out

Washing out is the process of removing the unhardened or softened coating from the plate. This is normally done by water spray, possibly assisted by gentle brushing. It is important that the unwanted coating is fully removed to avoid blemishes in the non-printing areas.

Desensitization

The non-image area is next treated with a solution based on gum arabic which performs the double function of protecting the aluminium surface due to its natural affinity and at the same time forming a water-receptive medium. This is performed by wiping over the plate with a gum solution, which will adhere to the non-image areas, but not to the image areas.

Inking-in

If the plate is not to be used immediately the image area should be protected with a purpose-made inking-in solution, which is applied to the plate by a wiping action and which will adhere to the image but not to the non-image areas.

Automatic plate processors

Automatic plate processors may be used for batch production or high volume work. The various steps of development, washing out, desensitization etc. are carried out in-line, in a fraction of the time taken to process plates manually. Automatic processing will also introduce a standard uniformity to processing as temperatures, times, chemicals and other variables may be more accurately controlled than with manual processing. Not all processors can cope with both positive and negative working plates, as these require different chemistry. Maintenance of the equipment, monitoring and replenishment of the chemicals, as well as the initial investment, must all be taken in to account when considering the purchase of an automatic processor.

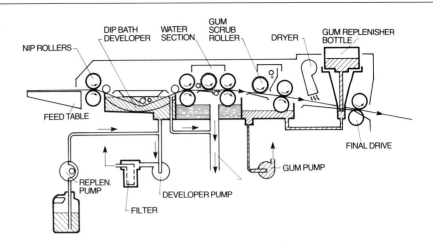

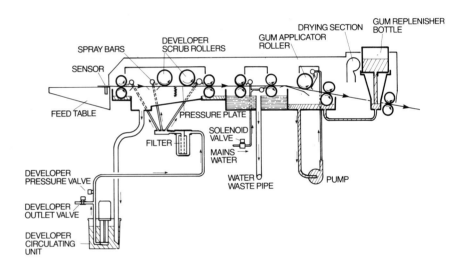

Figure 39 *Automatic platemaking. Presensitized litho plates can be processed automatically once they have been exposed to a film positive or negative. The chemistry and processing will vary, depending on whether the plates are positive-working or negative-working. (a) Flow diagram autopos. (b) Flow diagram autoneg*
Courtesy Howson Algraphy

Multimetal plates

A different approach to producing a lithographic image is based on the fact that different metals have varying degrees of receptivity to water and to printing ink. For instance etched chromium is water receptive and ink repellant; stainless steel has similar properties. Copper and brass on the other hand are ink receptive.

A typical multimetal plate might comprise a stainless steel base with a layer of copper formed by electrodeposition and a further layer of chromium electro deposited. A light-sensitive coating on top of the

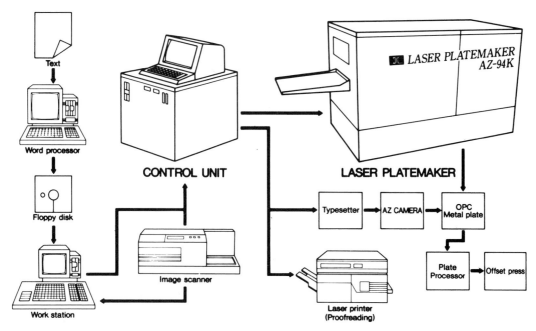

Figure 40 *Direct platemaking. Litho plates may be made directly, without the use of a camera or film. This illustration shows Polychrome's AZ laser platemaking system linked to a desktop publishing station*

chromium completes the plate in pre-sensitized form. Exposure to ultra-violet light, in a positive working situation, softens the coating, which may then be washed away to leave the chromium, non-image areas exposed, while the image areas are still protected. The chromium is then removed by a suitable etchant, to reveal the copper which will form the image. The coating on the remaining areas is then dissolved and removed to leave the plate ready for use.

There are a number of variations on this theme with various combinations of metals, but the main advantages of multi-metal plates are:

- The durability of the metal surfaces ensures long life of the plates, up to a million or more.
- The uncomplicated nature of the surfaces makes for cleaner printing with fewer problems.

Waterless plates   Another departure from the traditionally presensitized plate pattern is a lamination which includes a layer of siliconized rubber bonded to a photosensitive material on an aluminium base. The siliconized rubber will form the non-image areas and the photosensitive material will be developed to form the image area. Positive and negative versions are manufactured and the processing steps up to development are similar to those for other plates.

At the development stage the silicone rubber layer is removed from the image areas and the photosensitive layer is reinforced to form the ink receptive areas. The unique properties of the silicone layer cause it to reject ink, even without the presence of water; therefore this type of plate can be run on a lithographic press without need for a damping system.

Thermal hardening

Thermal hardening (baking) is the technique of heating the processed plate in an oven to harden the image area. This will increase the image life considerably, possibly up to two or three times the otherwise expected press life. It is important to have a totally 'clean' plate before baking, as the image becomes so permanent that any minor flaws will be difficult, if not impossible to correct subsequently. Plates should therefore be proofed and checked carefully so that any minor deletions or corrections may be undertaken before committing the plate to the oven.

Not all plates are suitable for baking, and there is no standard for time and temperature in the oven. Most manufacturers will supply guidelines for thermal hardening, including recommended oven temperatures and baking times, plus other considerations. In the absence of these, test plates should be tried with temperatures ranging from not less than 180°C to not more than 250°C, and times of not less than 5 minutes to not more than 15.

Proofs and proofing techniques

A proof is an intermediate document produced before the actual printing operation. There are various types and qualities of proofs depending on the purpose for which they are intended. They may be used *internally* as part of the planning, processing and quality control aspects of production, or they may be used *externally* for the information of the customer who may wish to have a preview of the finished work.

Simple proofs

Simple proofs are mainly monochrome or line work and could be the direct output from a desktop system, a text setter, a camera or other preprinting source. Where the text is intended to be checked for 'literal' qualities only, i.e., spelling, punctuation, arrangement, etc. a simple photocopy may suffice. However, where the 'image' quality is to be examined, i.e., definition, colour density or tonal properties, it may be necessary to produce an 'ink-on-paper' proof from printing plates.

Press proofs

Press proofs are produced on specially designed proof presses, which simulate the printing press conditions. The printing plates produced for this purpose may not necessarily be the plates to be used on the printing press, as part of the purpose of proofing is to check the quality of the work and to make alterations if necessary.

Proof presses

Proof presses have a different basic design from lithographic *printing presses*. On most proof presses the plate is laid upon a flat bed instead of a cylinder, as this allows for a wider range of plate sizes and types to be accommodated. Having the plate on a flat bed also allows for easier inspection by the proofer and better facility for altering and controlling variables as well as carrying out minor corrections.

On simple models it may be necessary to dampen and ink the plate by manual means, but it is more common to have travelling sets of rollers, under motorized control, which first dampen and then ink the plate as they pass along the bed of the press. The inked image is then picked up by a rubber blanket covered cylinder which traverses the bed on the return journey and transfers its image to the paper or other substrate, which is positioned at another bed in line with the plate bed.

Control of 'variables'

It is important that the proofer is able to adjust and establish as many variable factors as possible, in order to establish the best values in each instance, including:

- *Position* (register) of the plate and the substrate to the press and to each other. Calibrated, micrometer adjustment is essential for colour halftone work, combined with firm and positive location of the plate and substrate to the bed of the press.
- *Pressure* between the plate and the blanket, and between the blanket and the substrate is usually controlled by varying the height of the bed by means of a fine screw-threaded mechanism. Variations in pressure, in both instances, will affect the transfer of ink and the size of halftone dots; therefore the pressures should be quantifiable for future reference.
- *Inking and damping*. Precision setting of the inking and damping rollers to the plate is essential. The balance between the applied films of damping solution and ink is a critical factor in determining colour values and image strength. It is important that this information is quantified and recorded.

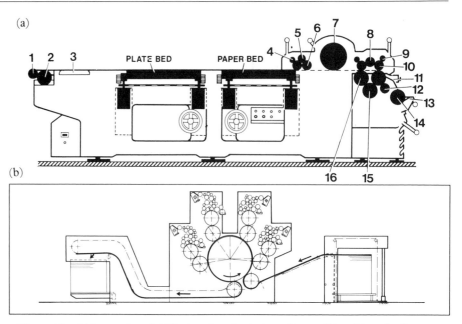

Figure 41   *Litho proofing. (a) Single-colour flat-bed proof press. Disposition of rollers:*

1	Water scavenger	9	Inking rider
2	Water roller	10	Inking roller
3	Damping table	11	Wash-up device
4	Damping rider	12	Transfer roller – optional
5	Intermediate damping roller	13	Ductor knife – optional
6	Damping roller	14	Ductor roller – optional
7	Blanket	15	Intermediate roller
8	Inking oscillator	16	Oscillating roller

(b) Four-colour rotary 'wet-on-wet' proof press
Courtesy Littlejohn Graphic systems and Fag SA Lausanne

Colour proofing

For colour halftone work it is essential to have the press set to the finest precision standards. The slightest variation in dot size due to different pressures, ink variations etc. will misrepresent the tonal values of the image. The tiniest false movement of the substrate, plate or blanket will result in visible misregister of the superimposed colours.

Substrates and inks

Substrates and inks should be matched to those of the production run. Although this may seem obvious to the layman, it is still not uncommon to see proofs which have been pulled on superior printing stock and 'special' inks to produce the best possible result, which the printer cannot possibly match under production conditions. Traditionally, proofs were seen as 'targets' which the machine printer aimed to reproduce. Current thinking is that the proof should attempt to give as realistic an impression as possible of the way the job will finally look when it comes from the printing press.

Colour sequence

The order in which the colours are superimposed will influence the appearance of the final result. There is no 'standard' sequence for printing the four colours – yellow, cyan, magenta and black. Some individual firms and other organizations have 'preferred' sequences, and it should be noted that there are often occasions where more than four colours are required. It may be necessary for the proofer to try a variation of sequences in order to achieve the best results to match the artwork.

Whatever sequence is finally decided, the proofer will produce a 'progressive' set of proofs showing the individual colours and their progressive superimposition. This will act as a guide to the machine printer who will print the work in the same sequence.

Control strips

Control strips will usually be included in the margins to enable both proofer and printer to measure factors such as ink density, trapping, dot size, register, etc.

Limitations of press proofing

At its best proofing can only *simulate* the press conditions. Even if the identical plates, inks and substrates are used there are variables which the flatbed proof press cannot reproduce accurately:

- *The printing 'cycle'* of damping, inking, blanket impression and substrate impression will be different in many subtle respects.
- *The dwell time,* or speed with which the blanket cylinder traverses the plate and then the paper will almost certainly be slower on a proof press and this will affect pick up and lay down of ink on paper and plate. A web-fed press will print several hundred times as fast as a proof press.
- *Overprinting* of colours on a proof press will take time. The proofer will normally produce a batch of proofs of the first colour down, once the optimum quality has been established; remove the first plate, wash up the press, re-ink for the next colour, put the second plate in position and start all over again. There will be a significant difference in time between first and subsequent printings, during which the ink will have had time to 'set' or dry. On a multicolour sheet-fed or web-fed press one colour is printed almost instantaneously upon another in a 'wet-on-wet' situation.
- *Curving the plate* around the cylinder of a printing press will cause a slight distortion in the image as compared with the flat plate.

Multi-colour proof presses

Multi-colour proof presses have been developed to overcome some of these problems. These come one step nearer to simulating the actual press conditions as plates are curved around cylinders and colours are overprinted wet-on-wet. Production time is improved on some by having automatic feed and delivery of the sheets to the press instead of the time-consuming hand laying method of the traditional flat-bed proof press. In effect, the more sophisticated this type of proof press becomes, the more it resembles a production press.

Non-press proofs

The production of press proofs is an expensive business; proof presses are major items of capital equipment, they are slow and they are labour intensive. The cost of producing a press proof may be more than a hundred times the 'per item' cost of the final print, and with all of this the end result may still be only an approximation of the job as it will be finally produced. For these reasons alternative methods of producing proofs have been developed, which have the advantages of lower capital cost, faster production and simplicity. Several have the facility to modify variables such as dot size, density, etc. Non-press proofs fall into the following categories:

Film laminates

Film laminates are based on sheets of light-sensitive coloured film matched to the same standards as printing inks. Exposure to the appropriate colour separations and subsequent development will produce four-coloured, transparent separations which can be laminated in precise register for viewing either against a white substrate background or in a transparency viewing booth.

Pigment/toner laminates

Pigment/toner laminates build up successive layers of coloured images on a white base substrate. A transparent, light sensitive film is laminated to the base and exposed to the first colour separation. This leaves the image area receptive to a coloured pigment powder matched to the appropriate printing ink, which is dusted across the film to adhere to the image. Any excess dust is removed. A second film is then laminated over the first, exposed to the next colour separation, dusted, cleaned and so on until the complete proof is attained.

Ink-on-paper proofs

Ink-on-paper proofs can be made on either a 'standard' base or the actual job stock. The base is first coated with a light-sensitive, water based ink of the desired colour. Exposure to the appropriate colour separation will fix the inked image areas to the substrate. The ink in the non-image areas can then be washed away leaving the coloured image on the base. A second coating then follows and the procedure is repeated until the complete proof is obtained. 'Special' colours or non-standard inks can also be used.

Ink-jet proofs

Ink-jet-proofs are based on the principles of ink-jet printing, whereby fine droplets of ink are forced through apertures and deflected to the appropriate areas on the substrate via microprocessor control. Practically any substrate can be used and computerized control makes this type of proofing system suitable for use in conjunction with colour scanners and studio systems. Ink droplets are just a few microns in diameter and they can be applied under high pressure at the rate of many thousands of droplets per second, per colour. Resolutions in the order of 100 dots per centimetre are currently possible.

Video proofs

Video proofs ('soft' proofs) give a preview of the work while it is in progress. A high resolution colour monitor is located at a suitable station in the system and programmed to display images in graphic arts terms with respect to dots, or lines per centimetre, and proportions of colours in terms of yellow, magenta and cyan percentages. These may be linked to cable or network systems for viewing at more than one point and may also have provision for hard copy printouts.

Electrostatic colour proofing

Electrostatic colour proofing is based initially on the same principles as monochrome electrostatic copiers, in that charged particles are deposited on a substrate with the opposite charge. However the definition and degree of control necessary to produce an acceptable colour proof are of a far higher standard than the normal office copier. Computerized, high resolution laser printers are the basis of these devices, and this makes them particularly suitable for use in conjunction with colour scanners, where the digitized information in the scanner can be used to produce the colour proof.

PRESSES

Most sheet-fed printing these days is by offset lithography. There is a superficial resemblance between the 'small offset' presses described in Chapter 3 and the larger versions used for commercial printing. The distinction between small and large offset is not clear cut, but in this chapter we are concerned with *larger sheet sizes*, A2 and above, *multicolour work* and *longer-run commercial production*.

A typical offset lithographic press will comprise three main elements:

1 The sheet feeder, which holds the bulk paper stock and issues sheets one at a time to the printing units.
2 The printing units, which will comprise plate, blanket and impression cylinders, plus inking and damping arrangements.
3 Sheet transport and delivery.

There may of course be a number of printing units in line, plus operations in addition to printing. This section deals first with the basic construction of a typical offset lithographic printing press, second with the ways in which they are put together and third with special considerations for particular types of presses.

The sheet feeder

The paper table

The first requirement is a paper table to hold the bulk stack of paper or board, etc. This needs to be sturdy and capable of supporting a substantial load, bearing in mind that a thousand sheets of A1 size carton board could weigh more than half a tonne, and a metre high pile could be consumed in less than 5 minutes at maximum speed.

For these reasons it is necessary to build in:

- An automatic pile raising mechanism, based on a sensing device which detects the position of the top sheet in the pile and raises the paper table as sheets are consumed.
- A quick changeover system as the stack is depleted. On most presses it is possible to truck in a press pile to replace the expiring stack, without stopping the press.

Sheet separator

The second requirement is a sheet separator. This is usually a set of pneumatic suckers and ancillary equipment, designed to separate the top sheet in the pile and forward it to the press. The most common technique is to blow air through the top few layers of the stack in order to give an initial separation; the top sheet is then isolated from the rest and the pneumatic suckers will pick up the top sheet and forward it to the press. For general-purpose work the separator may be required to cope with a variety of stock ranging from air mail paper to carton board.

Two basic types of sheet separators are in common use. First, the 'front separator' in which sheets are separated and forwarded from the front (gripper) edge. This is a simple and efficient system for smaller sizes of sheets, and can operate at up to ten thousand sheets per hour. However, this method does have a disadvantage when it comes to larger sheet sizes, as the suckers cannot pick up a second sheet until the first sheet has passed.

For this reason the 'back separation' technique is employed, in which the sheets are separated at the rear of the pile. The advantage here is that the second sheet can be picked up as soon as the first sheet has cleared the back edge. Sheets can therefore be forwarded to the presses in a continuous overlapping shingle. This type of sheet feeder is often referred to as a 'stream' feeder, which may be capable of feeding even the largest sheets at up to 15,000 per hour.

Having separated and forwarded the individual sheets, it is now essential to ensure that they are presented accurately to the printing unit. Standard practice is to locate the sheets firstly to a set of front stops or 'lays' and then to a side lay position. At this stage it is important to check that:

- Sheets are actually presented to the press; therefore a sheet/no sheet detector must be provided to avoid the press running on without paper in the system.
- Not more than one sheet is presented; therefore double or multiple sheet detectors are included.
- Sheets are located accurately at the stops, within the tolerance for the particular printing purpose, which in the instance of multicolour halftone printing could be less than 0.1 of a millimetre.

The printing units

There are three main cylinders in a typical offset litho printing unit: the plate cylinder; the blanket or offset cylinder; and the impression cylinder. An inking and damping system will complete the unit.

Plate cylinders

The plate cylinder must have provision for quickly and accurately locating the printing plate. This is normally by means of front and rear clamps which grip the ends of the plate and tension it around the cylinder. Provision for fine adjustment is usually necessary in order to accurately register one print with another, and a stud or pin locating arrangement may be provided for instant location of the plate, where this has been provided for at the planning and platemaking stage.

The emphasis on precision also applies to the caliper of the plate. Most presses have bearer rings at the ends of the cylinders and these indicate the pitch circle of the gears which drive the cylinders. The height of the bearer ring is a guide to the correct caliper of the plate plus any packing. It is worth noting at this point that if a plate should be under or overpacked by as little as 0.1 mm this could result in an overall circumferential variation of more than 0.3 mm, which is well outside the register tolerance for colour halftone printing.

Blanket cylinders

The blanket cylinder, as with the plate cylinder, must have provision for quickly and accurately mounting the blanket. Correct caliper is again essential, as the thickness of the blanket will affect the quality of ink transfer from the plate, as well as the image length. The bearer ring again gives a guide to the caliper of the blanket, together with its packing, and allowance must be made for the resilience of the blanket in order to ensure correct transfer of ink. Tensioning the blanket around the cylinder is also critical, as a slack blanket will give rise to faults such as slur and doubling, while overtensioning could stretch and distort the blanket.

The essential properties of a blanket need to be understood. The surface must be receptive to ink from the printing plate and at the same time easily release the ink to the printing stock. Tolerance of oils and solvents is important and rapid recovery from impressional force is essential. The blanket must be firm enough to receive ink from the plate and resilient enough to withstand the pressure which is necessary to transfer the ink.

Types of blanket

There are a number of types and makes of blankets, and choice depends largely on the class of work undertaken. Initially a blanket comprises a backing of fabric plies, usually cotton, bonded with adhesive to provide stability, plus a top layer of synthetic rubber to receive and transfer ink from the plate. The surface 'hardness' of the blanket is a critical property, and this is usually measured in degrees Shore, where a hundred degrees is glass hard and nought degrees is vacuum resistance.

A *soft blanket* would be graded at 70–75°S and is suitable for rough-surfaced papers, where light impression is required and for slower presses such as proof presses and where a wide variety of plates, printing stocks and types of work are undertaken.

A *medium blanket* would be around 75° and is the standard, general-purpose blanket, adequate for most commercial printing purposes.

A *hard blanket* would be from 75 to 80°S and would be chosen for best quality work, long runs, heavy solids, coated stock and high-speed presses.

Offset blankets may also be defined as either 'conventional' or 'compressible'. The conventional blanket, as described earlier, will distort under the pressure which is essential in order to transfer ink from the plate and then to the printing stock. This results in a travelling 'bulge' of surface rubber being formed around the printing nip area. Compressible blankets on the other hand contain a layer of spongy, cellular material which allows the blanket to be truly compressed rather than distorted out of shape. This type of blanket has the added advantages of fast response from impression on high-speed presses and rapid recovery from 'smashes' in the event of multiple sheets entering the printing nip.

Proper choice, care, maintenance and replacement of blankets is essential for good quality work and maximum efficiency, for it must be remembered that it is the blanket which finally places the inked image on to the printing stock.

Impression cylinders

The impression cylinder carries the sheets through the nip, where the ink is finally transferred under pressure to the printing stock. This is the moment of truth where the smallest dots, the finest lines, the lightest tints and the heaviest solids are laid upon the paper. The slightest variation in pressures, packings, inking, clamping, will be recorded. The tiniest judder of a gear, a pin prick fault in a blanket or plate, an imprecise setting of a roller or damper, will all be recorded at this juncture.

A set of grippers will take the sheet as it is presented to the impression cylinder and will release the sheet to the transport system after printing. The timing of the opening and closing of these grippers is critical in order to ensure accurate register and fault-free sheet transport. The grippers must hold the sheet firmly, but without damaging it and it should be noted that the section of the sheet held by the grippers cannot be printed upon – a factor which needs to be understood when ordering, designing and planning work for sheet-fed printing.

Inking

Lithographic inks are viscous liquids based on a resinous 'vehicle' which forms the body of the ink. Pigments are dispersed within the resin to give the ink its hue and additives such as solvents, and dryers to give the ink specific properties.

The ink supply on the press is normally held in a container called a 'duct' which in its simplest form comprises a flexible steel blade positioned at an angle to a metal roller. As the roller turns a thin film of ink is fed through the gap between blade and roller, and this gap can be varied laterally across the duct by screw thread adjustments to the blade. In addition to this lateral adjustment an overall variation in ink flow can

106 *Printing*

be arranged by varying the speed of rotation of the duct roller. Ink is then taken to the main roller train, usually by a rubber covered 'transfer' roller which travels between the duct and the first roller in the train.

The ink is then milled between a series of metal and rubber rollers, some of which reciprocate laterally across the press in order to completely break down the 'structure' of the ink. This will ensure that the ink is finally deposited on the plate as a thin, regulated film of just a few microns thickness, according to the needs of the image. The efficiency of this 'distribution' section of an inking system will depend to a degree on the number of rollers in the system and the total surface area of the rollers.

The final ink film is usually applied to the plate by at least two rubber covered plate inkers and more often by three or four inkers. These rollers will be of different diameters in order to ensure a complete and even coverage of the image without risk of a pattern developing which may give rise to the problems of ink repeat, ghosting and colour variation along the image. Press designers will use computer simulation techniques for determining the numbers, positions and diameters of rollers in an inking system in order to ensure maximum efficiency of ink film transfer with the minimum number of rollers.

A number of additional refinements may be included in the inking system such as automatic wash up on the system, cooling devices to avoid over-heating which may occur owing to the frictional forces involved in ink film splitting and remote control of the ink regulating keys.

Damping

The damping solution is applied to the plate in order to moisten the non-image areas sufficiently to reject ink, but not sufficiently to invade the image areas.

Conventionally the damping solution is carried to the plate by a series of rollers, starting with a metal 'fountain' or 'pan' roller revolving in the supply reservoir. Moisture is picked up from here by a transfer roller which travels intermittently between the fountain and the plate dampers. This roller is usually covered with a 'sleeve' of absorbent material such as the standard cotton 'molleton' material and the amount of moisture carried over will depend partly on the properties of the covering material and partly on the 'dwell' time between the transfer roller and the fountain roller, which can usually be varied to suit press conditions. Two plate damping rollers are usually provided, again covered with an absorbent material, and these are connected by a 'rider' roller, which receives moisture from the transfer roller. Care, maintenance and adjustment of all of these rollers requires meticulous attention if the damping of the plate is to be successful.

The conventional damping system, as described above, is quite adequate for most general purposes, but it does have some limitations. Maintenance and recovering of dampers is time-consuming and expensive;

loose particles from the molleton covering can invade the printing surfaces to cause minor blemishes or 'hickeys'. Under certain circumstances a 'surge' damping pattern will occur caused mainly by the intermittent action of the transfer roller. The traditional system is also slow to respond to changes in press conditions and the printing environment. For these reasons there is a trend towards simpler and more continuous damping systems which do not rely on molleton covered rollers or the intermittent travel of transfer rollers.

A typical continuous 'bareback' damping system may comprise only four rollers: a variable-speed chrome-covered fountain roller running in contact with a rubber-covered rider roller, which transfers solution to a second chrome roller, probably reciprocating laterally across the press and then to a single rubber-covered plate damper. Evidently if the fountain roller has a variable speed of rotation then the train of rollers cannot be in firm contact at all times. For this reason a slight gap is allowed between the damp supply rollers, sufficient to allow independent rotation of the fountain roller and its rider, but close enough to ensure moisture transfer across the gap. The amount of damping solution transferred will therefore depend first on the rate of rotation of the fountain roller and second on the precise settings between the rollers.

At this point it is important to emphasize that the damping solution is not just water, but a carefully balanced aqueous solution containing a number of additives which are necessary to the effective dampening of the plate. These include antifoamants and anticorrosives; salts and buffering agents to maintain the desired pH (acidity) of the solution, antibacteriants and, most important of all in some respects, alcohols and surfactants to reduce the surface tension of the liquid so that the plate is smoothly and evenly 'wetted'. The correct balance of these ingredients must be maintained at all times during the press run in order to ensure consistent results: open fountains may be affected by atmospheric and other conditions, alcohol will evaporate at a faster rate than the basic water solution and temperature changes will affect the rate of evaporation, flow properties, etc. For these reasons it is desirable to have a circulating supply system in which the solution is continuously pumped from a bulk supply, recirculated, filtered for cleanliness and 'dosed' as necessary in order to keep the balance right at all times.

Sheet transport   There are two basic mechanical methods of transferring the sheets from one part of the press to the next. The first is by chain and gripper trolleys in which the sheet is held in one set of grippers between transfers, and the second is cylinder to cylinder transfer in which the sheet is passed from one cylinder to the next.

The chain and gripper method has the merit of lower cost, simplicity and fewer transfers; however, sheet support is not always positive and 'flutter' could occur, which would be a particular problem with flimsy stock. The cylinder-to-cylinder method is more expensive from an

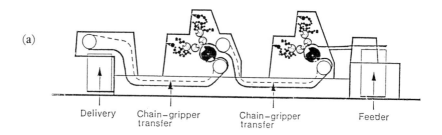

Figure 42 *Sheet transport. (a) Chain and gripper transport. (b) Cylinder-to-cylinder transport*
Courtesy Keonig and Bauer

engineering point of view, but it does ensure that the sheets are positively supported at all stages. However this system usually means more gripper changeovers, and where the 'wet' face of the work is presented to a cylinder it will be necessary to ensure that either the ink is properly 'set' or that contact with the cylinder is not so firm as to cause ink transfer with subsequent marking up and set-off problems.

For thicker and more rigid stock such as board, it is important that impression and transfer cylinders are not so small in circumference that sheets are distorted as they press around them. For this reason several manufacturers provide 'jumbo' size cylinders on their presses, which make them particularly suitable for carton printing and similar work.

Delivery

Sheets are finally deposited on to a delivery board, which is a mirror image of the feeder board; as the feeder board rises, so the delivery board lowers. Sheets are 'jogged' in to position by moving plates which push the sheets in to a neat pile, and arrangement is made for trucking out completed stacks of paper. Continuous 'non-stop' pile changing should also be provided for maximum production.

One essential requirement of a sheet delivery system is that the sheets should not 'set-off' in the delivery pile, i.e., wet ink from one sheet should not transfer to another. This can be arranged in a number of ways:

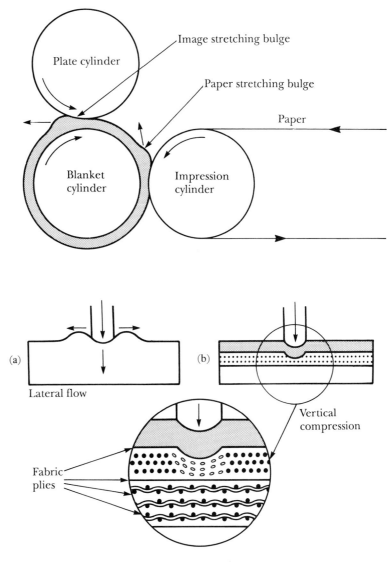

Figure 43 *Litho blankets. (a) Conventional rubber blankets will distort under printing pressure. (b) Compressible blankets are designed to give under pressure rather than distort Courtesy* Dunlop

1 Sheets can be taken out or 'boxed' in small batches before the weight of the pile is sufficient to cause set-off.
2 A fine 'anti-set-off' powder can be sprayed on to each sheet as it arrives at the delivery, and
3 'Radiation' dryers, such as infra-red, ultra-violet or electron beam can be sited prior to the delivery in order to 'cure' the ink before it is delivered to the pile.

The choice of technique will depend largely on the class of work being printed.

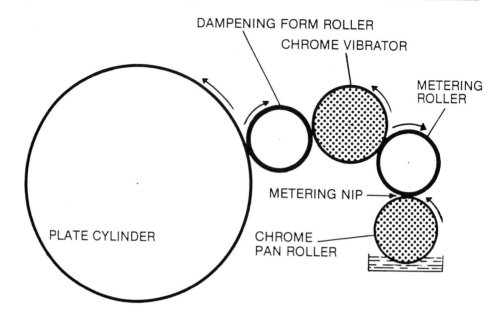

DAMPENING FORM ROLLER
CHROME VIBRATOR
METERING ROLLER
PLATE CYLINDER
METERING NIP
CHROME PAN ROLLER

Figure 44   *Damping. Typical arrangement of a four-roller 'bareback' damping system*

A second essential requirement of a delivery system is that sheets must be constantly available for inspection. Mere 'sighting' of the sheets as they arrive at the delivery pile is not sufficient. Arrangements must be made for sheets to be extracted from the delivery for detailed inspection both visually and by electronic inspection devices. On some presses an in-line electronic inspection system can be installed to constantly monitor the sheets as they reach the delivery area.

Types of presses

There are four basic types of sheet-fed press: single-colour; perfector; multicolour (more than one); and convertible.

Single-colour presses

Single-colour presses are 'maids of all work' in that they may be required to cope with every class of work from single-colour one-side work to two-sided printing and multicolour-process work. Sheets may be put through just once for the simplest type of work, such as a monochrome poster; they may be turned over and printed on the reverse for publication work; or they may be passed through the press several times where multicolour work is required. Two or more single-colour presses may be used in 'batteries' for quicker backing up or for speedier production of multicolour work.

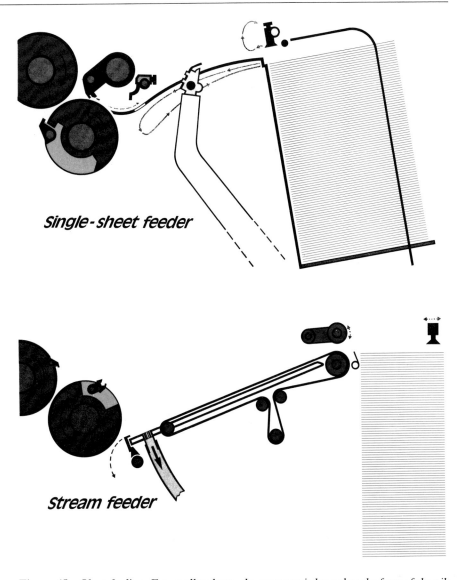

Figure 45 *Sheet feeding. For smaller sheets, the separator is located at the front of the pile and will forward one sheet at a time to the press. For larger sheets it is more efficient to locate the separator at the rear of the pile and feed the sheets in an overlapped stream to the press* *Courtesy* Heidelberg

Perfectors

Perfectors are the obvious choice where work needs to be printed on both sides of a sheet, such as monochrome publications, magazines, books and similar work. Since 'wet' work is being backed up instantaneously it is important to ensure that ink from the first side printed does not transfer to the impression cylinder of the second unit to cause the problem of 'second impression set-off'.

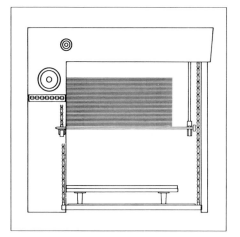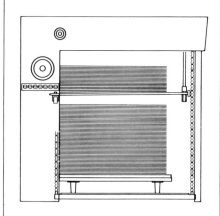

Figure 46 *Continuous pile changing on MAN/Roland presses. (a) Residual pile taken over by carrier rods with pile carrier plate lowered. (b) Pile change while machine is running*

A common design arrangement is to have the first printing unit as that for a single-colour press and the second unit designed in a reverse manner in order to print on the opposite side of the sheet. Sheet transport and delivery need to be carefully considered, bearing in mind that both sides of the sheet will be 'wet'. Only one side of the sheet will be visible in the delivery, therefore an efficient sheet inspection arrangement is essential. This type of press is only really justified where the majority of its time is spent on printing monochrome publications or similar types of work. The development of convertible presses (described later) has led to a decline in the demand for perfectors.

Multicolour presses

Multicolour presses come in a variety of designs. The most obvious method is to arrange a series of single-colour units in line, and to take the sheets from one unit to the next in progression. An alternative and not uncommon method is to arrange the press in 'pairs' of units in which two blanket cylinders print upon a 'common' impression cylinder; this has the advantages of compactness and fewer changeovers. Two two-colour presses working in tandem may be a useful arrangement to cope with a wide variety of work such as multicolour publications and allow flexibility of production, particularly where production capacity is limited and the breakdown or stoppage of one unit would be critical.

Convertible presses

Convertible presses are multi-unit presses which can be converted from one-sided, multicolour work to two-sided, perfected work. There are a

Figure 47 *The 'convertible' press. Sheets may either pass straight through the press to print two colours on one side, or the 'perfecting' mechanism may be engaged to enable two-sided printing*
Courtesy Miller-Johannesberg GmbH

number of variations on this theme and most major manufacturers now include convertibles in their 'stable' of presses. The basic idea revolves around a mechanism between given printing units, which reverses the direction of travel of the printed sheet so that it is presented tail-end first to the next unit for perfecting purposes. The benefits of this technique are particularly advantageous to printing houses which undertake a variety of publication work, requiring quick and frequent changes from multicolour printing to perfected work.

Convertible presses are sometimes criticized for the fact that the reverse edge of the sheet is fed in to the perfecting units, which is against the basic principle of always feeding sheets in to the same 'lay' edges. This requires in the first instance, precision cutting of the sheeted stock to ensure that there is no variation in register owing to changes in paper size from one batch to the next. It is also necessary to accept that the 'back-up' register, between one side of a sheet and the other, is never quite so critical as that between subsequent multicolour printing on the same side of the sheets.

Wet-on-wet printing

The technique of multicolour printing in line, requires the understanding of a few basic principles.

Optical principles

The optical effect of multicolour halftone printing depends on two ink/paper relationships:

1 'Process' printing inks are transparent and are laid as a series of 'films' on the substrate. The observed colour in 'solid' areas is therefore the result of looking at white paper through the overlaid coloured ink films, and not as a result of the physical mixing of the inks.

2 In the lighter tonal areas, the 'image' comprises many small dots, often of varying sizes and possibly more than a hundred to each square centimetre. In this instance the human eye is unable to discern individual dots and therefore observes the overall effect of the mixture of white paper and coloured dots as a range of hues, shades and tones.

Physical ink properties

The ability to lay one transparent ink film upon another depends not only on optical and chemical properties, but physical properties as well. Critical among these is the factor of ink adhesion or 'tack'. It is obvious that the first ink laid down must have a greater affinity for the substrate than for the offset blanket if it is to transfer efficiently to the stock. The second ink may not transfer entirely to the substrate, but must lay upon the first film of ink. To ensure efficient transfer the first ink film must be tackier than the second in order to 'trap' the second film of ink. Subsequent inks will also be tack graded to ensure that each subsequent film is efficiently transferred layer upon layer from unit to unit. It hardly needs to be said that if ink tacks were not strictly measured and controlled on multicolour presses, a reverse situation could occur in which ink transfers *to* the blanket *from* the previous printed film, resulting in 'back trapping' and a muddying of colour values.

Register tolerances

Bearing in mind that there may be more than 100 dots of varying colours in every square centimetre, it is evident that the margin which can be allowed for error is very small, and this applies as much to the machine printing situation as to the preprinting areas. Printed dots may be less than 0.2 mm apart and smaller than 0.01 mm in diameter. Printing presses and their components and accessories must be designed to work within these tolerances.

Substrate stability

It will follow from the previous paragraphs that the printing substrate needs to be stable within the tolerances prescribed. Unfortunately most paper and board stocks are 'hygroscopic', i.e., they will take in moisture from the atmosphere, and this will affect their physical dimensions. The most critical atmospheric property is relative humidity (Rh) which refers to the actual amount of moisture in the air expressed as a proportion of the maximum amount that could be held. The Rh may vary as temperature and other factors change. A 5 per cent change in Rh may cause an RA1 sheet to change by more than 5 mm, which is 100 times the register tolerance for colour halftone work. The lesson here is two-fold: one, ensure that printing stocks are not subject to undue atmospheric variations and two, install an air-conditioning system to keep atmospheric conditions stable.

Physical stress my also distort the substrate. The pressure on a sheet of carton board, for instance, as it presses through the printing nip, may be sufficient to compress it to a smaller caliper and spread it to a larger area, not necessarily in a straight-line proportion. With careful product testing for given substrates, this distortion may be predicted and taken in to account at the pre-press and planning stages, and allowed for when setting up the press.

Non-printing operations

As with the smaller presses described in Chapter 3 it may be desirable to carry out in-line operations such as slitting, numbering, perforating, etc. Several manufacturers also offer the facility of a 'coating' unit which will protect the final printed sheets with a liquid polymer film for added protection and superior finish. This adds even more to the final 'wet' ink film weight and will require specialist drying facilities in line. Radiation drying by means of infra-red, ultra-violet or electron beam radiation will need to be installed between the final coating unit and the delivery in order to ensure that sheets are fully dry before being laid one upon another.

There is also an increasing emphasis on keeping the press moving and not stopping the whole operation in order to carry out minor tasks such as cleaning blankets, washing impression cylinders, picking detritus from inking rollers, etc. For these reasons, manufacturers will provide blanket washers, etc. which will carry out these operations while the press is 'idling', i.e., running without sheets passing through, but still allowing the functions to be maintained. This will allow an immediate re-start of printing without going through a complete fresh start-up programme.

Press controls

Early offset litho presses had no control 'panels' as such. There were, of course, electrical provisions somewhere on the press for starting and stopping, as well as speeding up and slowing down. Most other operations such as feeding sheets, stopping sheet feed, applying damping solution, setting ink flow, applying ink, putting printing cylinders into pressure, adjusting lateral and circumferential register, and the myriad of other adjustments had to be performed manually at the appropriate press location. As a result, much of the printers' time was spent running up and down the press line, pulling levers, pushing buttons, adjusting keys, depressing pedals and making other physical adjustments to the press in order to maintain an equilibrium between the multiplicity of press variables.

On single-colour small offset presses, making adjustments locally is not unreasonable; but on large multicolour installations it is now essential to have a centralized control system whereby the printer can; in the first instance initiate all of the electromechanical functions of the press, such as sheet feeding, damping, inking and impression and, in the second instance, exercise control over print variables such as register, ink film thickness, damp film feed and so on for each variable on each press unit. The ideal location for a centralized press control panel is at the delivery end of the press, where the printer can examine a sheet as soon as it has reached the end of its travel, and initiate any corrections immediately variations are observed.

There are four distinct levels of press control:

Level 1   The printer physically carries out the adjustments to each variable, locally at each station along the press.

Level 2   Remote control facilities are provided whereby the printer can examine sheets and initiate corrections from a 'central' point. This may apply to some or all press variables.

Level 3   The delivered sheet is presented for electronic examination by comparison with predetermined quality factors, such as a 'pass sheet'. The printer observes any deviations from the standard and initiates correction procedures via remote control.

Level 4   Electronic inspection devices are installed at the delivery of the press to compare the delivered copies with the approved standard. Any variations observed will automatically be corrected, unless overriden by the printer.

Evidently level 3 and level 4 press control systems will require a high degree of sophisticated electronic equipment to be included, not only at the control desk but also integrated into the press structure. At these levels it is also possible to include additional factors such as:

- Presetting of all variables prior to the press run.
- Automatic sequencing of operations for rapid start-ups.
- Recording press-run information for repeat runs.
- 'Prediction' of corrections to variables, due to changes in press and environment conditions as the run progresses.

PRINT FINISHING

Having printed the job, the sheets now pass to the print finishing department, (often referred to as the 'warehouse'), for treatment and make-up in to the final form for dispatch to the customer. It is worth noting at this point that this department has a role to play prior to printing, as it is here that paper and other stock are ordered, stored and issued to the machine room. Close liaison is essential between the estimating, printing and finishing departments to ensure accurate ordering of stock, avoiding wasteful overordering or underordering. Careful storage and handling of stock is equally essential to avoid loss, damage or distortion of papers and boards.

The major operations in this area include: cutting, folding, assembling and make-up into books, magazines, etc. In addition to these there is a multiplicity of operations including: foil stamping, thermographing, embossing, varnishing, laminating punching, drilling, perforating, numbering, gumming and so on.

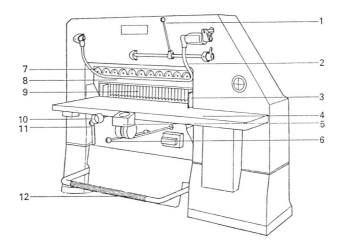

Figure 48 *Basic construction of a guillotine*

1	Starting handle	7	Knife beam
2	Sweep away guard	8	Knife
3	Side plates	9	Back gauge
4	Bed or table	10	Fine adjustment control
5	Magnifying tape reader	11	Backgauge locking lever
6	Back gauge control handle	12	Clamp foot-control pedal

Courtesy Arthur Martin

Cutting

Cutting or trimming single sheets of paper can be done by simple, hand-operated devices which are comparatively uncomplicated and inexpensive. However the cutting of bulk quantities of paper requires the use of a power guillotine.

Power guillotines

Guillotines are heavy-duty machines of solid construction capable of cutting through thick piles of paper with great precision and consistency. Safety precautions are important and all guillotines are required by law to include mechanical, electrical and/or photoelectrical devices to ensure that the machines cannot function when the operator's hands are in the cutting zone.

The basic parts of a power guillotine are:

The paper table

The paper table, which is a solid steel base, accurately machined and levelled to provide a stable working surface for the cutting operation. The table may be provided with an 'air cushion' in which ball-bearings are sunk below the bed level and supported by air pressure to ease the movement of piles of paper around the table.

Plates

Back and side plates are provided to locate the piles of paper accurately in position for cutting. These should be stable and adjustable to a fine degree, consistent with the required tolerances.

Paper clamp

The paper clamp firmly secures the back edge of the pile of paper prior to cutting, to ensure that no movement occurs during the cutting action.

Knife

The knife is a heavy-duty blade which cuts the pile once it has been clamped in position. The profile of the knife, and its cutting action are critical to the efficient and continued performance of the operation. Most guillotines now employ the 'dip-shear' action, in which the knife approaches the pile at an angle slightly out of the horizontal to slice through the stack with a slight lateral movement to finish up parallel with the cutting table. The knife does not finish up in contact with the steel table, but on a 'cutting stick' of wood, plastic or fibre which is inset in to the table, and can be changed as wear occurs.

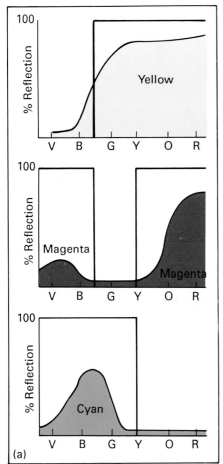

Colour plate 1 *(a) Spectral reflectance of standard process inks (curved line) compared with the ideal requirement (bold line).*

(a)

(b) Principle of colour separation and masking technique to compensate deficiencies in the printing inks

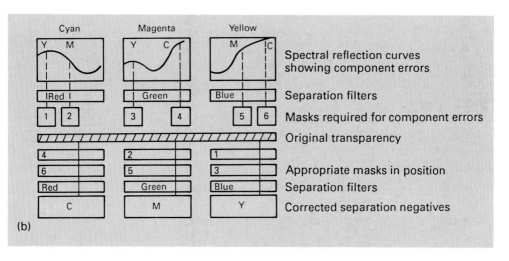

(b)

Colour plate 2 *Typographers use specific terms to describe the various parts of type characters. This illustration shows the terms most commonly employed*

A Em-square	3 Bowl
B Cap-height	4 Link
C x-height	5 Hairline
D Ascender	6 Terminal
E Descender	7 Bar
F Baseline	8 Counter
1 Ball	9 Stem
2 Serif	

Courtesy Mergenthaler Type Library

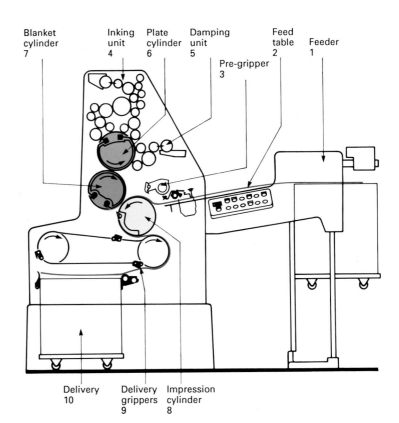

Colour plate 3 *Basic construction of a sheet-fed offset litho press*
Courtesy MAN Roland

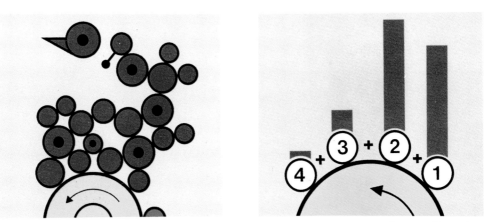

Colour plate 4 *Inking. It is not uncommon to have twenty or more rollers in a litho inking train. The purpose of the roller train is to break down the stiff, viscous litho ink to a thin film of a few microns in thickness. This system from Heidelberg is designed to lay the major film of ink on the plate with the first two plate inkers, while the third and fourth plate inkers smooth out the film and provide ultimate finish*

(5a)

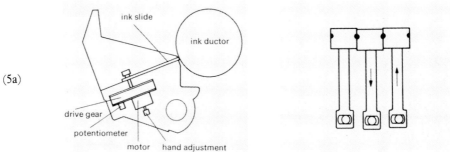

Colour plate 5 *Remote control of inking. Sectional duct blades or ink 'slides' are used for remote ink control by some manufacturers, such as the MAN/Roland system shown in (a) and (b). Others, such as Miller, prefer to stay with the conventional one-piece duct blade, as shown in (c) overleaf*

(5b)

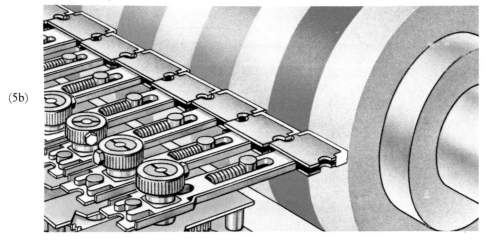

(5c)

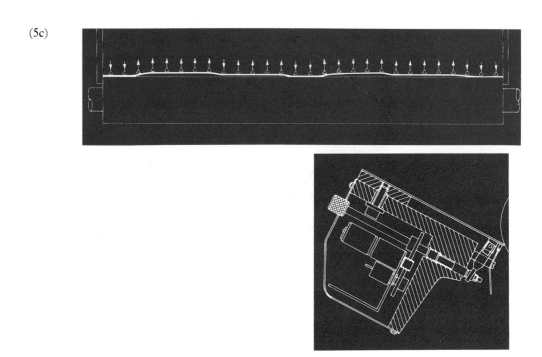

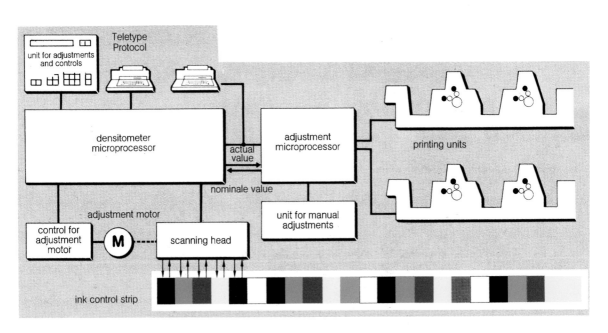

Colour plate 6 *Automatic ink control. Koenig and Bauer's densitronic system*

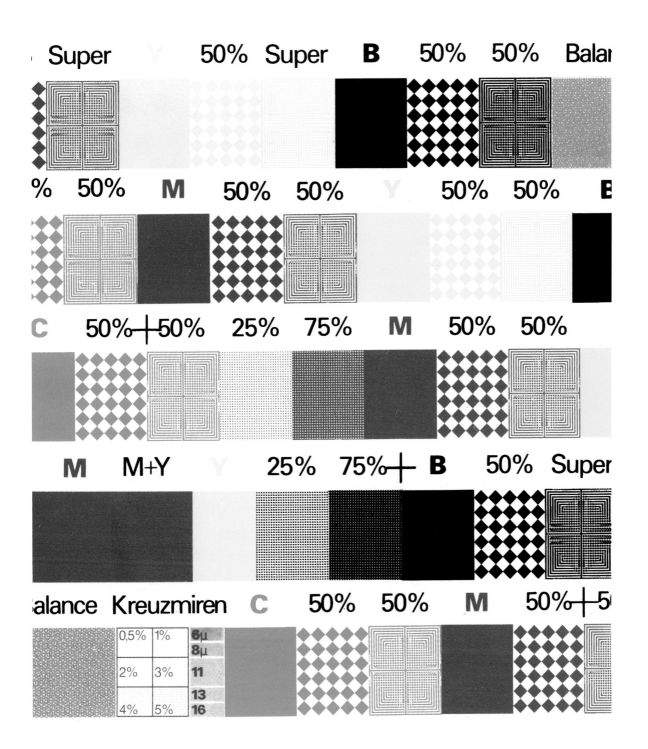

Colour plate 7 *Enlarged detail of system Brunner quality control strip*

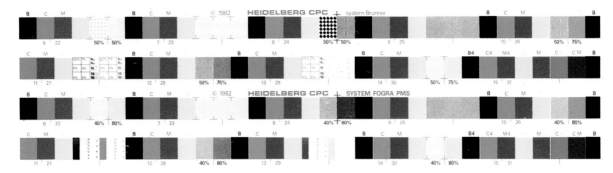

(above)

Colour plate 8 *Quality measurement and control via QC strips. Eight seconds is all it takes for a measuring pass across a 70 × 100 cm sheet. In this run, up to 208 measuring fields are read for quality control of all colours.*

Shown are sections of Heidelberg CPC quality control strips, system Fogra and system Brunner in four-colour versions

Colour plate 9 *Plate reading. (a) Plate readers can be used to predict the ink control settings on the press. A record of the settings can be stored to enable settings to be preset for repeat runs Courtesy* Heidelberg

(a)

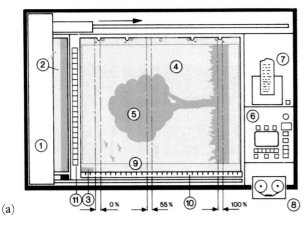

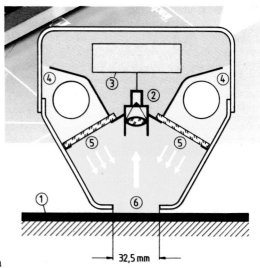

1 Measuring carriage
2 Calibrating strip
3 Calibrating field
4 Printing plate
5 Image area
6 Control panel
   and display

7 Printer
8 Cassette drive
9 Limit of maximum image area
10 Scale for width
11 Scale for length

(b) Sectional view of measuring carriage
1 Printing plate
2 Photoreceiver with convex lens
3. Electronics
4 Light sources
5 Diffusion glasses
6 Measuring diaphragm of ink zone
   width

```
HEIDELBERG CPC          DAY/MONTH/YEAR: 17.01.1985          TIME: 16.49

JOB:    MO BROSCHUER / SIDE 1        COLOR STRIP     : Heidelberg/FOGRA/4
PRESS   001      NAME :  ...........  COLOR SEQUENCE  : B-C-M-Y
                        ********       FILTER          : 1 2 3 4
RUN SUMMARY             MAGENTA        REF.VALUES      : STANDARD 1 (COATED)
---------------         ********       TOLERANCES      : STANDARD 3 (WIDE)

     SOLID DENSITY         SD     ] DEVIATION OF MEAS.VALUES ( DSD
     DOT GAIN              G (%) ]   FROM REF.VALUES         ( DG (%)
     REL.PRINTING CONTRAST C (%)
     SLUR                  S (%)


              AVERAGE MEAS.VALUES            DEVIATION DIAGRAM

            TIME    SD    G    G    C    S      DSD              DG 40
                          40   80   80          -- -   + +     -- -    + +
                                                 ! !   ! !     ! !     ! !
STARTING REF.VAL.16.48  1.50   15   9         0
STARTING TOL.    16.48  0.12   4    3         7

SHEET NO.    1  16.49   1.49   5    5   50    2        *        ((010*
             2  16.52   1.48   6    5   48    2        *        ((009*
             3  16.58   1.49   6    6   48    2        *        ((009*
             4  17.01   1.46   6    5   47    2       (*        ((009*
             5  17.03   1.45   7    5   47    1       (*        (008*
             6  17.05   1.47   7    5   48    4        *        (008*
             7  17.06   1.44   7    5   48    2       (*        (008*
             8  17.09   1.51   8    6   48    4        *        (007*
             9  17.17   1.48   6    5   49    2        *        ((009*
            10  17.24   1.50   7    6   48    3        *        (008*


AVERAGE VALUES          1.48   7    5   48    2        *        ((009*
STANDARD-DEV.           0.02   1    0   1     1


RUN-
AVERAGE VALUES          1.48   7    5   48    2
STANDARD-DEV.           0.02   1    0   1     1
```

Colour plate 10 *Information systems. Data relating to press conditions for each job, or each phase of a job as it progresses, can be recorded on tape, disc or via hard copy print-out*
Courtesy Heidelberg

Controls

Controls may be manual, motorized or 'programmed':

Manual control

Manual control on simpler guillotines requires the operator to physically manipulate the back and side stops, the pile clamp and, in some instances, even the knife – as well as manually handling and positioning the piles of paper.

Motorized control

Motorized control enables the operator to position the back and side gauges by remote push-button control, prior to positioning the paper pile. Clamping and cutting can then be carried out as a matter of course by pressing the appropriate buttons.

A high proportion of the operator's time may be taken up with:

- Working out the sequence of operations for cutting large sheets down in to smaller sizes for, say, pages, labels or coupons.
- Moving the back and side stops of the guillotine after every cut, in readiness for the next cutting sequence.
- Physically moving the cut piles of paper from one position to the next.

Programmed control

For these reasons the major manufacturers of power guillotines offer versions in which the operator can 'program' the machine to make sequential movements of gauges, clamp and knife, in conjunction with paper movement. Programming is usually by means of a push-button panel at the face of the guillotine, and control can be by tape, disk or microprocessor, according to the make and model of the guillotine. Standard or repetitive programs may be stored and re-used for subsequent occasions. Automated guillotines may also include disposal of unwanted trim and assisted movement of paper piles.

Folding

Where several pages are printed on one sheet of paper it may be necessary to fold the sheet down to page size, before trimming and making up in to final form.

At least one fold is necessary for a 'fly' sheet or 4 page leaflet. This may be printed on the sheet true-to-size, folded and need no further operation. For 8-page work a second fold will be necessary and this will result in a 'closed' end, which will need to be either slit or, more commonly, trimmed, in order to open the pages. Further folds for multiple pages will complicate the folded section and require three-side trimming to present neat edges for the final product. Hand folding is sometimes used for simple, irregular or short-run work, but for any real volume of production a folding machine will give quicker, more accurate and consistent results.

Folding machines

Folding machines will vary in size according to the size of sheet to be folded and the number of folding operations needed to arrive at the final page size. They will also vary in complexity according to the number of folds per sheet and the variety of folds and page sizes required.

Most folding machines have automatic feeders, similar to those on printing presses, which feed the sheets one at a time to 'stops' which locate the sheets to pairs of folding rollers. The sheets are then either pushed between the rollers by a blade or 'knife', or deflected in to the rollers by an induced buckling action as they reach the stop plate. Combinations of *knife* and *buckle* folding actions may be incorporated into one folding machine.

The simplest technique is to fold the sheet in half across its largest axis at every folding stage (cross folds). However, there are many occasions where it is desirable to fold the sheet again across the same axis as the previous fold (parallel folds). The arrangement or 'imposition' of pages on a printed sheet needs to be determined at an early stage of production in order to ensure that the sheets are folded and finished in the most efficient way.

The more folds in the sheet, the thicker the section becomes, and the more difficult to fold, particularly for buckle folding. Under these circumstances it may be helpful to perforate the sheets at certain fold locations before folding. This will assist the fold and allow trapped air to escape.

Folding machines can be noisy and most makers provide baffle enclosures which can cover the machine while it is operating. If this is not available, employees may be advised to wear ear muffs.

Assembling

For short run work, small unfolded sheets may be assembled into order on a bench, either by hand or via simple mechanical aids as described in Chapter 3. Folded sections may also be assembled by hand, but where the run is of any significant length it is preferable to use machinery. There are two basic techniques.

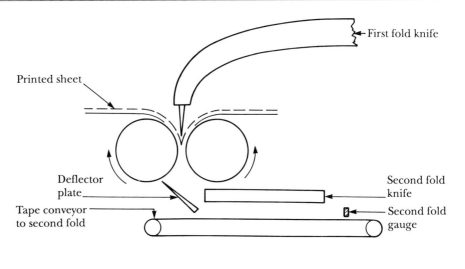

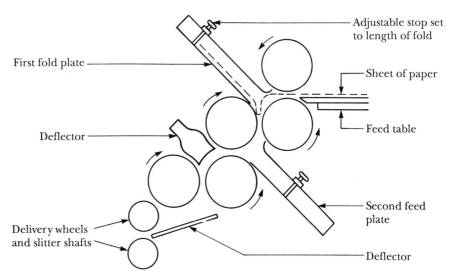

Figure 49 *Machine folding principles. (a) Knife folding. The sheet is pushed between two knurled rollers by a blade or knife. (b) Buckle folding. The sheet is fed into a narrow channel until it meets a stop. As the feed rollers continue to propel the sheet, a buckle is formed which becomes nipped by a second set of feed rollers and so on*

Insetting

Insetting is where the folded sections or 'signatures' are located one inside another. This is a comparatively quick and simple method, provided there are not too many sections or too bulky a publication. The inset sections are then stapled or 'stitched' together through the spine, and trimmed to give a neat finished edge. For regular volume production a 'flow-line' combination of insetter/stitcher/trimmer units may be used.

Here the various sections are loaded into 'hoppers', dropped astride a travelling chain to fall in order on to each other, then transported to a multiknife trimmer for finishing and waste disposal.

Gathering

Gathering refers to collecting sections side by side. This is generally preferred for thicker publications and where a square or rounded back is required. The sections then need to be joined to each other or 'secured' before covering or binding.

The simplest method of securing a number of sections is stapling through the side of the back edges (side stitching or stabbing) for a limited number of pages. Another simple method is adhesive binding in which the gathered sections may be trimmed to form individual sheets and a purpose-made adhesive applied to the spine to hold the sheets firmly together.

Covering

Covers for insetted work may be of the same stock as the rest of the publication and printed as part of the main run ('self cover'). Alternatively, a special 4-page cover sheet may be printed on a superior stock to give better protection and improved appearance.

Gathered work may be covered by 'wrappering' in which a one-piece cover is wrapped around the gathered sections and glued at the spine. For more permanent and positive protection the 'drawn on' cover technique may be employed in which the cover is glued to the outer blank sheets of the publication as well as the spine.

A variety of different options exist for specialized areas such as loose-leaf or lay-flat publications. These include: spiral wire loops, plastic combs, metal rings or prongs and interlocking screws, each of which requires its own appropriate equipment and techniques.

Casing

Paperbacks

Paperback books are usually produced via the gathering, adhesive binding and wrapping method.

Hardbacks

Hardback books, as their name implies, have a firm 'case' within which the gathered sections are enclosed and attached. The gathered sections are usually secured at their spines by sewing and/or adhesive taping for positive joining and flexibility of opening. After securing and trimming,

Figure 50 *Print finishing techniques. (a) Mechanized gathering. (b)*
A perfect binding line
Courtesy Kolbus GmbH & Co. Ltd

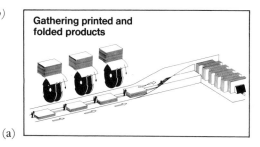

(a)

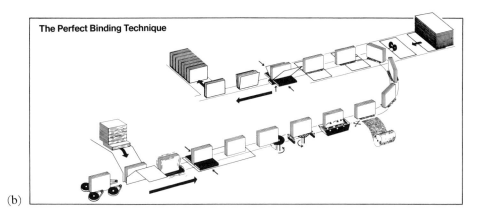

(b)

the book is mechanically 'rounded' in order to give the characteristic curve to the spine and fore-edge.

Cases

The case is made from boards cut to size and covered with bookcloth or other material. Individual or small-volume cases may be made up by hand, but for any reasonable quantity a casemaking machine will be used. 'Hoppers' will contain bulk supplies of boards and covers; the adhesive will be applied to each cover as it is fed to the assembly station; boards and spine reinforcements will be pneumatically located on to the covers; and the ends of the covers will then be turned around the boards to complete the case.

Casing-in

Casing-in completes the bookbinding operation. The spine of the case is first rounded via a curved former bar to conform with the curve of the book block. Adhesive is then applied to the outside pages ('end papers') of the book, then book and case are brought together under pressure.

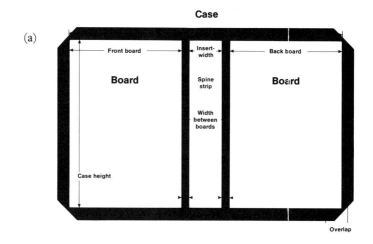

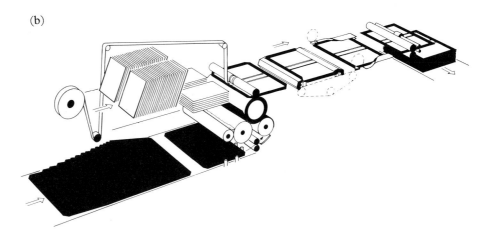

Figure 51 *Casemaking. (a) Make-up of a typical case for a hardback book. (b) An automatic casemaking line*
Courtesy Kolbus GmbH & Co. KG

Ancillary finishing operations	**Hot foil stamping**

Ancillary finishing operations

Hot foil stamping

Hot foil stamping (blocking) refers to the application of metallic foil to a substrate via heat and pressure. Early craft bookbinders used heated relief 'tools' to apply gold leaf to the covers of books, etc. and this technique may still be used for specialized and individual purposes.

Modern foils are based on a polyester film which carries either a thin, tinted aluminium layer, or an 'atomized' deposit of metallic material which will transfer to the substrate under suitable conditions of heat and pressure. Foils are usually supplied in roll form for feeding through the 'blocking' press.

The press itself comprises a heated bed or cylinder holding the engraved relief block, and an opposing bed or cylinder to receive the impression. The foil roll and the substrate pass between the two beds or cylinders, and as they close together under impression the heated block presses the foil on to the substrate to form the metallic image.

Embossing

Embossing is the technique of deforming the paper or board substrate to form a relief image. This practice requires first, an etched or engraved 'die' which is a recessed image of the desired design, and second, a 'force' which is a relief image fitting snugly in to the die. The die and force may be located on opposing flat beds of a press or on the cylinders of an embossing unit. As the substrate passes through the 'nip' of the embossing press the material is deformed to give the raised image.

The image to be embossed may be preprinted to give a three-dimensional effect to the illustration, and care must be taken to ensure that the image is not ruptured or otherwise damaged during the embossing operation.

'Blind' embossing refers to the production of a raised image without relating to a relevant printed image.

Die stamping

Die stamping also produces a relief image on the substrate via a die and a force. In this instance however the die is flooded with ink, then the surface of the die wiped clean, leaving ink in the recessed area. As impression takes place ink is transferred and the substrate embossed at the same time. Fine detail can be held in the engraved recesses and multi-colour work (not halftone) is common. Although this is a comparatively expensive and time-consuming operation, the die stamped effect is generally considered to be the sign of a good quality product.

Thermographing

Thermographing is sometimes, rather unfairly referred to as 'imitation die stamping' as it achieves a relief effect without the use of an engraved die and force. In this process a print may be made by any normal printing process and the inked image dusted with a resinous powder while still 'wet'. The dusted image is then exposed to a source of heat, which causes the resin to swell and fuse giving the raised effect.

Transparent powders may be dusted over coloured inks, or coloured powders over specially formulated colourless inks which are designed to enhance the thermographic effect. Metallic or fluorescent powders may be used to give special effects. Mobile thermographing units may be used in-line with the printing press so that dusting and fusing can take place as the sheets are delivered.

Varnishing

Varnishing is the coating of printed sheets with a film of clear transparent liquid medium. This is applied as a semi-viscous liquid via a train of rollers, either to the sheet as a whole or to selected areas as 'patch' varnishing.

The purpose of varnishing is two-fold; first to give added protection to the print and substrate and second to improve its appearance by the added 'gloss'.

Whichever method is used it is essential to ensure that the previously printed ink film is completely dry in order to avoid a reaction between the wet ink and the wet varnish, which could result in the inks 'bleeding' in to the varnish and causing discoloration.

The physical and chemical properties of the inks and the varnish must be taken in to consideration, and it is advisable that the same supplier be used for both in order to ensure compatibility.

Drying of the final coated film may be accelerated by using infra-red, ultra-violet or electron beam radiation to speed up production and ensure a solidified film which will avoid further complications.

Laminating

Laminating is the application of a clear transparent plastic film to the printed substrate. As with varnishing the intention is to both protect and improve the appearance. Laminators may be simple hand-operated machines in which the sheets are fed one at a time for covering with film or they may be part of a 'flow-line' production system.

Where the laminate is to be secured by an adhesive it is essential that the ink is thoroughly dry and also compatible with the solvent in the adhesive to ensure that the dyes and pigments in the ink do not 'migrate' or 'bleed' in to the laminate.

Non-adhesive lamination is possible with the choice of suitable plastic films which will adhere to the substrate merely by the application of heat and pressure.

Where the sheet is laminated on both sides and sealed at the edges for complete protection the term 'encapsulation' is often employed.

Punching

Punching refers to making holes, slots or other shapes in the substrate, usually by means of appropriately formed relief punches engaging with recessed dies or matrices. These may be used for ring, prong, spiral or loop binding, plastic comb work, etc. Flat-bed or rotary systems may be employed according to the type and volume of work.

Drilling

Drilling may be a more efficient way of making holes in the substrate as punching devices can only penetrate a few sheets at a time. However this is limited to the production of round holes and these will be of limited size. Positive control of the sheets is essential for accurate drilling.

Perforating

Perforating may be by means of punching a series of small, close holes in a sheet, as with postage stamp perforation. A pattern of steel punches and matrices will be necessary for this operation, made to precision tolerances and with provision to remove the waste 'confetti'.

An alternative is to cut a series of slots in the sheet by means of a sharp steel disc with appropriate gaps, cutting against a steel 'anvil' cylinder as the printing stock passes between them. The ratio of 'cut' to 'tie' will determine the efficiency of the perforation.

Slitting

Slitting requires the use of a continuous sharpened steel disc cutting against an anvil cylinder as the substrate passes through. An alternative is to use two flat, overlapping discs working against each other as a pair of rotary 'scissors' to ensure that the sheets are cleanly and positively separated.

Rule cutting, perforating, creasing and scoring

Where more complicated shapes such as cartons, envelopes or folders are to be made from the substrate it may be necessary to make up a 'forme' from specially designed steel rules.

Cutting

Cutting of the basic outline will be by means of sharpened steel rules, curved to the appropriate shape and held within a base frame or board. This will cut the outline from the substrate as it is forced between the cutting forme and an opposing bed.

Perforating

Perforating rules are of a similar profile to cutting rules, but have regular slots cut in them to avoid complete severance, while allowing easy separation when required.

Creasing

Creasing will allow the material to be folded easily along a predetermined line. This is undertaken by a rounded steel rule, slightly lower in height than the cutting rule, which forces the substrate in to a narrow channel in the opposing bed.

Scoring

Scoring is a simpler method of making a folding line. A sharp rule is carefully set to cut part way through the substrate, so that it may be readily folded at a later stage. This has the disadvantage of weakening the substrate and risking rupture of the fold.

Numbering

Numbering is normally carried out by 'boxes' which comprise a set of steel engraved wheels with the numbers 0 to 9 cut in relief around the periphery of each wheel. The wheels are ratcheted to turn one way only and interlocked so that when the first wheel has completed its sequence, the next wheel is engaged and so on. The wheels can be referred to as: units, tens, hundreds, thousands, ten thousands, hundred thousands, and so on.

For individual numbering of a few sheets the box may be hand held and inked by an impregnated ink pad, similar to a date stamping device.

Volume numbering will require a number of boxes to be mounted around a cylinder and inked by a roller inking system as sheets pass between the numbering cylinder and an impression cylinder.

Where the work is printed and numbered more than one to view, it will be necessary to use numbering boxes in which the 'unit' wheels do not have consecutive numbers. For example, in two-up printing the first numbering box will have a unit wheel with odd numbers only, while the second box will have a unit wheel with even numbers only. Higher multiples of sheets to be numbered will require more complicated numbering box patterns.

6 Web-fed production

Web-fed printing

Sheet fed production has its practical limitations including:

- Throughput is restricted to an absolute maximum of 15,000 sheets of paper an hour.
- Certain materials such as thin plastic films, textiles and metallic foils are difficult to handle in sheet form.
- Continuous designs, as for wallpapers and textiles cannot be achieved.

Web-fed production is an obvious alternative as it offers:

- *Higher throughput*: up to 50,000 metres of printed matter per hour, printed in multicolour on both sides if required.
- *Multi-web presses* enable complete products to be printed in full colour on both sides, assembled, cut, folded and delivered in final form.
- *Greater flexibility* in press design is possible; i.e., printing units may be built vertically, horizontally or 'stacked' around a common frame.
- *Ancillary operations* such as folding, cutting, laminating, perforating, punching, trimming, numbering and rewinding can be readily incorporated in web press design.
- *'Difficult' substrates* such as films, foils and textiles may be more easily handled in roll form.
- *Continuous cylinders* allow 'endless' designs to be achieved for wallcoverings, textiles, wrappers and adhesive tapes, etc. Computer listing paper and continuous stationery can only be produced from a web.

Limitations do exist, of course, and these must be fully understood before entering the web-printing field. Web presses are definitely not 'general-purpose' machines which can accommodate a wide variety of substrate types, sizes and calipers in order to print the almost infinite range of printed products accomplished via sheet-fed production.

A degree of specialization is an essential feature of web presses, which may be purpose built to mass produce practically any specified printed product from books to brochures, cartons to canisters, mail shots to magazines and tickets to timetables.

Other printing processes are also quite commonly used for web printing, and indeed a mixture of processes is not uncommon on one press. Offset litho may well be used for colour publications, but photopolymer relief (letterpress) plates have economic advantages for books and newspapers which are predominantly monochrome. Photogravure has a strong presence in long-run multicolour publication and packaging work, where its depth of colour, continuous printing area and tough surface come in to their own. Flexography, printing from rubber, plastic or laser-cut plates or cylinders is one of the simplest, economical and most versatile of all printing processes, currently printing practically everything from drinking straws to national newspapers.

Each process is described separately in this chapter.

Basic principles of web-fed production

All web presses comprise three main elements:

1 *Pre-printing* sections containing the reels, reelstands, infeed and web control mechanisms.
2 *Printing units* and associated equipment which put the inked image on the substrate.
3 *Post-printing* areas which take the printed webs and convert them to the end product.

There are certain common principles to all web-fed presses as follows:

Reelstands

Reels are supported by means of a shaft passing through the centre core of the reel or, for large reels, by a pair of cone-shaped wedges gripping each end of the core. The reelstand needs to be of sturdy construction as full-sized reels, in newspaper production for instance, may weigh the best part of a tonne. The reel support must hold the reel firmly, yet allow it to rotate freely. Pneumatic 'expanding' reel shafts are often used for fast and positive grip of the core, while cones may be inserted under pneumatic or hydraulic pressure for precise control. Reelstands on smaller presses are usually located in-line with the printing units, but for larger installations and multiweb presses they may be located in a basement below the printing units.

Reel control

Reel control is an essential requirement. A half tonne roll, revolving at a circumferential speed is excess of 10 metres per second has a considerable dynamic potential. A reel braking device is usually fitted to avoid the reel overrunning in the event of the press slowing down or stopping, and to ensure efficient feed of paper to the press.

Reel brakes may take many forms including shoe or disc brakes operating on a boss at the end of the reel shaft; straps or bands working by friction on the reel surface; or motorized, variable speed drives to the reel.

Whichever type of brake is employed, it is essential to have a finely graduated control of the force applied to the brake in order to maintain a consistent tension in the substrate as the reel unwinds. A reel weighing half a tonne when first loaded in to the press will weigh less than a kilogramme by the time it is completely unwound, and this constant change in mass will need to be reflected by changes in the brake control system as the run progresses.

Infeeding

Infeeding to the press may in some primitive instances be simply by presenting the web to the nip of the printing cylinders. However, it is more common to have an infeed device which will be responsible for unwinding the reel and feeding it to the printing units at a controlled rate. This is achieved in its simplest form by means of a pair of 'gripper' rollers directly geared in to the press drive. More sensitive and flexible control is obtained by variable speed infeed drives which can control the unwinding of the reel, and at the same time feed the material in a constant state of tension to the printing units.

Web tension control

The thread of paper or other material unwound from the reel is referred to as a web. On smaller and simpler presses the web may be threaded through the press by hand, but larger and more complicated installations will have an automatic web-feeding device as a standard feature.

Accurate control of web tension is essential for efficient production: a loose or flapping web may give rise to creasing, wandering, snatching and misregister, while too much tension will stretch the material, distort the image and run the risk of web breakage. Control of tension initially requires a sensor, such as a spring-loaded roller or a strain gauge which can measure the stress in the web and record the information. This information can then be used to modify the web tension control devices such as the reel brake and the infeed system so that the web or webs are maintained within predetermined tension tolerances as they progress through the press.

Web guiding

Web guiding devices may be used to control the lateral movement of a web and either maintain it in a central position on the press or align one edge to a lateral position, according to the needs of the particular type of work. Edge guides may operate on mechanical, pneumatic or photoelectric principles, depending largely on the type of stock and the nature of the work.

Reel changing

On the simplest of presses, as the reel nears completion the press is gradually slowed down and stopped, just before the expiry of the material. The web is then broken out, the reel core removed and a fresh reel installed. The beginning of the new reel is taped to the end of the previous one, the press re-started and printing resumed as soon as optimum conditions are achieved.

Time can be saved by having a spare reel shaft and a second reel position on the press, so that the new reel can be mounted and prepared while the press is running. Changeover is reduced to a matter of seconds while the press is stopped and the webs 'spliced'.

Non-stop splicing

Stopping the press to change reels may take anything from a few seconds to a few minutes, but this can be significant in terms of lost production. Apart from time taken to change the reels, there is loss of time and materials as the press is slowed to a halt and again as it is restarted and accelerated to the production speed. It may take a high-speed publication press half a minute to slow down and stop and the same time to resume a satisfactory printing state. At a production rate of a thousand copies per minute this is a loss that can be ill-afforded, particularly on a multi-reel press where the reels may well be unequal in size and will expire at various times.

For these reasons non-stop splicing devices are standard features on most high-speed web presses, and these fall in to one of two basic categories.

Butt join splicers

Butt join or 'zero-speed' splicers are based initially on a 'festoon' arrangement, comprising a series of loops of paper between the reel and the infeed unit, which act as a reservoir of material during the splicing period. Double reelstands are employed and the ends of the webs are joined statically, in a few seconds, as the press draws paper from the festoon.

This type of non-stop splice is better for thicker substrates, such as cards and boxboard which require a 'butt' splice rather than the normal overlapping join, in order to avoid a thick wedge of material entering the printing nip and damaging the plate or blanket.

Flying splicers

Flying splicers are fully automated systems in which a new web can be joined to the tail of the old one at full press speed. These are usually based on revolving 'magazine' reelstands which hold two or three reels at a time.

As the reel running in the press diminishes, the front edge of the next reel can be prepared with adhesive or tape, ready for the splicing operation. At an appropriate time the new reel is located close to the web speed. Then, at a critical moment the new reel and the expiring web are brought in to firm contact, the splice made, and the expired web severed, leaving the new reel running in the press. The used core can then be replaced with a new reel, and the whole cycle repeated.

Automatic splicers need to be extremely efficient devices, with better than 99 per cent efficiency. One bad splice on a multicolour, multiweb press, outputting at more than 60,000 copies per hour, could bring out all the other webs, cause wrap-rounds of printing cylinders, etc. and hold up production for hours.

The time and expense required to repair the damage to plates, blankets, rollers etc. and to re-thread the webs and resume printing could be a very costly exercise. For this reason it is standard practice to instal web sensors at critical positions along the web path. These may be either photoelectric or electromechanical devices linked in to the press

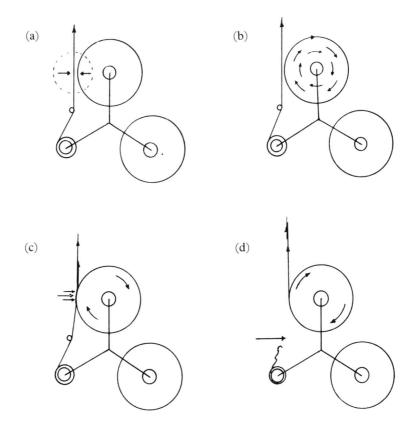

Figure 52 *High-speed reel changing. (a) Location. The relationship of the web to the reel must be precisely determined. (b) Rotation. The reel to be spliced must be rotated to match the web speed. (c) Splicing. The web must be brought into firm contact with the adhesive lip on the reel. (d) Severing. The expired web is cut to leave the new reel running in the machine*

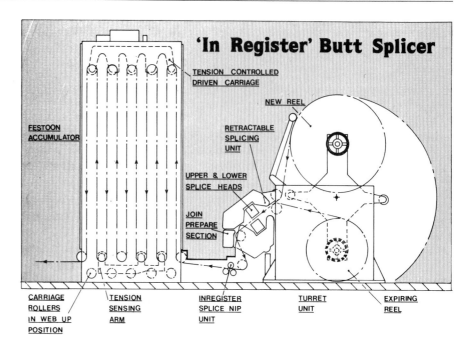

Figure 53   *Principle of festoon splicing*
Courtesy Hurley Moate Engineering Co. Ltd

control system, to take the printing cylinders out of pressure, stop the press and initiate any other safety precautions that may be necessary.

Printing processes

The previous chapter referred to the fact that offset lithography is the most common commercial printing process in use today for sheet-fed production. The developments which led to the ascendancy of sheet-fed offset litho have also influenced the web-fed sector, particularly in publication printing where the majority of titles are now printed by this process, which is usually referred to briefly as 'web offset'.

However, there are a number of limiting factors to web offset production. Start-up and running waste is high compared with the letterpress system and this may be important for long run work, plate life is limited compared with that which may be obtained by other processes, press design, particularly the printing units themselves is more complicated and expensive than with other processes, and there are some substrates which are difficult to print by offset litho, which is particularly important when looking outside the publication field at, say, packaging, which requires printing on a variety of materials from plastic films to corrugated board.

The other printing processes which have significant sectors of the web market are:

- *Photopolymer relief printing*, a modern version of the traditional letterpress process.
- *Flexography* relief printing which is currently the most rapidly expanding printing process.
- *Photogravure*, which has a strong foothold in the long run and quality process colour sector.

'Hybrid' presses, which employ more than one printing process are not uncommon.

WEB OFFSET LITHOGRAPHY

The number, nature and arrangement of the printing units in a web offset press can vary considerably, depending mainly on the requirements of the particular end product.

Local newspapers of moderate circulation, for instance, may be produced by printing units designed on the blanket-to-blanket principle. Here the web travels horizontally and the printing units are placed above and below the web, with the blanket cylinders on either side of the web acting as impression cylinders for each other, so that both sides are printed simultaneously.

A single unit may print, say, eight newspaper pages, and the more pages required, the more printing units will need to be installed in the press line.

Mass produced national newspapers may require bigger printing units to accommodate larger plates carrying more pages, and these are more likely to be arranged with the web running vertically between the blanket cylinders and the printing units arranged in an arch form either side of the web for convenience and accessibility. These are usually three-tier installations with the webs coming up from a reel room in the basement plus a comprehensive superstructure above the printing units to assemble and organize the webs before folding and delivery.

Colour printing may be undertaken by running the web from one printing unit to the next. In a typical instance, a four unit, in-line, blanket-to-blanket press could print four colours on each side of a single web. Alternatively, the four units may take two webs and print two colours on each side of both webs, and so on, making full use of this versatile arrangement.

Satellite units may be employed where multicolour printing is a standard feature of the publication. In this design a number of blanket cylinders are grouped around a common, central impression cylinder. This technique ensures impeccable registration of the colours as the web remains on the one impression cylinder during the full printing cycle. If colour is required on both sides of the web, then two satellite units may be employed.

Combination presses will contain a mix of blanket-to-blanket perfectors

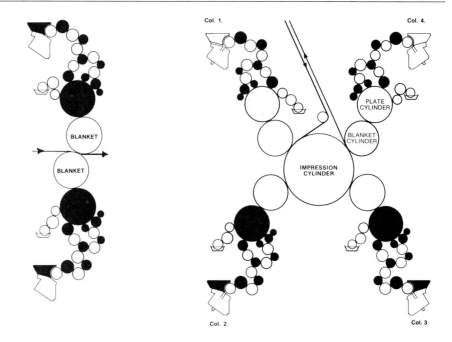

Figure 54 *Arrangement of web-offset printing units. (a) Blanket-to-blanket system. (b) Satellite system, with four units arranged around a common impression cylinder*
Courtesy Baker Perkins

for the monochrome work, plus a satellite unit for colour. This is an ideal arrangement where the majority of pages are monochrome and colour is required only on a limited number of pages.

Design of printing units

The basic principles of offset lithography are similar for both sheet and web printing. Plates are produced in much the same way, although the high volume requirements of web production are more likely to require direct camera-to-plate systems and automated platemaking lines.

The design of the printing units will also need to be modified for web printing as the intermittent pattern of sheet-fed production is replaced by the continuous flow of a web, and this will influence practically every element in the printing unit.

Dimensions

Cylinder dimensions are usually of a fixed diameter, therefore at every revolution a certain amount of substrate will be fed through the press, corresponding to the cylinder circumference, and this will relate to the final end-product size. This is in contrast to the sheet-fed situation where various sizes of printing stock can be fed in to a press, up to the maximum sheet size. There are no recognized international standards for

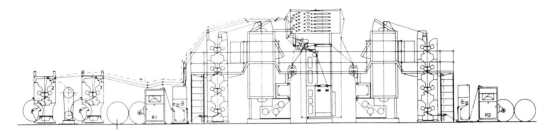

Figure 55 *Web-offset publication press. This schematic diagram of a Goss 'community' press illustrates how a compact design can be achieved by stacking printing units vertically either side of a central folder. Drying ovens are sited between the printing units and the folder, with full web-turning facilities arranged above the folder*

web press circumferences, although there are certain 'recommended' cut-off sizes for periodicals. This can give rise to problems where publications are to be printed simultaneously in more than one centre on presses with different cylinder diameters.

On some smaller and specialized presses, designed for say the forms or packaging markets, it is possible to have interchangeable units or 'cartridges' to cater for different sizes of product; but this technique is not appropriate to publication work.

Plate cylinders

Plate cylinders will be designed with the minimum possible gap to hold the ends of the plate. This will enable the maximum surface area of the cylinder to be available for printing. This does give rise to some technical problems, as the ends of the plates which enter the gap must be accurately formed to enter the limited space available. The plate locking system must be simple, quick and ensure that the plate conforms accurately to the cylinder circumference, without imposing undue stresses. Poor design of plate lock-up will lead to edge cracking, which is probably the most common cause of plate failure on web-offset presses.

Blanket cylinders

Blanket cylinders will also need to be designed with a minimum gap for gripping both ends of the blanket. A bulge in this area will give rise to a number of printing and web-control problems, not the least being the likelihood of web breaks. On some simpler web offset presses 'stickyback' blankets are used, whereby the blanket is held on the cylinder by an adhesive backing. However, this technique is not recommended for high-speed publication presses.

Impression cylinders

Impression cylinders do not need to have a provision for grippers to hold the substrate, as in sheet-fed production, and these may in their simplest form be continuous steel cylinders geared in to the press drive, which in turn drive the other cylinders in the printing unit.

Inking systems

Inking systems on web offset presses will be designed on the same basic principles as for sheet-fed presses, except that a more continuous flow of ink will be required as against the intermittent flow on sheet fed machines. A bulk supply of ink is also a common feature, pumped to the appropriate station in order to cope with the high volume demand. Remote control of inking is standard on most web-offset presses, together with automatic monitoring and correction.

Damping

Damping will also need to be continuous, and precautions must be taken against the feed-back of ink into the damping system. Conventional damping techniques, similar to those on sheet-fed presses are often employed, plus 'non-contact' methods such as sprays or brush damping which apply moisture without direct roller contact to either the inking rollers or the plate cylinder. Whichever system is used there should be continuous circulation from bulk storage, with automatic filtering, replenishment and 'dosing' of additives, etc. to maintain a clean and consistent solution.

PHOTO-POLYMER RELIEF PRINTING

This is a modern version of the original letterpress process in which the image to be reproduced is raised in relief above the base material. Metal type and plates have long since been replaced by photopolymer materials which can use photographic input to produce flexible, one-piece relief plates which can be wrapped around a printing cylinder in much the same way as a litho plate.

Relief printing has several advantages when compared with lithography:

- The *ink/water balance*, essential to the lithographic process, no longer applies. The moisture variable is eliminated, leaving only the ink level to be determined. This makes for faster start-ups, quicker make-readies, lower wastage, less maintenance and lower materials costs.

- *Direct printing* from plate to substrate is possible, without the need for an intermediate first cylinder, thus simplifying press design and lowering costs.
- *Image quality* is consistent. Once established the image is less likely to fluctuate than litho with its ink/water balance problems and three-cylinder system.
- *Durability of the photopolymer* material is superior to most litho printing surfaces. Runs in the order of millions are quite common, compared with the tens or hundreds of thousands expected from a typical litho plate.
- *Plate size* will correspond to the printing area. A one centimetre square patch will only need a one centimetre square plate and not a full cylinder size plate as with litho.

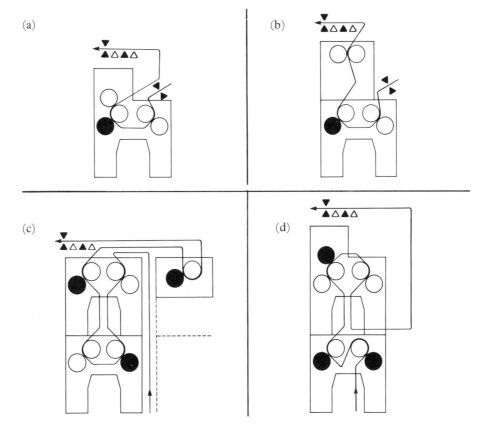

Figure 56 *Variations in colour capacity for publication printing. (a) Five cylinder configuration. In tight slip-in situations a colour cylinder requires fewer modifications to the superstructure so that colour can be available where it is needed. (b) Six cylinder configuration. A reversible halfdeck is ideal for flexible colour placement in an all-new pressline or in a slip-in application where there is plenty of room. (c) Eight cylinder configuration. Four colours can be laid down in close proximity for best register, picking up black on the back side of the web from a halfdeck over an adjacent unit. (d) Nine cylinder configuration. Four colours over one colour can be accomplished in one unit space to conserve page capacity*
Courtesy Motter Printer Press Co

Photopolymer relief plates

Photopolymer platemaking systems can be quite varied in their applications. Small 'desktop' versions can be purchased for producing the 'rubber stamp' type of plate, or for making relief plates for the imprinting units of litho printing presses. At the other extreme, in-line production systems are available for high-volume production such as books, magazines and newspapers.

The 'hardness' of photopolymer plates may be varied to suit the needs of the work in hand.

Hardness is measured in degrees Shore, on a scale which runs from zero hardness – 0°S to 'glass' hardness at 100°S. A 'soft' plate could be less than 40°S and may be used for run-of-the-mill work such as paperback book work or business forms. Harder plates of 60°–70°S will be used where finer definition is required, such as fine line work and halftone printing.

There are two basic types of photopolymer relief (p.r.) plates:

1 The 'solid' plate which is provided by the manufacturer in a range of base sizes, calipers and hardnesses for subsequent processing.
2 The 'liquid' plate which initially comprises a molten resin mixture which can be extruded from its reservoir to a required size and caliper prior to processing.

Both types may be used either as unsupported plates which can be secured to the printing cylinder by adhesive, or fused on to plastic or metal bases to provide better stability and rigidity and mounted via plate tensioning and clamping systems.

Solid plates

Solid plates usually comprise a stable metal or plastic base with the light-sensitive photopolymer material keyed firmly to it, plus a thin protective film to avoid premature exposure.

A 'flash' exposure may be given in the first instance in order to 'wake up' or presensitize the material prior to the main exposure.

The protective film is then removed and the main exposure made in a vacuum frame, with the plate material in firm contact with a negative. Exposure to ultra-violet light hardens the photopolymer and determines the printing image areas.

The plate is then passed to a processing unit in which it is 'washed out' or sprayed with a solvent to remove the unexposed polymer, thus forming the relief image. Some systems employ an aqueous-based wash-out solution which may be an advantage where environmental and pollution problems are of consequence.

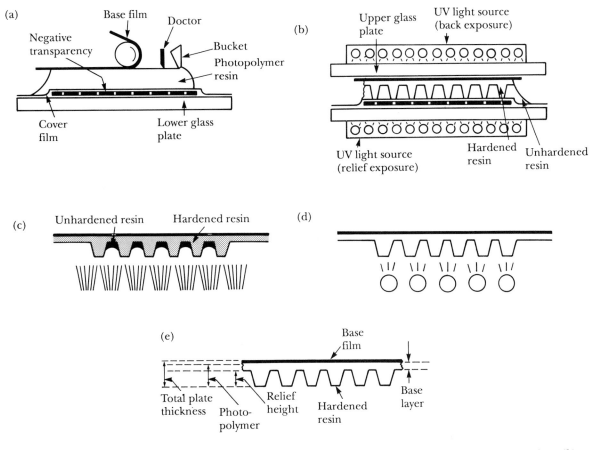

Figure 57 *Photopolymer relief plates – the liquid resin system. (a) Preparation. (b) Exposure. (c) Wash-out. (d) Post-exposure. (e) Finished APR plate*
Courtesy Asahi Chemical Industry Co. Ltd

A final drying and curing unit will solidify and finalize the plate ready for forwarding to the printing press.

Liquid plates

Liquid plates operate on similar principles to the solid version, except that the polymer is kept in a molten form, in a resin tank, until it is required to make a plate. The polymer is then extruded on to a light table holding the negative, which is protected by a thin cover film, and 'doctored' to the required thickness. The resin sets rapidly and at this stage can be exposed to ultra-violet light to establish the image areas.

Washout is similar to that of a solid plate, plus final drying, curing and hardening. In most liquid systems, surplus resin may be returned to the bulk supply and recycled.

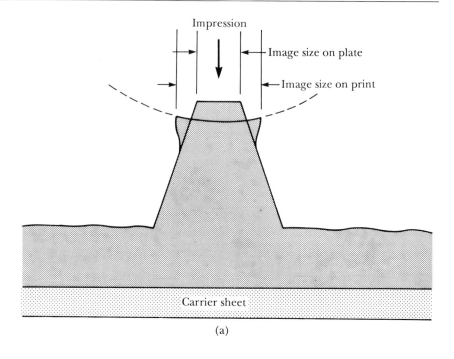

(a)

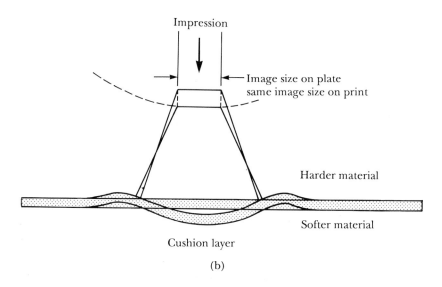

(b)

Figure 58 *Distortion of rubber and plastic relief plates. (a) illustrates the distortion which occurs when a 'standard' rubber relief plate is subjected to printing pressure. Distortion occurs at the printing surface, thus changing image values. (b) illustrates the use of a cushion layer of resilient material to absorb the pressure and allow the printing surface to remain undistorted*

Proofing

Proofs for photopolymer printing may be obtained in three ways.

Soft copy proofs

Soft proofs may be viewed on VDU terminals, at the makeup stage. The copy may be 'okayed' without further approval being required, and sent to press. This type of situation is most likely to occur where the content is mainly text or monochrome production, and where copy-to-print time is short, as in newspaper production.

Hard copy proofs

Hard copy proofs may be obtained prior to platemaking, either via photocopying or an output device, such as a laser printer linked directly to a page planning system, or as contact proofs from the negatives which will be used to make the printing plates, or the 'paste-up' copy prepared at the page make-up stage.

Pre-press proofs such as these are a speedy and economical guide to the final appearance of the printed work.

Press proofs

Press proofs, from the actual printing plates may be called for to give a true 'ink-on-paper' reproduction. Unlike the majority of litho press proofs, these will be printed on rotary proof presses, where the plates are curved around a cylinder of a similar circumference to that of the production press.

Rotary proofing

Rotary proofing is preferred owing to the fact that photopolymer plates are significantly thicker than litho plates and will distort more when curved around a cylinder. In other words, the print length will be shorter if the plate is proofed flat compared with printing on the curve. The significant factors in determining the final print length are plate caliper and cylinder circumference.

Photopolymer plates may be less than a millimetre in thickness or more than 5 mm for certain purposes. A typical 2 mm plate wrapped around a 60 cm cylinder may print more than 5 mm longer than it would if printed on a flat bed proof press.

Ideally, whenever accurate print length is of importance, photopolymer plates should be exposed, processed, proofed and printed all on cylinders of the same circumference.

Design of printing units

Design of printing units for photopolymer plates is similar to that for the letterpress web-fed presses which they have now largely replaced.

There are three main component areas in any relief printing unit and these are: plate cylinder, impression cylinder and inking system.

Plate cylinders

Plate cylinders are designed to take the wrap round plates and hold them firmly and accurately on the cylinder either under tension, or by magnetic force.

Tension systems require the plates to be gripped head and foot and put under stress to ensure accurate conformation to the cylinder. The clamps gripping either end of the plate must be below the cylinder surface and the gap or slot into which the ends of the plate are inserted should occupy the least possible area of the cylinder in order to allow the maximum possible circumference to be available for printing. A rapid or automatic plate locking mechanism should be employed, particularly where time is limited as on multiplate, multi-unit, multiweb publications presses.

Magnetic systems are appropriate where the plates have a ferrous base, such as steel. The printing cylinders will have either built in permanent magnets or electro magnets which can be switched on and off as required. This technique has the merit of speedy location on the cylinder without the need for plate clamping devices.

Pin or stud registering will also aid quick and accurate mounting of the plates on the cylinder. In this technique the leading edge of the plate is punched with precision holes at the planning/plate making stage to coincide with locating pins on the plate cylinder.

Impression cylinders

Impression cylinders may be plain, continuous steel cylinders which serve to support the web and act as a counter force for the plate. This is acceptable where the softer grades of plate are used, but where harder grades are employed for more precise image definition, it is more common to use an impression blanket on the cylinder to (a) soften the effect of printing pressure (b) reduce wear on the plate and (c) permit an element of tolerance in the impression zone.

Blankets usually comprise a number of plies of fabric and rubber or plastic material. The ideal structure is to have a resilient base which will compress under pressure from the printing plates, but a firm surface layer to ensure accurate reproduction of the relief image.

As with plates, the blankets need to be secured at both ends and tensioned around the cylinder, with the least possible loss of printing surface. Overtensioning will risk stretching and damaging the blanket, and could alter its effective caliper. Undertensioning will allow the blanket to move under printing stress and cause bulges, particularly in the area of the blanket gap, which will affect the printing quality and increase the risk of web breaks.

Pressure between the plate and impression cylinders can usually be finely adjusted to allow for different calipers and types of web material. For the most precise control the cylinders are provided with hardened steel bearer rings at either end as an integral part of the cylinder. The height of the bearers will be equivalent to either the plate caliper or the blanket caliper respectively, plus any allowance for underpacking.

Non-bearer cylinders are also used where the need for really precise cylinder circumferences and minute pressure control is not quite so critical.

Inking system

Inking of photopolymer plates is by means of roller trains, not dissimilar to those on litho presses. The nature of the ink varies from 'paste' to semi-liquid consistency and is generally somewhat less viscous than litho ink.

In the simplest systems the ink is metered to the rollers from a 'duct' where the ink flow is controlled by keys acting upon a flexible blade making near contact with a rotating steel roller, as in sheet-fed systems. For high volume production the ink may be held in a bulk store and pumped to the individual units, then metered to the roller train. Manual control of ink metering may be employed on the simpler presses, but remote control via a central control panel will be a standard feature on high-volume presses.

Arrangement of printing units

The arrangement of the printing units will depend on the nature of the work and the particular end product.

Arch-type units

Arch-type perfecting units may be used for multiweb and monochrome publication work, where the webs are fed in from below the units. These will differ from the web-offset versions in that they do not operate on the blanket-to-blanket principle as there are no offset cylinders. The webs are therefore fed from one printing 'couple' (i.e., plate and impression cylinder) to the next. Good control of the webs is ensured as they wrap around the impression cylinders, but care must be taken to ensure that ink from the first side printed does not transfer to the second impression cylinder and cause 'set-off' on subsequent impressions. To minimize this problem, blankets may be coated with a silicon layer which will refuse to accept ink from the web.

Extra 'spot' colours may be obtained either by additional printing couples, possibly situated above the main units, or more simply by adding a second plate cylinder with its own inking system to impress against a common impression cylinder.

Reversible couples are designed to give greater flexibility for colour printing and versatility of web patterns. By this technique units may be used either for perfecting in black and white or for adding extra colours simply by reversing the direction of travel of the units and re-threading the web in a different route.

In-line units

In-line units will be used where the web travels horizontally and several colours are to be printed on one side of the material, as with the majority of packaging work. The plate cylinders and their inking systems will usually be above the web for convenient accessibility and the impression cylinders below the web.

Printing on the underside of the web may be by means of specially designed reverse printing units or by the reversible unit technique, where the printing couple is mechanically reversed and the web re-routed.

Multicolour units

Multicolour units may be used where precise register is essential, as with colour halftone work. Four or more plate cylinders, each with its own inking system will be arranged around a central impression cylinder to provide a compact but efficient unit. This arrangement is particularly suitable where the majority of a publication is monochrome and a colour section is required. Care must be taken in ink formulation to ensure first that the inks lay or 'trap' correctly one on top of the other and second that the superimposed ink films are sufficiently dry before being subjected to the stress of folding, cutting, rewinding, etc.

FLEXOGRAPHY Flexography is a relief printing process with some similarities to photopolymer relief printing. However, its origins and applications are fundamentally different. Flexo, as it is commonly called, was developed in the early part of this century for the cheaper quality web-fed packaging market and was originally known as 'aniline' printing due to the nature of the liquid ink which was based on methylated spirit and aniline dyes.

The original process was based on hand-cut rubber plates or rubber duplicates made from letterpress originals, with the fluid ink applied from a trough by a simple two-roller inking system. The process adapted naturally to printing on cellulose and plastic substrates as well as aluminium foils, which enabled it to become a major force in the packaging field. In the early 1950s the term flexography was coined in

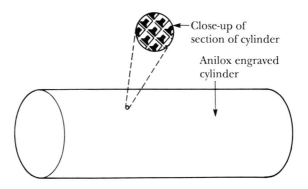

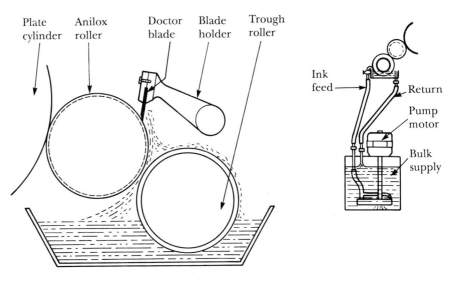

Figure 59 *Principles of flexography (a) The anilox system. (b) Reverse angle doctoring. (c) Principle of circulating ink system*

the USA and the Flexographic Technical Association came in to existence.

Flexo's basic advantages of low all-round cost coupled with simplicity of operation enabled it to move in to other markets such as books, textiles, wallpapers and children's comics, and it has more recently established itself as a viable process for newspaper printing.

Flexographic printing surfaces

Hand-cut plates

Hand-cut plates or cylinders may still be obtained from specialist houses where simple and straightforward designs are required, but most flexo surfaces are now either duplicate rubber plates, photopolymers or laser engraved.

Duplicate rubber plates

Duplicate rubber plates require a letterpress 'original' to be made in the first instance. This is usually produced via a negative which is exposed to a light-sensitive coating on a zinc plate. Light passing through the negative hardens the coating in the image area, and subsequent development washes away the coating from the non-image area, leaving the hardened coating as an acid resist. The plate is then etched in an acid bath to produce a rigid, flat original plate with an appropriate etch depth for duplicate platemaking. The image will be 'wrong-reading', i.e., laterally reversed, as in all direct relief printing processes.

A mould or matrix is then made from the 'zinco' by placing it in contact with a sheet of matrix material such as a thermosetting plastic and subjecting it to heat and pressure in a moulding press. Heat will soften the matrix material and pressure will force it in to the recesses of the relief plate. This is a critical operation as temperature, time, pressure and the dimensions of the materials must be accurately measured and controlled to obtain predictable results.

To produce the final printing plate the matrix is now placed in contact with the plate material and again subjected to heat and pressure in the moulding press. Any number of plates within reason may be taken from the matrix and matrices may be saved indefinitely for future reprints.

The plate material is usually a compound of natural rubbers and synthetic materials such as copolymers, plus additives such as sulphurs, carbons, plasticizers and resins, each with a special purpose either to aid the moulding process or to give particular properties to the final plate.

Plate hardness (durometer) will vary from 30°S (soft) to 65°S (hard), depending on the purpose for which they are intended. Soft plates make for easier and quicker setting up although they are more likely to distort under printing pressure, which will affect the reproduction of fine lines and dots. For this reason plates intended for accurate reproduction of detail work, such as colour halftone printing will tend to be of harder durometer.

Care must be taken at every stage of production to ensure that the plates are accurate to a caliper of plus or minus a few hundredths of a millimetre and within the prescribed tolerances for the printing image dimensions. Most rubber compounds will shrink in the moulding process, and where this is known to occur an allowance can be made at the origination stage. It should also be noted that rubber plates are made flat and will distort when curved and mounted on to the printing cylinder. Where final print length is critical this too can be compensated for at the origination stages, provided that the degree of distortion is known in advance. As mentioned under photopolymer relief plates, distortion is a function of plate caliper and cylinder radius.

Photopolymer flexo plates

Photopolymer flexo plates are similar in their make-up and methods of production to the plates earlier described for photopolymer relief printing, but with some significant differences. Flexographic photopolymer plates need in the first instance to be resistant to the solvents commonly used in flexo inks, and this will affect the choice of polymer. They are generally thinner than moulded rubber plates which may be several millimetres in caliper, whereas photopolymer plates rarely exceed 2.5 mm and plates of 1 mm or less are obtainable. To avoid distortion of the relief image under printing pressure the plate may be composed of layers of material of varying hardness – the printing surface layer being of a comparatively hard durometer to resist distortion, while the base layer may be of a much softer durometer to absorb the stress of printing pressure. It is also possible to coat photopolymer material on to a cylinder or sleeve for the purpose of printing continuous designs for packaging, wallpapers, textiles, etc.

Earlier, photopolymers were criticized owing to their poor ink receptivity when compared with rubber, but modern compounds have improved this situation and photopolymers are steadily replacing moulded rubber plates due to their simpler techniques, lower overheads, faster production and the fact that there is no need to produce an original zinc plate or thermosetting matrix. Where print length is critical it is quite practicable to expose and process photopolymer plates on the curve and thus avoid the distortion problems which occur with rubber duplicates.

Laser engraving

Laser engraved plates and cylinders are produced via computerized scanning equipment in which a helium/neon laser beam examines the

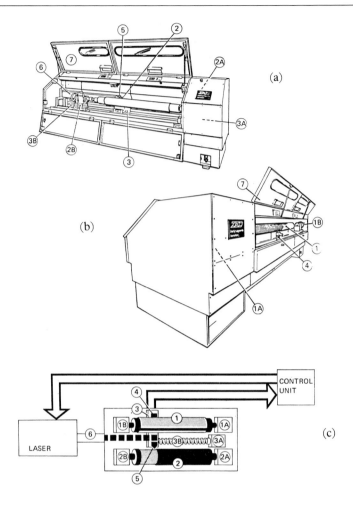

Figure 60 *Laser engraving of flexographic plates and cylinders. (a) Engraving side. (b) Scanning side.*

1	Artwork cylinder (unjointed copy)	3	Cross-slide assembly
1A	Headstock drive and encoder	3A	Lead screw
1B	Tailstock	4	Scanning head
2	Engraving cylinder (seamless)	5	Engraving head
2A	Headstock, drive and encoder	6	Laser guard
2B	Tailstock	7	Guards

Courtesy ZED Instruments Ltd

artwork as it revolves below the beam on a 'copy' cylinder. The scanner relays digitized information to the central computer which analyses the information and initiates the cutting of the image by means of a CO_2 laser beam located above an 'engraving' cylinder rotating in synchronization with the copy cylinder.

This is the fastest means of producing flexo printing surfaces as it is a direct 'copy-to-cylinder' system, without the intermediate stages required in other systems. Not surprisingly the initial capital investment is higher than for moulded rubber plates or photopolymers, but as well as speed, computer control allows a great deal of flexibility of image reproduction. Repetitive designs or images can be 'stepped and repeated' from a single master; continuous designs can be 'seamlessly' joined and the 'profile' of individual dots and lines, etc. can be cut to provide the strongest support coupled with the ideal printing image.

Rubber is the preferred image medium as it is easily vapourised by the CO_2 laser and will receive and release ink readily. For economy, plate 'patches' may be mounted upon a carrier sheet so that only those parts of the cylinder which contain a printing image will be engraved.

Proofing

Flexo plates are usually proofed on specially designed proof presses which will take the actual cylinders or sleeves which will be used on the printing press. Printing cylinders are easily removable on most flexo presses to allow for changes in print length and for pre-proofing. It is also possible to store complete sets of cylinders with their plates intact for reprints.

Most proof presses print one colour at a time using modified inks and inking systems to allow for their slower rate of production and the time interval between colours.

Individual plates

Individual plates are normally fixed to the cylinder by means of a double-sided adhesive. The first set of plates is placed in position by reference to a 'key' layout which shows the location of each element in the design. A proof is then taken and used as a basis for the location of subsequent sets of plates by cross referencing to the key layout. As each set of plates is mounted, further proofs are taken and superimposed on the previous images until the work is complete.

Complete cylinders

Complete cylinders as in the case of continuous photopolymer designs or laser engraved cylinders are quicker to proof as there is no need to mount individual plates for each element of each colour on each cylinder.

Most mounter/proofer devices are intended primarily to ensure accurate registration and image size of the plates on their various cylinders. Other values such as colour and image qualities relating to such factors as dot gain, ink film density and ink trapping will be only approximate.

Design of printing units

Flexo printing units comprise a plate cylinder, an impression cylinder and an inking system of two rollers only, plus an ink trough.

Plate cylinders

Plate cylinders are traditionally solid steel or alloy cylinders upon which the plates are mounted with a double-sided adhesive. The cylinders are removable to allow for different circumferences of cylinder to be employed to cater for different print repeats and pre-mounting and proofing prior to printing. This is in contrast to the pattern with web offset and photopolymer relief presses previously described, which have fixed cylinders of a standard size.

Continuous design cylinders

Continuous design cylinders will also have a metal base, but the photopolymer or rubber will form a complete overall layer in which the image is contained, as distinct from the conventional multiplate system.

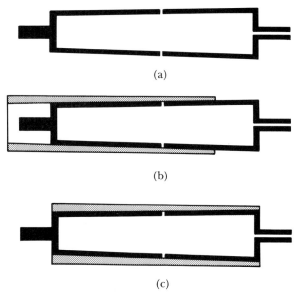

(a)

(b)

(c)

Figure 61   *Sleeve systems for flexography. The Strachan and Henshaw 'Speedwell' system. (a) Special base mandrels are supplied to suit existing printing unit. Each mandrel has a shallow tapered body, and includes piping and air outlets arranged radially in one position on the body. (b) The sleeve has an internal diameter with corresponding taper but of smaller diameter. This allows easy feed of sleeve to mandrel to a point when initial interference takes place between sleeve and mandrel. (c) Air is applied at nominally 150 psi which expands the sleeve, allowing easy positioning of sleeve in printing position. When air supply is switched off the sleeve contracts uniformly and positively grips around the mandrel ready for printing*

Sleeves

Sleeves are a simple and inexpensive alternative to solid cylinders. These are, typically, fibre glass tubes upon which the printing image is held in any of the ways previously described. The sleeve may be simply slipped over a body cylinder or mandrel on the production press or proof press and locked in to place. Sleeves have the advantages of light weight, quick mounting, low cost and easier transport when compared with solid metal cylinders, provided that the press has been specially designed or adapted to accommodate them.

Impression cylinders

Impression cylinders are usually plain steel cylinders geared into the press drive. Their circumference is not necessarily the same as that of the plate cylinders as is the case with web offset and photopolymer relief presses, and they do not have blankets. Their main function is to act as a support for the web and as an impression resist for the plate cylinder as well as providing a drive to the other cylinders in the unit.

Inking system and ink trough

Inking systems on flexo presses comprise two rollers only. A rubber covered trough or fountain roller sits in the ink tray containing the fluid ink and feeds the second roller which in turn applies ink to the printing cylinder. There are no ducts or keys as with other systems.

Ink is metered first by adjustment of the gap between the two rollers and then by a cell pattern engraved on the applicator roller surface. This cell pattern is referred to as the 'anilox' screen and will determine the ink film thickness which is laid upon the printing surface. Various shapes, sizes and depths of cell patterns may be used according to the type of work and the substrate in use. For solids and line work on absorbent paper stocks a coarse, deep pattern of 25–30 cells per centimetre may be used, whereas colour halftone work on non-absorbent plastic film may call for anilox rollers with more than 150 cells per centimetre.

The two-roller inking system on its own will give satisfactory results in many instances, but for the finest ink control a 'doctor' blade will be used. This is a fibre or metal blade which rides on the surface of the anilox roller against its direction of travel. The function of the blade is to shear the surplus ink cleanly from the surface of the roller leaving a precise quantity of ink in each cell to be deposited on the web.

Ink is normally pumped to the trough from a bulk supply and constantly re-circulated to keep it clean and of consistent quality. An independent variable-speed motor drive is often fitted to the inking rollers to control the initial ink flow, which may vary with press speed, ink viscosity, etc. The motor drive to the inking system may also be used to keep the rollers 'idling' during press stops and to avoid ink drying on the rollers.

Inks

Flexo inks have three main ingredients – colouring matter, resins and solvents – plus certain additives for specific purposes.

Colour

Colour is usually provided by means of dyes or pigments, or a combination of these. Dyes are usually transparent and dissolve completely in the solvent, whereas pigments may be opaque, have a definite particle size and form a 'suspension' in the solvent in combination with the resin to give the ink its 'body'.

Resins

Resins are usually synthetic materials used to give a substance to the ink and the final printed image. It is the resins which will key the ink to the substrate and the choice of resin will depend largely on this factor. For absorbent stocks the resin will need to give the ink sufficient body to prevent it penetrating through to the other side, causing the fault of 'strike through'. For plastic films the resin must have a chemical affinity for the substrate in order to ensure good adhesion.

Solvents

Solvents are used to dilute the ink to a consistency which will enable it to flow through the inking system, fill the anilox cells and transfer easily to the web. The proportion of solvent to pigment/resin content will determine the flow property or 'viscosity' of the ink. This can be measured in the laboratory by special purpose viscometers, or more simply at the press side by measuring the time a given quantity of ink takes to flow through a known aperture in a 'flow cup'.

Solvents are chosen for their ability to dissolve the resins and carry the pigments and for their compatability with the rubber or photopolymer printing surface and the substrate. For these reasons the number of solvents which can be employed in flexo inks is quite limited. Most are classified as alcohols, ranging from the traditional methyl and ethyl spirits to propyl and butyl alcohols. Various other solvents may be added to the ink to give it or the final printed film particular properties.

The solvent may comprise more than 80 per cent of the volume of an ink, but once it has fulfilled its function of carrying the pigments and resins to the substrate, it is no longer required and may be allowed to evaporate or be forcibly evaporated by means of accelerated drying devices on the press.

There are two safety factors which must be taken in to account when using evaporative solvents: The first is that most of the solvents referred to are flammable and a concentration of fumes can ignite under certain conditions. The second factor is that random evaporation of solvents will pollute the atmosphere and could contravene Health and Safety requirements. Evaporation must therefore be contained and controlled; inking and drying systems should be enclosed and solvent extraction devices employed to remove the fumes. Ideally a solvent recovery system should be employed to recover the evaporated solvent so that it can be recycled for future use.

Water-based flexo inks

Water-based flexo inks are available from most ink manufacturers and these are environmentally acceptable and non-flammable. However their use is not universal. They are mainly used for printing on absorbent materials such as papers and boards where they are ideal, but satisfactory formulations for impervious substrates such as plastic films are still difficult to achieve.

Arrangement of printing units

Flexographic printing units are initially arranged in three basic ways; stacked, in-line, or around a central impression cylinder. Combinations of these arrangements can be used for particular purposes and specially designed units are obtainable for publication work.

Stack presses

Stack presses have their printing units positioned around a central frame, the web being threaded from one unit to the next. These are the most common type of flexo press, as they are compact, of moderate cost and versatile in use. Stack presses are normally used for single-side printing, but perfecting can be arranged by altering the gearing on one or more of the units and re-threading the web. Up to six units is quite common and more than this can be provided if required.

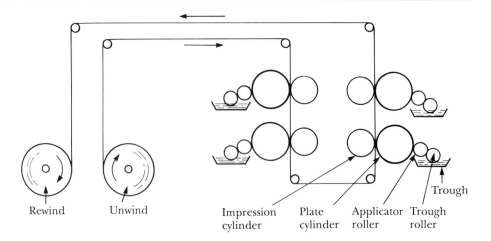

Figure 62   *Stack-type flexographic machine. A general-purpose machine suitable for a wide range of work on a variety of packaging materials*

In-line printing units

In-line printing units are a simple and logical way of arranging the press elements. All units are accessible and at convenient working height; any number of units can be included for front or back printing, and other in-line operations built in as and where required. Although in-line presses may take up more floor space than stack presses this can be a preferable arrangement for extra large presses printing on stiffer materials and where multiple in-line operations are undertaken.

Central impression presses

Central impression (CI) presses have several plate cylinders grouped around a single impression cylinder. This design is suitable for closer register work as the web is held firmly on one impression cylinder during the whole printing cycle. This is particularly advantageous when printing on extensible plastic films where stretch or slippage could occur when printing on separate units. CI printing units print on one side of the web only, therefore reverse-side printing will require an additional unit or units depending on the needs and nature of the work.

Publication presses

Publication presses are comparatively recent introductions and are based on the same basic principles as those for photopolymer relief publication presses. Arch-type perfecting units, etc. can be used, the main difference being that the simpler anilox inking system will be employed in place of the multi-roller trains traditionally used on relief presses.

PHOTO-GRAVURE

The photogravure process, or 'gravure' as it is commonly known, is a photographic version of the original 'intaglio' copperplate etching or hand-engraving processes, which may still be practised either as a craft form or for certain specialized purposes. In this technique the image is cut or etched in to the metal plate, most commonly copper, then rolled and filled with a viscous ink. Surplus ink is wiped from the surface, a sheet of paper laid over the plate and both plate and paper subjected to pressure in the intaglio press. Ink from the recesses is transferred to the paper according to the width and depth of the engraved lines. The result is a unique image with its own characteristics which make it distinctive from the other printing processes widely used for long-run publication and packaging work.

Applying the photographic principle to the intaglio process meant the introduction of a halftone screen and the replacement of continuous etched or engraved lines by a pattern of minute recessed cells. Flat plates are now replaced by cylinders, a liquid ink replaces the stiff copperplate ink and hand wiping is replaced by mechanical 'doctoring' with a metal blade. Instead of solid copper, the cylinders are electrodeposited with a 'skin' of copper which can be stripped at the end of the run and replated for the next job.

There are still two basic methods of producing the gravure image: etching and engraving.

Etching

Etched cylinders are the original form of photogravure and fall into two categories: conventional and halftone gravure.

Conventional gravure

The conventional method is largely manually operated, requiring a great deal of skill and experience to achieve the excellent results which are possible, as follows:

- A light-sensitive pigment or 'carbon tissue' comprising a coating of dyed gelatine on a stable paper base is exposed in a vacuum frame to a gravure screen, comprising a pattern of opaque squares separated by transparent cross lines. The exposure hardens the pigment paper in the transparent cross line areas and this will form the cell walls of the gravure image.
- The carbon tissue is then given a second exposure, this time to a continuous-tone positive. This exposure hardens the gelatine selectively to form an acid resist.
- The tissue is transferred to the prepared printing cylinder by wetting and rolling under pressure to ensure thorough adhesion.

- Etching with a ferric chloride solution determines the depth of each cell, depending mainly on the previous exposure. Cell wall areas will remain unetched due to the primary exposure to the gravure screen.

Conventional gravure gives the nearest approach to a continuous tone effect as the printed ink film is more or less continuous and the tonal efect depends on the depth of the ink film. However it does have some problems in that the very fine highlights may be difficult to hold and the slightest wear will affect them. This is particularly important when superimposing multicolour ink films. Fine detail may also suffer as the screen pattern is always present and fine lines or smaller typefaces can be reproduced only as a pattern of square cells.

Halftone gravure

Halftone gravure, together with more automated techniques, has largely replaced the conventional method, particularly for colour reproduction. Current systems have some or all of the following features:

- Pigment paper is replaced by presensitized film or by direct coating of the cylinder with a light-sensitive emulsion.
- Double exposure for screen and tone is replaced by a single exposure to a litho-type screened positive to produce dots of varying diameters rather than cells of constant area.
- Automatic etching machines and sequential production lines have replaced the traditional hand-bathing method. Flow rate, acid value, temperature, viscosity and other variables are accurately controlled and monitored during the processing cycle.
- Depending on the particular system dots may also be of varying depth as well as varying area to give a complete and subtle range of tones, coupled with a full depth of colour.

Electronic engraving

Etching of gravure cylinders either by hand or by automatic means is a time-consuming series of operations. For high-volume work, requiring speedy production of large numbers of cylinders it may be preferable to use a one-stage electronic engraving system which will incorporate the following features:

- A scanning unit will examine the copy via pulsed electronic light beams and transmit digitized information to a central computer console.
- A visual display station will enable the operator to examine the copy and modify the images to be engraved.

- The modified information will be used to drive an engraving unit in which diamond tipped styluses cut in to the copper surface of the printing cylinders at more than 4000 cuts per second.

The diamond stylus is designed to cut an 'inverted pyramid' cell in to the copper surface of the cylinder. This is an ideal feature in many ways in that the highlight tones will have a small area and shallow depth, while solids will have a maximum area and full depth. Computerized control also enables the electronic engraving system to save information for repeat work, cut multiple images from one master copy (step and repeat) and make 'seamless' images for continuous pattern work.

Whichever method is used, the continuous copper cylinders are capable of long runs in the order of several hundred thousand impressions. For extra long runs, in the order of millions, the cylinders may be chromium plated to give indefinite life.

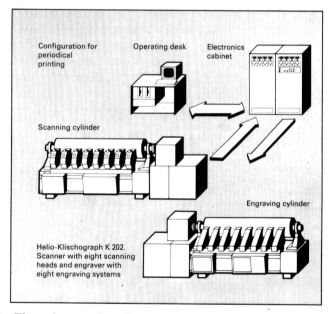

Figure 63 *Electronic engraving of gravure cylinders. The principles of Hell's Helio-Klischograph system are shown here*

Proofing

The flat-plate proofing technique commonly used for lithography is inappropriate to gravure, which is primarily concerned with the production of cylinders.

Proofing presses

Proofing presses for gravure are therefore highly specialized machines as they may need to cater for a wide variety of cylinder widths and diameters and to print on a wide variety of substrates. For small items such as stamps and labels the cylinder may be just a few centimetres in circumference and width, whereas larger publication presses can employ cylinders over a metre in circumference and up to three metres wide.

As with other printing processes the ideal proof press is one which most nearly simulates the production press situation. Few proof presses however can print at 500 metres per minute from several cylinders at the same time on a continuous web of material, therefore a degree of compromise is necessary.

Cylinders are usually proofed one at a time with modified inks to allow for the difference in press speed and the time interval between printing. The sheets or webs of paper are passed through the proof press the appropriate number of times and overprinted at each pass. With care and experience the proofs can give a good indication of the main image properties such as image location, register, relative ink film thicknesses, etc., sufficiently to determine whether any modifications are necessary before sending the cylinders to the pressroom. Corrections can be made either by further etching to deepen cells or by selective electrodeposition of copper to reduce cell volume.

Non-press proofs

Press proofing saves the expense of using a costly production press to predetermine the quality of the cylinders, but this is still an expensive and time-consuming exercise, which does not always produce results which accurately predict the performance of the cylinders on the production run. For these reasons a number of non-press proofing systems have been developed, similar to those described for lithographic pre-proofing in Chapter 5.

These systems usually simulate the build-up of subsequent colours by either overlaying transparent coloured films which have been made from the colour separations, or by building up successive layers of toner, pigment or ink on to a white base via photochemical means.

Ideally the base should be the actual stock on which the job is to be printed and the toner or pigment should be matched to the inks used for production. Control strips showing ink densities and percentage dot sizes, etc. should be included to enable accurate measurement of these factors at each stage of production.

As with press proofs, non-press proofs cannot claim to be absolute facsimiles of the production run, but with care and understanding they can provide a reasonably accurate prediction of the way the work will look when printed.

Design of printing units

Gravure printing units in their simplest form comprise the printing cylinder running in a trough of ink, a rubber impression roller and a 'doctor' blade to remove surplus ink from the surface of the cylinder.

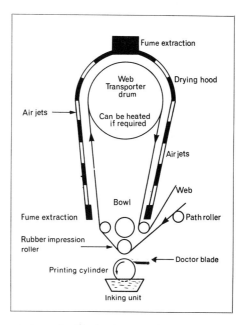

Figure 64 *Gravure printing unit. The basic parts of a typical gravure printing unit and its drying system are shown here*

Printing cylinders

Printing cylinders are usually one piece continuous cylinders containing the recessed, screened image which has been produced either by etching or engraving. The cylinders are designed to be easily removable for quick changeovers and to enable the cylinders to be proofed prior to printing and if necessary, stored for future use. Many gravure presses can accommodate cylinders of different diameters to allow for the production of work with varying print repeats, such as packaging work.

Ink container

The ink container may be a simple pan or trough in the most elementary types of press, but is more likely to be part of a complete circulating system where ink is pumped to the tray from a bulk supply and surplus ink returned, filtered and adjusted for solvent balance, etc., then re-pumped to the cylinder. The whole system should be enclosed as far as

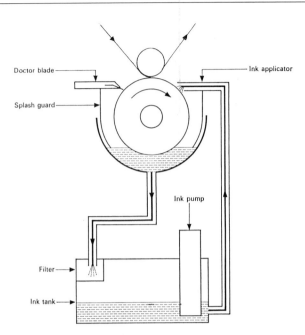

Figure 65 *A gravure ink circulating system showing spray rail application. Replenishment of the ink is automatic and surplus ink (after doctoring) is returned to the main ink supply for recirculation*

possible to ensure cleanliness of the ink and the avoidance of fumes escaping into the atmosphere.

Doctoring

Doctoring of the ink is by means of a flexible steel blade which is meticulously prepared to ride on the surface of the printing cylinder and remove surplus ink without damaging the surface of the cylinder or its image. Non-steel substitutes have been tried, but very few with any success. The slightest nick, burr or other imperfection in the face of the blade will either prevent efficient shearing of the ink from the cylinder surface or damage the fine cell structure of the printing image.

The doctor is normally located as near as is practicable to the printing nip in order to minimize the possibility of the volatile ink evaporating and drying in the cells between doctoring and impression. Adjustments can usually be made to the pressure and the angle of the doctor in relation to the cylinder to ensure the cleanest and most efficient 'wipe' of ink.

Impression

Impression is usually by means of a hard rubber covered roller in firm contact with the web and printing cylinder. Firm pressure is essential to ensure maximum transfer of ink from the minute cells of the gravure image. The impression roller is often backed up by a steel 'bowl' roller to reinforce its pressure and prevent deflection under the high stresses involved.

Electrostatic assistance

Electrostatic assistance may be employed to ensure efficient ink release. In this technique the impression roller is electrostatically charged, with the result that its electrostatic field attracts the oppositely charged ink in the cells of the printing cylinder. Electrostatic assist overcomes the problem of 'cell skip' where some cells fail to print, and at the same time permits printing with less pressure and consequently less wear on the image.

Arrangement of printing units for gravure is nearly always in-line, with the web being transferred from one unit to the next via a series of path rollers. Drying units are usually placed above each unit to ensure

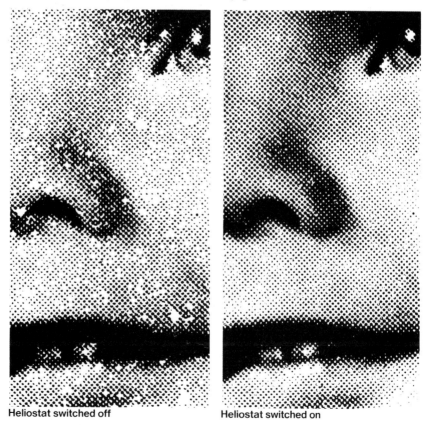

Heliostat switched off   Heliostat switched on

Figure 66 *Electrostatic assist. Uncontrolled electrostatic charges in the ink and the substrate may give rise to the problem of speckle of 'cell skip' where ink from certain cells does not transfer. The Heliostat device controls electrostatic fields at the printing nip to ensure that all the ink from each cell is released and transferred to the stock*
Courtesy Crosfield Electronics

that ink is sufficiently dry for overprinting or backing up, particularly on non-porous materials.

Inks

Gravure inks comprise three main ingredients: the colouring matter, resins and the liquid phase.

Colouring

Colouring is usually via dyes or pigments which must be of a small enough particle size to enable formulations which will easily enter and leave the cells of the gravure image.

Resins

Resins are synthetic polymers which combine with the colouring matter to give the ink its 'body' – the higher the proportion of resin, the 'stiffer' the ink. The physical formation of the final ink film depends largely on the properties of the resin content, therefore resins are chosen largely for their ability to dissolve in the solvent, carry the pigment and key to the substrate.

Solvents

Solvents are most commonly based on aromatic hydrocarbons such as toluene and xylene, which can dissolve most resins used in gravure inks and will evaporate quickly once the ink is transferred to the substrate. Other solvents may be included to either accelerate or slow down the drying rate, and specific alcohols may be incorporated to lower the surface tension of the ink which will assist flow into and out of the cells.

Hydrocarbon inks are ideal for printing on paper stock which initially absorbs a high proportion of the liquid ink. However, where gravure is used for printing of packaging materials such as wrappers, bags and other containers the residual odour of hydrocarbon solvents may be unacceptable and their evaporation rates may be too slow for films and foils where there is no absorbency to assist the drying. In these instances inks based on a specific range of commercial alcohols will be preferred, due to their faster drying rates and lower residual odour.

Whatever solvents are used it is desirable that the inking system is as closely covered as possible to ensure that flammable solvents are safely

Figure 67   *Multicolour gravure press by Windmöller and Hölscher*

contained and that their fumes do not escape to pollute the atmosphere. Where accelerated drying systems are used to 'boil off' the solvents it is also advisable to have an extraction system which will draw off the fumes and contain them safely. Ideally a solvent recovery system should be employed which will extract solvents as they evaporate and allow them to be recycled for future use.

WEB CONTROL DURING PRINTING

In all types of web printing the web must be kept under positive control before, during and after the printing process. The reel brake, web sensor and infeed system all play their parts prior to printing by ensuring that there is a constant tension in the unwound reel, and the feed through the printing units should ensure a similar consistency of control.

Cylinder circumferences need to be precisely determined in order to ensure:

- True rolling harmony between one cylinder and the next, particularly where ink is being transferred.
- Correct feed of the web from one unit to the next.

At each revolution a specific length of material will be fed through the press at a rate equivalent to the circumferential speed of the printing cylinders. If plate or blanket calipers are inaccurate, this will affect the passage of the web causing problems such as overfeeding or under-feeding, wrinkling, creasing, stretching, wandering or web breaks.

Web register

As the web passes from one printing unit to another it is essential to ensure that the printed images are laid upon the web in precise registration to each other. Minor adjustments to the fit can be made in two ways:

1 Varying the length of web between units by 'register' rollers.
2 Adjusting the relative circumferential locations of the printing cylinders via differential gearing.

Register rollers are a simple arrangement in which the web is passed over an intermediate roller which can be moved from its base position. Movement of the roller will alter the length of web between one unit and the next, and thus control the register.

Differential gearing allows the cylinders to be independently rotated, even while the press is running. This method is preferred where intermediate rollers are either undesirable due to the possibility of ink marking up on the rollers, or impracticable as with common impression cylinder machines.

Whichever method is used, very fine adjustment is required to achieve the fine register tolerances necessary for colour halftone work. The adjustment may be made either manually, by remote control or automatically.

Manual adjustment

Manual adjustment is by means of handwheels connected to the register rollers or differential gearing arrangements, as appropriate. The operator will observe a copy at the delivery of the press, note the need for adjustment, move to the appropriate stations, make the corrections, and repeat the sequence until a satisfactory state is attained. This is a simple and economic method for comparatively slow running presses or smaller, compact machines where all units and controls are within arms reach.

Remote control

Remote control is desirable for larger and faster presses where the delay in travelling from one station to another will result in an unacceptable waste level. Register controls will be extended mechanically or electro-mechanically to the central control area of the press where the print is first inspected and corrections initiated.

Automatic correction

Automatic correction is by means of photoelectric scanning heads situated between the units. These will inspect the moving web to check for accuracy of register, and at the same time send signals to the register control devices to initiate corrections as they are observed.

This technique requires specific 'register' marks to be included in the printed image and positioned on the running web in an appropriate manner for inspection by the scanning heads. Accuracy with these systems will be finer than that which can be determined by the human eye, and response to changes in register will be almost immediate.

Web turning

In the simplest of reel-fed presses the web passes in a direct line from unwind to delivery. However there are many occasions where the web is required to turn out of the normal web line and arrangements must be made for this. The main reasons for turning a web are either to meet a space problem or to make the press more versatile. The most common arrangements are:

- Right-angle turns via angle bars.
- Lateral displacement via turner bars.
- Inversion of the web via turnover sections.
- Exit and re-insertion via 'bay-window' devices.

Angle bars

Angle bars simply comprise a bar placed in the web path at 45 degrees so that the web can be wrapped around it and turned at a right angle. This enables manufacturers to build presses in which the web will 'turn corners'. The system is quite uncomplicated provided that the side of the web which contacts the bar is uninked. For instance, reelstands can be positioned at right angles to the printing units on a multiweb press to save space, or a web printed on one side may be turned over for perfecting on a second unit at right angles to the first.

However, where the inked side of a web is required to contact the angle bar there will be a risk of ink smudging as its rubs across the bar.

This is usually avoided by providing an 'air cushion' between the web and the bar by pumping low pressure air through apertures in the wrapped section of the bar.

Turner bars

Turner bars comprise a pair of bars at 45 degrees to the web path, so arranged that they will take a half web on a publication press and displace it laterally to run in line with the other half. This enables manufacturers to build 'double-width' presses, i.e., with webs twice the width of a standard newspaper, thus doubling the page capacity, but allowing the slit and turned webs to come to a single-width folder. As the webs have usually been perfected and are then passed over two bars it is desirable to have air cushion devices incorporated.

Web turnovers

Web turnovers comprise a pair of bars, one at 45 degrees and another at 135 degrees to web travel, plus an intermediate roller at 90 degrees. The web is thus turned over three times in all to finish up inverted, but travelling in the original web line. Air cushioning may be incorporated to avoid marking up, and mobile web turnovers can be used on multi-unit presses to increase versatility. For instance a four-unit press may print two colours on each side or three colours on one side plus one on reverse, etc.

Bay windows

Bay windows comprise an arrangement of angle bars and rollers designed to take a web or one strip of a web out of the press and re-insert it at another position. A basic method would be to pass the web over a 45-degree angle bar which takes the web to the side of the press; a 90 degree roller will then divert the web towards its new location and another 90 degree roller will redirect the web back in to the press where a second angle bar will re-align it in its original direction, but with a different relationship with the other web strips.

Web drying

Once the ink is deposited on the web it needs to change quickly from its free-flowing paste or liquid state to a plastic or solid form, firmly anchored to the substrate.

Paste inks

Paste inks used in litho and relief printing will have been reduced to films of a few microns in depth, and exposure to oxygen in the atmosphere will cause them to polymerise and thus form a cohesive body on the surface of the substrate.

Liquid inks

Liquid inks used in flexographic and gravure printing will also be reduced to thin films as their initially high solvent content evaporates to leave the resin/pigment body as a residual film adhering to the substrate.

Failure to dry thoroughly may give rise to a number of problems. Tacky, undried inks may cause layers of material to stick together, which is particularly undesirable where work is to be rewound; residual odour from unevaporated solvents may be offensive or even legally questionable under Health and Safety or Food and Drugs legislation; trapped solvent may cause dyes and pigments to 'bleed' in to the substrate, causing unpleasant halo effects around the image areas.

The drying process can be accelerated in a number of ways including forced air, heating and radiation curing.

Forced air drying

Forced air is helpful where solvent-laden fumes are to be removed. The rapid passage of air over the ink-laden web will speed the removal of evaporated solvents. Increased oxygen will also assist the polymerization of residual resin-based ink film.

Heating

Heating of the environment around the web will also accelerate the evaporation of solvents, and at the same time speed up the polymerization of the resinous material forming the base of the ink film.

Radiation curing

Radiation curing is used to convert resinous ink films from a semi-fluid or viscous condition to a stable plastic or solid state by means of selective radiation. Infra-red, ultra-violet and electron beam radiation may be employed, depending on the specific need, and it may be necessary to

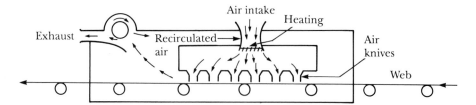

Figure 68   *Principle of hot-air drying system*

use inks specifically formulated for the particular method of radiation curing.

Location of the drying devices will vary according to the needs of the job, the printing process and the press design.

Intercolour drying units

Intercolour drying units are used on some simpler gravure and flexo presses, particularly when printing on non-porous films and foils. These are usually hot-air blowers aimed at a section of web between two printing units and the aim is to drive off sufficient solvent to enable the first ink film to 'set' to a plastic stage, sufficient to receive the next layer of ink. Controls for temperature and air will be included to allow for variations in substrates, press speed, etc., so that each ink film successfully 'traps' the following layer. A final dryer may be included when all colours have been printed, to ensure that the overlaid films are sufficiently dry before finishing operations such as folding, cutting and rewinding.

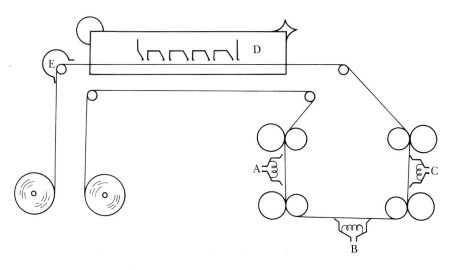

Figure 69   *Integrated drying system on a flexographic machine. A, B and C are intercolour hot-air blowers. D is the main drying tunnel and E the final cold air blower*

Drying hoods

Drying hoods are often preferred for the larger gravure and flexo presses. Here the drying equipment is located above the printing unit. Immediately after printing the web is passed around either a large drum or a bank of rollers and subjected to high velocity pre-heated air. The air is then extracted, with its evaporated solvent content, and the web continues to the next station with the ink in a virtually dry condition.

Oven dryers

Oven dryers will be used on multicolour web offset and relief presses, particularly when printing on coated papers which do not assist drying by absorbency to the same degree as non-coated stocks. The inks will initially 'trap' each other, wet-on-wet, in a similar manner to sheet-fed printing, then pass to the heated chamber for completion of the drying process. Hot air may be used, as on other types of press and it is quite common to use direct gas flames to heat and polymerize the ink.

Gas flame drying is often preferred as it is easily controlled and quick to respond. Electrically heated ovens take time to heat up and cool down, whereas gas ovens react almost instantaneously. Care must be taken to ensure that the gas flames only operate while the press is running at speed, and safety cut-outs will be incorporated to shut off the gas jets in the event of web breaks or sudden press stoppages.

Maximum temperatures in the oven must be strictly controlled to avoid singeing or burning the web, or blistering of coated stock. Temperatures may be reduced by using longer ovens or by zigzagging the web through the chamber where space allows for this arrangement.

Web cooling

Cooling of the web is essential after heat-assisted drying, as the web emerging from the drying system will contain hot, tacky ink which could cause marking-up problems on press rollers and other moving parts and cause the web to stick to itself or other items with which it comes in contact. Cold air blowers are sometimes used, but 'chill rollers' are considered more efficient, where the web is passed around a series of hollow rollers or drums containing continuously circulating refrigerated water.

This is the final operation to ensure that the ink on the substrate is sufficiently solidified to enable it to be subjected to the web finishing operations.

WEB FINISHING OPERATIONS

After printing and drying the web passes to the final part of the press for finishing. These operations may include folding, cutting, rewinding and a variety of ancillary operations.

Folding Folding may be either along or across the web.

Length folding

Length folding, as typified in broadsheet newspaper production is most commonly performed by a vertical, triangular 'former' plate, around which the web is wrapped and pulled by 'drawing' rollers to the cross fold and cutting sections. Several webs can be wrapped around one former, and the technique has the merit that, apart from the feed rollers there are no moving parts.

An alternative method of length folding is the 'plough' folder, so called for its superficial resemblance to a ploughshare. This technique makes the fold around a horizontal former and is used more in packaging work than for publications.

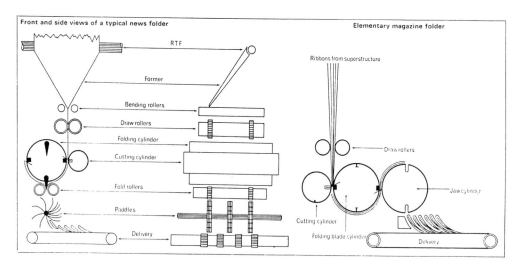

Figure 70 *Basic web folding system*

Cross folding

Cross folding usually requires the web to be pushed in to the nip of a pair of rollers by a metal blade. In most instances the web will by this stage have been cut in to its final print length. More than one cross fold may be made in order to achieve magazine, pocket book, digest or diary page sizes.

Concertina folding

Concertina or zigzag folding is a technique for cross folding uncut webs for such items as business forms (continuous stationery) pack labels and computer listing papers. The web is usually pre-perforated laterally as an aid to precise and positive folding.

Combination folding

Combinations of these techniques are often necessary to produce a final completed product such as a newspaper or magazine, and to lend versatility to the end-product provision.

A typical newspaper folder, for instance, may start with a set of feed rollers which propel the combined webs to the former plate. A second set of feed rollers, at right angles to the first, will 'draw' the webs around the former to make the length fold on a 'broadsheet' paper.

The webs may then be cut to length (hence the term 'cut-off') and passed to one or more sets of folding cylinders or rollers for cross folding. Finally the completed papers are delivered via an endless belt delivery system for counting, batching and despatching to their destinations.

Tabloid newspapers are produced in the same manner except that the webs are slit before folding in order to produce the final page size.

An additional 'quarter page' fold may be provided to produce a magazine-size product.

Ribbon folding

'Ribbon' folders employ a different approach in that the full width web is first slit in to page-width strips, which are then diverted around angle bars and associated before cutting to length and cross folding. This is a particularly versatile method for publications in which page sizes and numbers of pages may vary from one run to the next.

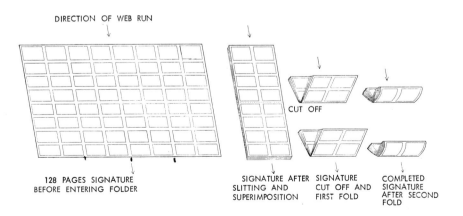

Figure 71 *Web folding. The folding sequence of a printed signature for pocket book production*
Courtesy Strachan and Henshaw Ltd

Cutting

Cutting the web to its final size is usually by means of a rotating blade cutting against either a counter-cylinder or another blade. Where a 'wad' of paper is to be severed and the quality of cut is not too important, a saw-toothed blade may be used, cutting into a resilient 'buffer' on the counter cylinder. This produces the typical newspaper-type cut-off being efficient and economical and requiring simple maintenance. In some instances such as magazine and sectional production, a saw-tooth cut may be used on press for fast delivery from the folder, with the final trimming taking place at the finishing stages.

More precise cutting will be by two finely-set and sharpened steel blades, usually one rotating and one fixed. To avoid a heavy load on the two blades as they make contact a slight 'scissor' action is made so that the rotating blade passes across the fixed blade from one side to the other. This requires the cutting section to be set at a slight angle to the web to ensure that the final cut is at a true right angle to the edge of the web.

Rewinding

There are many occasions where the web is required to be rewound rather than cut to length and folded. For instance the end product may be required in roll form, such as adhesive tapes, wallpapers, snap-off bags, wrapping papers, etc.; or it may be that rewinding is an intermediate stage for further operations as in the case of preprinted colour work for newspapers, overprinting, varnishing, laminating, bag and sack making, etc. There are two basic approaches to rewinding.

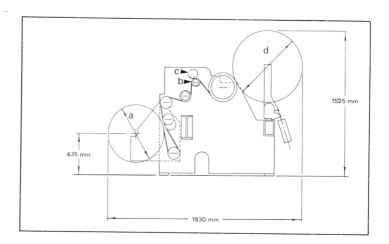

Figure 72   *Basic arrangement of a typical slitter/rewinder*
a Unwind diameter (610 mm maximum)
b Female shear knives or grooved roll
c Male shear knives or razor blades
d Rewind diameter (762 mm or 1060 mm maximum)
Courtesy Fords Dusenbery

Surface drive rewinds

Surface drive rewinds have the web wrapped around a core and driven by a drum or roller acting on the surface of the material. This gives a positive and efficient drive to the rewind and it is essential to ensure that the ink is thoroughly dry before it touches the rewind drum.

Centre drive rewinds

Centre drives work directly on the rewind reel shaft to provide a variable-speed drive which does not rely on physical contact with the reel and which can be adjusted to ensure correct tension in the web as it is rewound.

Whichever method is used it is essential to ensure that the ink is dry before rewinding to avoid the problem of 'blocking' where successive layers or rewound web stick to each other.

Web finishing

One of the advantages of web printing is that a number of non-printing operations, including finishing can be undertaken in-line on the press. In fact there are many instances in flow-line and batch production where there is no clear line between the web press operations and the finishing equipment.

Folding and cutting have been quoted as examples of in-line finishing operations on publication presses where delivery is to an endless belt arrangement. From here on the copies may pass via a specially designed conveyor system to other forwarding and finishing operations before despatch.

Once cut to size the work emanating from the web press can in many ways be treated in a similar manner to sheet-fed production, with the provision that the increased volume may require specially designed equipment and flow-line production techniques. Assembling, stitching and covering may take place in line with printing operations and three-knife trimmers may be used to cut the edges of the publication.

Batch counting devices

Batch counting devices may be included to identify quantities of newspapers or magazines in bundles. Traditionally these are 'quire-count' arrangements, whereby a 'kick copy' is slewed or displaced every so many copies to indicate the completion of a quire. (Originally a quire was defined as one-twentieth part of a ream. The number of sheets in a ream has varied from time to time, but is now standardized at 500. Thus a quire is 25.) More sophisticated arrangements are available if required where papers can be batched according to the quantities required by the eventual destination such as the distributor or retailer.

Bundling devices

Bundling may include strapping, tying or wrapping the bundles to assist further handling. Hand bundling is still practised for comparatively simple production conditions, or where labour costs are not of great significance. Automatic bundling is more common for modern high-volume production to wrap either standard size bundles or variable quantities by means of programmed control.

Labelling devices

Labelling devices may be linked to the batch counter to state the destination and route of the particular bundle or group of bundles. Ink-jet or laser printers are commonly used for this purpose as they can be computer programmed with each label printed and produced on site at the point of application. Pre-printed labels may be used where there is a standard pattern and where the publication is to be individually wrapped and mailed.

Inserting

Inserting ('stuffing') is the technique of placing loose sheets, cards, leaflets or other items of promotional material in to each publication before bundling, labelling and despatch. As with other operations this could be performed manually for comparatively low-volume production, but automatic equipment is more efficient for high-volume, fast-turnround work.

Reel handling and storage

Where work is rewound the reels need to be handled with care to ensure that the printed image is not damaged and the reels themselves not distorted out of shape to make them unfit for further processing.

Ideally, printed reels waiting for further processing should be supported through their centre cores so that no pressure is brought to bear on the substrate or the printed image. If this is not practicable then reels should be stored with their cores in a vertical position so that the weight of the reel is borne on its edge. Printed reels should not be stored horizontally as this will put pressure on the base of the reel, possibly causing problems such as ink transfer and sticking (blocking) as well as distortion of the image and substrate.

Where space is limited and it is necessary to stack reels one upon another, vertical stacking should be used rather than horizontal, for the same reasons stated above. In this instance it may be advisable to employ fork lift or clamp trucks designed specifically for the purpose of lifting transporting and stacking reels, especially where heavy or bulky materials are concerned. Unprinted reels may be stored horizontally and even stacked horizontally in limited quantities and for limited amounts of time. It may even be permissible to roll unprinted reels along the floor, provided it is clean and free from debris. Printed reels, however, should never be stacked horizontally or rolled along the floor.

Web collators

Web collators are used for assembling multipart sets for business forms, computer listings, continuous stationery, etc. Reel-to-pack collators take the printed reels, interleave them (possibly with one-time carbon) and present the assembled webs to the zigzag folder. Paper feed is usually via the pre-punched 'sprocket' holes used for form feeding.

Pack-to-pack collators are used where the individual webs have been pre-folded as they come from the press; otherwise the collating principle is similar to that for reel-to-pack collating.

Slitter/rewinders

Slitter/rewinders are used in many instances where a full width reel needs to be cut into narrower ribbons and rewound. These may be used before printing where mill reels are cut down to size for press use or after printing. Typical post-print instances are adhesive tapes, labels, stickers and ribbons. Precision slitting is essential plus fine control of unwind and rewind stations to ensure consistent quality of rewinding.

Waxer/coaters

Waxer/coaters work on a reel-to-reel basis to give additional protection to the substrate and its contents, as well as improving the appearance. Coating with molten wax or synthetic coating substances may be undertaken at the simplest level by dipping the web in a trough of coating material and shearing off the surplus by doctoring rollers or blades.

More precise coating thicknesses will be obtained by measured application from flexographic 'anilox' rollers or more directly by gravure-type applicator cylinders. A drying system will need to be included to solidify the coating before rewinding and other processing.

Hot-air impingement, ovens or radiation drying may be used according to the nature of the coating, the substrate and the speed of the machine.

Tests should be carried out at an early stage to ensure that the coating material, inks and substrate are compatible and will not give rise to any subsequent problems.

Laminating

Laminating requires one or both sides of a printed web to be brought into permanent contact with another layer of material, usually a transparent film. A thorough understanding of the various substrates involved is essential before deciding upon the appropriate method.

Adhesive lamination ensures efficient bonding by means of an appropriate liquid fixative, usually applied to the laminating film prior to being brought in to contact with the printed substrate. An efficient drying system is essential to ensure that solvents contained in the adhesive are fully evaporated and not trapped between the print substrate and the film laminate.

Thermal lamination can be used where materials are known to be compatible. The combined plies are subjected to heat and pressure and will bond without the need for an intermediate adhesive. Several layers may be combined in this way and care must be taken to ensure precise tension control in each web from unwind to rewind, as well as accurate temperature control, including efficient post-laminating cooling arrangements.

7 Non-publication printing

The main thread of this book so far has centred around commercial printing and publication work in particular and the communication industries in general, as do the other books in this series. However there are far more applications of the printing processes than the production of books, newspapers and other journals.

It is not possible in one volume to go into all of the specialist techniques required for the production of printed items varying from aerosol cans to art reproductions, beer mats to bank notes, charts to calendars, diaries to dictionaries, envelopes to encyclopedias, and so on through to video cases, wall tiles, x-ray prints and zip-a-tone transfers. What can be done is to home in on a few of the more general areas of non-publication printing, such as screen process, packaging, business forms and security work.

Screen process printing

Screen process printing is based on the stencil principle, which ante-dates all other modern printing processes. The reproduction of images by dabbing ink or paint through shapes cut out of thin sheets of material was practised in the far east more than a thousand years ago, and in Europe as early as the thirteenth century.

The modern process, however, dates only from the early years of this century when it was found to be commercially practicable to mount the stencil in a fabric mesh or screen which would allow the stencil to remain intact, while ink could pass freely through the mesh. This technique avoided the need to provide 'ties' to hold the various parts of the stencil together and thus improved the quality of printing dramatically. The application of photography enabled photostencils to be made, boosting the quality and versatility of the process even further.

Although screen printing cannot at present compete with the other printing processes in terms of speed and volume, particularly in the fields of publication work, it is in many ways the most versatile of all printing processes. It can print on practically any material from conventional papers and boards to metals, glass, fabrics and plastics as well as printing directly on to irregular-shaped objects such as bottles, cans, T-shirts and ceramics.

The equipment for screen printing can be essentially quite simple. The screen mesh is stretched taut across a rectangular frame which is hinged to a base board on which the material to be printed is placed. The stencil containing the image to be printed is attached to the screen either manually or by photomechanical means. A quantity of ink is placed at one end of the frame above the stencil and the ink forced through the mesh by a rubber or plastic 'squeegee' blade.

Screen meshes

Screen meshes were originally made from silk or similar fabrics, hence the traditional term 'silk screen' printing. Modern meshes are more likely to be made from synthetic fibres such as polyamides (nylons) or polyesters which are tougher, more stable, easier to clean and can be manufactured to very close specifications and tolerances. For specific purposes metal meshes of stainless steel wire or phosphor bronze may be used where absolute dimensional stability is essential or for extra long runs and thicker ink films.

The thickness of the fibres and the number of fibres per centimetre will determine the fineness of detail which can be reproduced and the depth of ink which will be laid upon the substrate. Choice of mesh will therefore depend on the type of work in hand. For road signs on metal where heavy ink films and solid areas are to be printed, thicker filaments will be used with good spacing between them. Fine detail on the other hand will require thinner filaments and closer spacing to ensure that the most minute information is recorded.

Stencils

Stencils may be produced manually or photomechanically. The simplest technique is to paint over the screen mesh with a suitable medium which will set hard to form the non-image area. This method however is mainly used for creative and artistic purposes and is rarely employed commercially.

Hand-cut stencils

Hand-cut stencils are used for simpler types of work where the original artwork can be transferred to a suitable stencil medium and cut by means of a scalpel to provide a clear, clean outline for attachment to the screen without the time and expense of photographic processing. Early paper stencils had to be glued to the mesh with an appropriate adhesive, but modern materials contain an adhesive backing which can be pressed or ironed directly on to the screen.

For high-volume work automated stencil cutters are available which can be linked to computerized image plotters which direct the scalpel to cut the base material.

Photostencils

Photostencils are used for the majority of screen process purposes. These comprise light-sensitive coatings which can be exposed to a master and developed to produce a stencil which will allow ink to pass through the image areas but not through the non-image areas. Photo-stencils can be processed in a darkroom and then transferred to the screen (the 'indirect' method) or the screen itself may be coated with the light sensitive material and the stencil formed directly in the screen mesh (the 'direct' method). Combinations of these two basic methods are also possible depending of the type and quality of work undertaken.

Frames

Frames for the simplest of screen machines may be made of wood or even plastic, but for larger installations or precision work aluminium is more likely to be used or even steel. It is essential that the frame be stable and rigid as the screen will be mounted under tension and any distortions of the frame will be reflected as an instability in the mesh. The tension in the screen is critical to good results and care must be taken to ensure that it is correctly stressed before it is secured to the frame. This may be done by separate screen tensioning devices or by incorporating a tensioning system in the frame.

The base needs to be flat and perfectly level to ensure accurate transfer of ink through the mesh. For paper substrates the base may contain a number of small holes through which air is drawn by a vacuum pump to ensure that the stock is held in firm contact during the printing cycle.

Squeegee blades

Squeegee blades were originally made from natural rubber and these can still be obtained where required for special purposes. Plastic blades, however, have now largely replaced rubber as they are tougher, more resistant to abrasion and can be produced in a consistent range of hardnesses. The length, thickness and hardness of the blade will influence the way in which ink is forced through the mesh as will the angle at which it is operated, as well as the speed with which it traverses the screen. Wear on the blade may alter its profile. It is therefore essential to ensure that all of these variables are controlled and maintained at all times if consistent results are to be obtained.

Inks

Inks for screen printing must be fluid enough to pass through the screen mesh and at the same time sufficiently cohesive to form a solid, continuous film on the substrate. Adhesion qualities are also important for printing on non-absorbent bases such as glass, metals and plastics.

These are the main constituents in a screen printing ink: pigments which provide the colouring matter, liquefied resins which form the body of the ink, and solvents which dilute the ink to enable it to pass easily through the screen mesh and then evaporate to leave the main body of the ink in firm contact with the substrate. A variety of additives may also be included in order to aid flow, drying and adhesion, or to improve properties such as gloss, scuff resistance and flexibility.

Printing

Adaptations of the basic screen process principle are quite common and the technique may be varied to suit the type of work in hand. The simplest equipment is manually operated but automatic versions are quite common and multistation versions available where several colours are to be printed. The printing stations may either be arranged in-line or in 'carousel' form, whichever is the most appropriate.

For printing on cylindrical objects such as bottles and cans the frame may be arranged to traverse the container as it revolves below the screen during the printing cycle.

Textiles and wall coverings etc., may be printed by means of a cylindrical screen where the ink and squeegee are contained inside the cylinder. The continuous web of material will pass between the screen cylinder and a counter-cylinder with ink being forced through the stencil as the cylinders revolve.

Drying

Drying of the screen printed image requires special attention as the ink film is usually far thicker than that of other printing processes and there is often a high solvent content. Further time must be allowed for the solvent to evaporate or an accelerated drying system should be employed.

For shorter runs it may be possible to place the sheets individually in a drying rack until they are sufficiently dry to be handled in bulk. When printing on metal or glass it may also be necessary to heat the finished work in an oven to dry and fuse the ink to the substrate. Specially designed racks and drying systems are made to take work as it comes from the printing station so that work flow is continuous, and completed dry work is delivered at the end of the line.

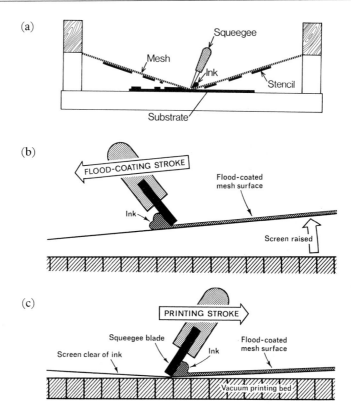

Figure 73   *Principle of screen process printing*
Courtesy Autotype

Screen inks may also be formulated to dry by exposure to infra-red or ultra-violet radiation. This reduces the need for a high solvent content as the radiation affects the photochemistry of the polymer resins in the ink to 'cure' or solidify them by forming cross-polymer links. In addition to the infra-red or ultra-violet lamps there is usually some need for extraction of residual solvents and cooling of the finished work. Care must be taken to ensure that the lamps are properly shielded, and that the ozone given off by ultra-violet lamps is safety extracted.

Packaging and converting

The packaging industry in the UK alone is estimated to account for more than a billion pounds worth of printed matter per annum out of a total estimated turnover of just over five billion pounds. The list of printed products which come under this heading includes bags, wrappers, cartons, boxes, pouches, packs, sacks, tins, bottles and other containers, each of which has its own subcategories and special requirements.

This area is also allied to the fields of 'identity marking' which includes such items as tickets, tags, badges, stickers and labels; as well as 'decorative products' including textiles, wall and floor coverings, printed tiles and 'decals' or transfers.

The range of substrates in this field is far greater than that for commercial printing and publishing. Special techniques and machinery may be required for printing on materials which range from multiple-ply sacks to corrugated box boards, flexible films, rigid plastics, metal sheets, metallic foils and on to glass, ceramics and textiles

Paper bags and wrappers

Paper bags and wrappers are usually printed from reels of machine glazed (MG) bleached sulphite paper, a cheap, white stock, glazed on one side only and receptive to the liquid inks usually employed for this type of work. The most common printing process for the cheaper ranges and short-to-medium runs (say, up to a million) is flexography, which can print at low initial cost and include quick and simple changes of information such as addresses, prices, dates and other variable data. Gravure may be used for longer runs and where thicker films of ink are required, such as metallics or fluorescents. Combination presses are not uncommon where the main colour illustrations are printed by gravure and changeable data printed by flexography. Continuous designs for wrappers, etc. can be printed by either process.

Wrappers may be either rewound after printing and distributed in rolls of various sizes to agents, wholesalers, etc., or they may be cut to sheet size to be sold by the hundred or thousand sheets.

Bags will need to be converted either 'on press' by means of folding, gluing and cutting stations to produce batches of finished bags, or the printed webs can be rewound and finished later on a bag making machine.

Overprinting machines, usually flexo, may be used to print local or update information at the rewinding, bag-making or sheeting stages.

Plastic bags and wrappers

Plastic bags and wrappers are printed on web-fed presses, again mainly by flexography or gravure depending on the length of run, type of image and quality of reproduction required. Extensible films require delicate control of web tension to avoid distortion of the substrate and to ensure accurate registration for multicolour work. Where colour halftone work is to be printed the common impression type of press is preferred, where all printing cylinders print against one impression cylinder as the web passes around it.

Most plastic films have an 'inert' surface which does not readily accept printing ink. The surface can be made receptive to ink by either gas flame impingement or 'corona discharge' treatment in which the web is subjected to a high voltage source which renders the surface more receptive to printing inks. Reels of film may be supplied 'ready treated' on one side or both and it is essential to check which side is treated in the event of one-sided film. In cases of doubt a quick check can be made by dabbing ink on both sides to see which will best receive it.

For high volume production the film may be 'blown' from an extruder, printed and finished in line. A complete tube of film may be blown for in-line bag making and flattened or gusseted prior to the printing stations. In this case surface treatment must take place in line and before printing. As with paper bags and wrappers, the printed work may be rewound for further processing or completed in line to produce cut bags or 'snap apart' sets.

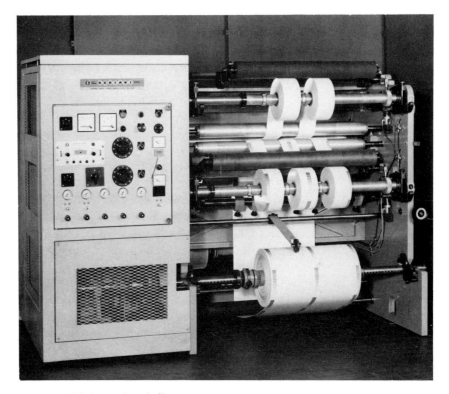

Figure 74 *Slitting and rewinding*
Courtesy Cesare Schiavi

Films

Films fall into a number of basic categories:

Cellulose films

Cellulose films are made from regenerated cellulose and are among the most widely used and versatile of packaging materials, being transparent and naturally proof against contamination by dust, grease and oil. They can be coated to make them moisture-proof and airtight or tinted for practical or economic reasons. Flexible grades can be obtained for 'twist wraps' such as sweet wrappers; they can be sealed by heat and pressure, are bio-degradable and can by recycled for future use.

Polyethylene films

Polyethylene, or polythene as it is commonly called, is one of the most commonly used plastic films, being of low cost, comparatively tough, flexible and easily heat-sealed. It is almost completely inert chemically, unaffected by most common solvents, acids and alkalis and is not affected dimensionally by atmospheric conditions. Bulky, irregular-shaped articles are often packed in polyethylene due to its properties of strength, flexibility and elasticity.

Polypropylene films

Polypropylene is tougher, clearer, glossier and more versatile than polyethylene; offering better protection against greases and oils as well as being less permeable by gases and odours. It is as clear as most cellulose films, though not as odourproof as the best of them, and requires a higher temperature than cellulose film or polyethylene for heat sealing.

Polyester films

Polyester films are clear, stable and durable, with high resistance to chemicals, gases and solvents. Although they are comparatively expensive, polyesters can be produced in extremely thin gauges – less than one-hundredth of a millimetre in thickness – which may be tougher than much thicker films of other plastics due to its extremely high tactile strength. These films are often used as laminates for wood-grain surfaces and other articles which must withstand hard wear, and as polyester is not unduly affected by high or low temperatures, it is particularly suitable for food packs which may be stored under refrigeration and subsequently boiled-in-the-pack before opening.

Polystyrene films

Polystyrene is more rigid than most other plastics and the thicker gauges can be moulded to form fancy-shape box tops, blister packs or complete boxes. It is comparatively expensive and not easily heat sealed. In its expanded form polystyrene can be 'blown up' to form a cellular material containing many air pockets. This is a white material of very light weight, extremely good for insulating purposes and may be cut and creased to form a carton, moulded to form a box, used as an insulating jacket or as a liner for other cartons.

Metalized films

Metalized films are metallic coatings which can be applied to cellulose and plastic films to improve their appearance and properties. These are not thin sheets of pure metal but a deposition of 'vapourized' metal upon the substrate. Most of the more commonly used packaging films can be obtained in metalized form and a wide variety of colours and effects can be achieved. To prevent damage by scratching or scuffing the metalized layer may be sandwiched or laminated between two other films for protection.

Laminates

Laminates of two or more films may be necessary to obtain the ideal properties with a degree of economy. For instance, if the high protection, clarity and surface properties of polyester film, which cannot be heat-sealed, need to be combined with the economy and sealability of polyethylene, then a laminate of the two films may be the answer. Another instance might be where ink rub-off cannot be risked; therefore the film is 'reverse printed', i.e., on the underside of the film, and yet under health regulations the ink may not contact the food product inside; here again a lamination may solve the problem.

Cartons

Cartons may be printed either on sheet-fed presses or on specially designed web presses, and the design and origination stages will vary according to which method is to be used. For sheet-fed production the designer must bear in mind that the cartons will be cut from a rectangular sheet of carton board of a given size and that any unused board will be waste. Allowance must be made for the sheet to be gripped at the front edge and space allowed around the cutting area where the image is to bleed off the edge of the carton. Provision should be made for register marks, control strips and other guides such as cutting and folding indicators, and these may be located either in the trim areas of the sheet or at folded-in areas such as glue flaps.

Offset lithography and relief offset are the most common sheet-fed printing processes and origination, planning, proofing and platemaking will follow standard procedures as described earlier. Presses for carton printing will need to be robust machines, particularly in the larger sizes, capable of handling the stouter carton boards firmly but without damaging them. Impression cylinders and sheet transport systems should not unduly bend, stretch or scuff the boards. Automatic non-stop changeovers should be included at feeder and delivery, as a metre high pile of boards will only take a few minutes to process. Drying systems such as ultra-violet curing are commonly located at the delivery to ensure that the ink is thoroughly dry on each sheet before the next is super-imposed.

After printing, the boards will go to the finishing department for cutting into carton blanks. A 'forme' is prepared comprising cutting rules to form the outer shape of the carton, creasing rules which are less sharp and slightly lower to form the folds in the cartons and perforating rules for tear-off tabs, etc. The forme is contained on the bed of a press to which the sheets are fed one at a time, and cutting takes place against a specially prepared, steel jacketed flat bed or cylinder. Accurate alignment between the printed image and the forme is essential and it is advisable to prepare the forme well in advance and have it checked with proofs, preferably before platemaking to ensure an accurate fit. Forme production is a skilled precision technique and modern forme-making systems employ computerized plotters to ensure accurate positioning of the rules. After cutting, the waste is stripped and the cartons may be folded and glued either manually or automatically ready for filling and closing.

Reel-fed production of cartons provides a higher throughput and ensures a continuous supply of ready-cut carton blanks. It is usually advisable to standardize on a limited number of web widths and cylinder circumferences for maximum efficiency and there may be a limit to the minimum run which is practicable when compared with sheet-fed production. Printing, cutting and stripping of the waste can all take place at the same time, leaving the blanks ready for the erection, gluing, filling and closing operations.

Although offset printing may be used for web fed carton production, flexography and gravure are more commonly employed; flexo for its economy and ability to change patches of information quickly and as often as necessary, and gravure for its long-run ability and the depth of colour which is difficult to achieve with the other processes. Flexo and gravure also have continuous printing surfaces and the ability to change print-length as quickly as a cylinder can be changed. This gives the carton designer more scope and greater flexibility for creating interlocking shapes, continuous patterns and overall background tints, coatings etc.

Bar codes

Bar codes are printed on many cartons and other containers to indicate the manufacturer, contents and type of pack, and in some instances the price. The codes comprise a series of lines and spaces printed to a precise specification, plus a numerical code. The intention of a bar code is to give instant information relating to the pack and its contents by scanning with a light pen or other device. Manufacturers can register with the Article Numbering Association to obtain their individual codes and can then code up to 100,000 different products for the purposes of stock control and retail distribution.

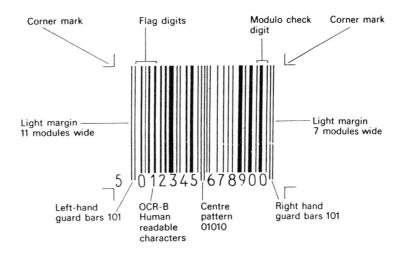

Figure 75 *Bar coding. Bar codes give rapid information relating to a product. This diagram shows the basic components of the European Article Number (EAN) System*

Two main systems are in use: European Article Numbering (EAN) and the American-based Universal Product Code (UPC). Both have similar features and are in many respects compatible with each other and with code-reading devices.

The codes need to be printed with great accuracy as any thickening or sharpening of the lines could result in incorrect information being recorded. The production of master codes on film is a specialized field and printers need to use high quality masters if codes are to be printed within the required tolerances. Inks must be sufficiently dense to be read by the recording device, ideally black on white, but any reasonably dark colour ink on a light background may do. A yellow bar code printed on a green background will certainly be unsatisfactory and it is advisable for printers to use light pens as part of their quality control programme to ensure that codes are being printed to a satisfactory standard.

Labels

Labels may be printed on sheet-fed presses for short runs and where the work forms an occasional part of the work pattern of a general commercial printing house. However, for specialized production web-fed presses are more commonly used. The development of the self-adhesive label revolutionized that sector of the industry in the 1960s and 1970s and improved base materials continue to be introduced together with purpose-designed machines which can produce labels of high quality combined with versatility.

The basic substrate for self-adhesive label printing is a laminate comprising a base of stable carrier paper (or sometimes card) coated with a siliconized 'release' layer and label paper itself with its adhesive backing. Various grades of label paper can be obtained depending on the printing process to be used and the quality of work expected. Metallic and metalized plastic printing substrates are also available. Adhesive backings may also vary according to the purpose for which the labels are intended.

Practically all of the main printing process may be used for label printing depending on the customer's preference, and it is quite common to mix printing processes on one press in order to obtain the appropriate quality or effect. Other operations such as die stamping, embossing, thermographing and foil stamping can be employed in line, plus hole punching for, say, tractor-fed computer labels, as well as perforating and slitting.

After printing, the labels pass to the finishing stations where the die-cutting unit will cut the individual label shapes out of the paper layer. This is a precision operation as the cutting blades must cut completely through the paper but not the silicon coated base. The next operation is to strip the non-label waste from the base leaving only the labels in contact with the silicon layer. The web may then be either rewound, folded into packs or cut in sheets.

Metal containers

Metal containers may be printed initially from flat sheets of tinplate or aluminium which are first coated with a suitable medium to receive the printing inks. Screen printing is often used for short runs, specialized work and where thicker ink films are required, but offset is more commonly employed for longer runs and in flow-line production.

Presses for metal printing are purpose-designed to handle the heavy, rigid sheets or rolls of metal. A straight line printing path is desirable to avoid bending or cracking the metal and continuous feed and delivery systems are essential to avoid frequent stoppages.

Base coatings and inks are specially formulated to suit the needs of metal printing as well as overlay lacquers which may be used to protect the printing image from abrasion and scuffing. The coatings, inks and lacquers also need to be compatible with the drying system which may range from racking and 'stoving' of small batches in individual ovens, to in-line drying ovens or radiation 'curing' systems. The inks, etc. must also be sufficiently pliable to withstand shaping and forming into the finished article.

Cylindrical containers

Cylindrical containers such as tubes, cans and bottles are usually printed after they have been formed and shaped. As with sheet-fed metal printing the main processes are screen, for batch work, and relief or litho offset for longer runs. Offset printing presses are often designed on the common blanket principle, where a number of printing plates deposit ink on a single blanket cylinder. This enables several ink films to be transferred to the container at the same time as they rotate in rolling contact, thus saving the need for them to travel from one printing unit to another in order to receive each subsequent colour.

This technique is ideal for line images where colours do not overlap. However where colours do overlap it is important to ensure that the inks remain as cohesive layers by correct adjustment of their 'tack' or adhesion properties. In choosing the sequence of colours the printer will bear in mind that the last film of ink laid down on the blanket will be the first and lowest film transferred to the container. The final visual effect will therefore depend on the successful 'trapping' of the ink layers and their degree of transparency or opacity.

Business forms production

In an increasingly bureaucratic age the creation and usage of business forms is now a major sector of every industry. The 'paperless society' mooted in previous eras has proved to be a myth, and it is estimated that stationery and business forms of one type or another account for up to one fifth of all printed matter. While the production of the odd letterhead or invoice is a standard part of the jobbing printers' repertoire, mass production of these items requires specialized techniques and machinery.

Web-fed presses

Web-fed presses are most commonly used especially for the production of continuous forms for computers and data processing purposes. Offset litho is the main printing process, although relief offset may be employed for longer runs and direct relief printing for imprinting and numbering.

The basic construction of a typical forms press would be an in-line arrangement comprising a reelstand, infeed, printing units, ancillary units for perforating, punching, numbering etc. and finishing stations for either rewinding, cutting or pack folding. Multiweb presses may be used for high-volume production of multipart sets, but it is more common to print individual webs and collate the parts at a later stage.

Fixed-size presses

Fixed-size presses are the simplest, cheapest and most efficient machines, allowing continuous production and rapid changeover from one job to the next. This does, however, require a measure of standardization on a limited number of form sizes as they must correspond to the circumference of the printing cylinders, plus a guarantee of sufficient work to keep the press fully occupied. The larger business forms producers may be able to support a number of fixed-size presses catering for most of the common form sizes, but the odd non-standard order must either be rejected or printed on a variable-size press.

Variable-size presses

Variable-size presses are designed to cater for a number of form sizes and this is most commonly accomplished by changing the main printing cylinders for cylinders of different diameters. In offset printing this will mean changing the plate and blanket cylinders only, as the impression cylinder on a web press is usually a continuous drum. The two cylinders are contained as a 'cartridge' which can be withdrawn and replaced in a matter of minutes. Some additional adjustment may be necessary to the inking and damping roller settings to compensate for the change in cylinder diameter. For direct relief printing only the plate cylinder needs to be changed. It may also be necessary with change-size presses to make similar adjustments to ancillary units such as perforating, punching, numbering, cutting and folding in order to accommodate the change of size.

Ancillary operations

Ancillary operations are probably more prolific in forms production than any other class of printed matter. Hole punching is necessary for form feeding through computers or other automated equipment as well as for filing and storage; slitting is used to cut webs of paper to single-form width and to remove unwanted trim; perforating is used for separating forms and indicating tear-off slips or tabs; numbering is required on a high proportion of printed forms; stapling, crimping or line gumming will join sets of forms together; spot carbon patches may be printed on the reverse side of the form where information is required to pass through to subsequent parts of the set only at discreet positions. The additional operations may be undertaken either in-line with printing or

Figure 76 *Business forms printing. Timson T24 press with unwind, web aligner, infeed control, three printing towers, and ancillary operations including perforating, punching and slitting with the option of sheeting, rewinding or zigzag folding*

as separate operations when the form sets are gathered and collated together for finishing.

Collators

Collators are machines specifically designed to gather the individual webs as they come from the printing press and complete the sets ready for despatch. Most webs will already be printed, punched and perforated, leaving other operations such as numbering, imprinting, stapling, crimping and gumming to be performed as the webs are collated, plus the insertion of carbon sheets when required. An advantage here is to 'crash' number or imprint from relief plates completely through the set at one operation.

Overprinting machines

Overprinting machines may be used to add information to preprinted or even unprinted packs. This enables the forms printer to mass-produce part-printed or blank forms for overprinting with individual information at a later stage. Thus a standard form set may be overprinted with a customer's individual information in quantities as and when required. It is also possible for local printers to take advantage of this technique by purchasing bulk supplies of blank form packs and overprinting them on their own premises. In this instance the overprinting machine may be either a purpose made device or an adapted sheet-fed press such as a small offset, which will allow the local printer to offer customers the benefit of personalized multipart form sets.

Papers for forms

Bond papers

Bond papers are good quality printing stock of substances up to and above 100 grammes per square metre (100 gm^2), surface sized for good ink reception and retention and often having a watermark denoting the mill or special making. These are used as letterheads, top copies of form sets and other documents which need to be substantial, long lasting and of a presentable appearance.

Bank papers

Bank papers are similar in structure to bonds but thinner, usually less than 60 gm^2 and are used for multipart sets to reduce bulk and cost.

Manifold papers

Manifold papers are even thinner than banks, having a substance of less than 40 gm^2 and are used to reduce bulk where there are many parts in a form set.

Tinted papers

Tinted papers are available in all of the above types and are useful to immediately identify different parts in a set as well as saving a printing operation or a colour change. An alternative is to use a tinting device on the press, which will apply a dye to one or both sides of the stock. The thin, liquid dyestuff used dries almost immediately to allow for overprinting as an in-line operation.

Carbon papers

Carbon papers are thin-base tissue webs with a pressure-sensitive carbon coating on one side. These are used as interleaves between parts of a form set and are usually intended to be used one time only, hence the term OTC (one time carbon). Coatings may be obtained in varying degrees of pressure sensitivity to suit variables such as the type of paper, number of parts in the set and whether the forms are to be handwritten or completed by machine. The most common colour is black although other colours can be obtained if required.

Carbonless papers

Carbonless papers are used to transfer written or typed information as the form set is completed, through the top sheet to lower sheets without the need for carbon interleaves. Various types are available from 'coated back' papers in which a pressure-sensitive coloured coating is applied to the reverse side of a web to transfer the information in a similar manner to that of carbon paper, to 'chemical transfer' papers coated with colourless chemicals which produce visible images when impacted by a ball point pen or typewriter key. The types and grades of carbonless papers need to be chosen carefully according to the number of parts in the set, the position in the set of each part (top copies may have different requirements from intermediate or bottom copies) and the method of completing the form.

Sizes

Form sizes for cut sets should normally conform to the ISO A series from A3 at 297 mm × 420 mm to A5 at 148 mm × 210 mm. Continuous forms, however, are still tied to the original 'imperial' sizes which were measured in inches, and still are in many parts of the world. The reason for this situation is that the vast majority of the original machinery and equipment for printing and processing continuous forms was conceived, developed, manufactured and installed before the introduction of the ISO sizes. 'Sprocket' punch holes for feeding paper were specified as one-eighth of an inch in diameter and spaced at half-inch intervals, centre to centre, along the edge of the form. Perforations were arranged to cut precisely half-way between a given pair of holes and form sizes were thus established.

With the advent of metrication it was not found practicable to convert continuous forms immediately to the ISO A sizes. A compromise was therefore agreed in which the imperial sizes were accepted as standard and converted to the nearest appropriate metric size, the one-eighth holes are now specified as 4 mm in diameter and the half-inch spacing becomes 12.7 mm, etc.

In practice this causes few problems as web or form widths can be specified in either millimetres or inches, and form depths or cut-off sizes can be chosen to fit the nearest ISO size within a few millimetres.

Design

Form design needs at least as much consideration as any other product, yet there is never a shortage or badly designed forms. A poorly planned set of forms can be unnecessarily expensive in terms of wasted materials, equipment and time. Forms designers should address themselves to three basic areas and a number of questions.

1 *Reason* for producing the form. Is it intended to *obtain* information as in the case of a questionnaire? To *give* information as in the instance of an invoice? *Record* information as with a file card? Perhaps a combination of all three? How many people need copies of the form? What is the purpose of each part and where will it finish up?

2 *Processing* of the forms. Will they be hand or machine filled? Posted, circulated or filed? Separated and distributed? Will the punch hole selvedges need to be removed? Do they require tear-off reply slips or window envelopes? Will they be folded, file hole punched, perforated or numbered?

3 *Printing* considerations. What are the minimum and maximum form dimensions possible? What area of the form can actually be printed? Can the back of the form be printed? What substrates are available? Are there any technical limitations to the position of printed matter, numbers, perforations, etc.?

Forms design packages are available for most computer-based systems, allowing these and other questions to be considered. A number of trial formats and designs can be tested and evaluated before the finalized document is put into the production sequence.

Security printing

The term 'security printing' encompasses a number of obvious areas including bank notes, stamps, credit cards, cheques, postal orders, vouchers, travel tickets and coupons, as well as printed matter coming under the headings of 'classified', 'confidential' and 'private', which can include many types of document from examination papers to top secret government information.

There are three main concerns for the security printer:

1 To secure the confidentiality of the documents through origination and production, from the preparation of artwork to proofing, platemaking and printing.

2 To ensure the authenticity of the documents and make them readily identifiable by all concerned.

3 To make copying, duplicating and forgery of the documents as difficult as possible.

In-works security

In-works security depends on three main factors:

1 Premises security in the form of solid buildings, guarded doors, limited access and positive storage of valuable artefacts in safes, strong rooms, etc.
2 Recruitment of reliable staff whose record shows that they can be relied upon and who are prepared to conform to stringent working procedures and security requirements.
3 Strict observance of procedures for working methods, stock control, storage of materials, waste disposal and the reception and despatch of goods.

These requirements do not necessarily mean a regimented, distrustful environment, but in many ways the opposite, for example an environment which is orderly, regulated and predictable, in which members of the organization understand their individual duties and reponsibilities and work together to achieve common objectives.

Currency printing

Bank notes are typical of the security printing situation as they must be instantly recognizable, simply identifiable, durable and difficult or impossible to reproduce illegally.

To achieve these aims bank notes are printed on a specially tough rag-based paper produced under conditions of high security. The paper contains its own individual watermark, which could possibly be different in design and position for each denomination. Some bank notes comprise more than one layer of paper which enables metal, or plastic strips and other devices to be incorporated to aid identification and deter forgery. The 'feel' of the note as well as its appearance helps to make its characteristic quality.

The design of a bank note is usually based on a hand drawn or engraved image which is difficult to copy or photograph. Standard typefaces or photographs are rarely, if ever used and 'Guilloche' patterns are commonly incorporated. These are complicated line patterns produced by mechanical or computer-driven plotters, often in several intertwined colours and difficult to copy or reproduce by conventional printing techniques. Micro images and subtle hidden or 'secret' patterns may also be included to aid the detection of forgeries.

Cheque printing

Although credit cards, bank giro systems and other forms of credit and money transfer have increased dramatically in recent years, there are still many millions of cheques made out and encashed every day.

Unlike bank notes, cheques themselves have no particular value – it is the personalized information written on the cheque which gives it value. The 'security' factors for cheque printing are therefore centred more around the problem of fraudulent issue of cheques rather than copying or forging.

Figure 77   *Examples of guilloche patterns which may be used in security printing systems*
Courtesy Jens Scheel

The information to be *printed* on a cheque falls in to a number of diminishing categories including:

- The name of the bank or other financial institution.
- The address of the individual branch.
- The code of the branch and bank.
- The account number.
- The name(s) of the account holder(s).
- The individual cheque number.

Provision must also be made for the individually typed and/or written instructions.

The printing process chosen may vary according to the nature of the information to be printed and the numbers required. For instance, the basic cheque form may be required by the million and could be printed by any of the standard printing processes, but more localized information such as the branch, account and individual cheque numbers may need to be inserted at a later stage by either relief overprinting devices or ink jet printers. The main production run may therefore be on web-fed presses, with 'localized' information superimposed in batches via either sheet-fed printing or individual 'imprinting' machines.

The hand-filled or typed individual instructions are usually contained within a background 'tint' area, often comprising the name of the issuing institution printed in minute lettering and repeated in closely spaced lines. The ink used for this feature is normally of a 'fugitive' nature in that it is water or solvent based and easily disturbed if attempts are made to erase, obliterate or otherwise modify the information typed or written upon it.

The individual cheque number and other coded information may be printed with an ink containing minute ferrous particles which can be detected by a magnetic ink character recognition (MICR) system. This is not so much a security precaution as a means of identifying and sorting cheques for re-routing information to individual branches and accounts. To aid rapid recognition the characters are printed in a distinctive, stylized form so that the magnetic reading head can distinguish each character by recording the levels of ferrous material present as the characters pass below the reader. Ink film thickness, character size and spacing, and the position of the coded information on the cheque must be precisely controlled to ensure that MICR cheque sorting and data recording function efficiently.

Credit and charge cards

Plastic cards were originally used for obtaining or transferring money from one account to another, or to obtain credit within predetermined guidelines. These basic functions are still central to the plastic card economy although they are now capable of recording far more information and performing a greater variety of functions.

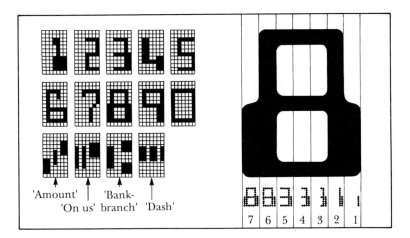

Figure 78 *Magnetic ink character recognition (MICR). Magnified view of the E13B MICR system. The varying thicknesses in the strokes of the characters will result in differing wave forms as the characters pass below a reading head. This coded information can then be used for computer sorting of cheques and other items*

The cards are usually multilayer laminates on a poly-vinyl-chloride (PVC) base, printed on both sides, with a protective film layer and containing additional material such as magnetically-encoded strips, embossed information and holograms.

Caliper and dimensions

Caliper and dimensions of the cards must conform to the appropriate ISO standards in order to function correctly with the relevant machinery and processing equipment. Printing may be by screen process or litho depending on the quality and effect required; screen will be preferred for solid lay down and thicker films of ink, whereas litho may be used for more subtle images and halftone reproductions.

Protection

Protection of the printed image may be by means of a final coat of varnish or lacquer; or for more complete protection a plastic film may be used to complete the lamination on each side.

Embossing

Embossing is by physical deformation of the laminate, requiring an individual master die to be made for each card. The embossed image is then formed by heat and pressure in a stamping press. The relief height of the image needs to be precisely controlled in order to 'register' correctly in the recording equipment. Too shallow an embossing will mean that the digits may not be fully recorded, whereas too high an image could mean that the card may not be received, or premature wear and distortion of the image could occur.

Magnetic strip

The magnetic strip is usually bonded to the card *prior* to final lamination. This is subsequently 'encoded' with invisible magnetic information which can only be decoded in an appropriate reading device. Information from the magnetic strip can be used to activate automated machinery in cash dispensers, credit recorders, communication devices, security entry doors, etc.

Signature panels

Signature panels are a feature of many plastic cards. These panels or strips are bonded to the card *after* final lamination. The card holder is required to make a signature across the panel, which usually has a printed background image to avoid the possibility of an altered or substituted signature.

Holograms

Holograms are often included in plastic cards as identity markers and security devices. An original hologram is produced by photographing an object with laser light from different angles and superimposing the image optically to reproduce the original with a three-dimensional effect. There are several different types of hologram, but for printing purposes the most relevant is the 'embossed' hologram.

An embossed hologram is a lamination of several film layers including a base of stable polyester material and two or more layers of 'metallized' foil containing the printed and embossed images, plus a protective film layer or coating.

Metallization is the deposition of vapourized metal on to a plastic base to give a pure, even film of metal, just a few microns in thickness.

Embossing of the foils is usually from a metal master derived from the original hologram or three-dimensional design. Embossing in this sense is not to be confused with the palpable relief image seen when papers or boards are deformed by a die and force to give a visible raised image, but more in the form of a subtle variation in the surface structure of the metallized films, which themselves are only a few microns in thickness. Superimposition of the printed and embossed films will give the unique three-dimensional effects obtainable only by embossed holograms.

Holograms are difficult, if not impossible, to photograph or photocopy, which makes them ideal for security purposes. The specialized techniques required to produce holograms in the first instance makes forgery an equally unlikely possibility.

8 Quality control

Assessment of quality

There are two basic approaches to the assessment of printing quality: the *subjective approach* and the *objective approach*.

Subjective assessment

Subjective assessment is based on an individual's perceived opinion of the quality of an object as being 'good', 'bad' or otherwise. This is a simple and inexpensive method of defining quality, but it can lead to difficulties where a 'bad' judgement is given without specific reasons for the decision. Simply saying 'I don't like it' will not necessarily convince a client that the work is not of an acceptable standard. In the event of a difference of opinion it will be advisable to look at the work in a rational manner to establish whether it has met certain acknowledged standards of production, and if it has failed to do so, what can be done to improve or correct the situation.

Objective assessment

Objective assessment is based on the premise that quality factors can be identified, measured and controlled. This requires a number of steps to be taken. First, an agreement must be made on the quality factors which need to be assessed; second, the method of measurement of each factor should be established and a 'norm' or agreed standard accepted; third, the question of 'tolerance' may be determined, in which it is agreed how far each quality factor can stray from the norm and still be commercially acceptable.

Specifications

The basis of any quality control system is the initial specification. This is usually in the form of a contract between the print-buyer (the customer) and the printer or his agent. This will list in detail the nature and particulars of the materials to be used throughout the production, such as films, papers and inks, and the quality factors to be observed in relation to each individual area such as origination, typesetting, proofing, printing and finishing.

A standard specification may be adopted, as recommended by publishers, printers and/or buyers organizations, or the 'spec' may be individually drawn up between the buyer and the printer.

Figure 79 *Examining a proof sheet for quality*
Courtesy Proofing Technologies

Materials

Quality control starts with the checking of all materials; first, to ensure that what was ordered has been delivered in both quantity and quality, and second, to check that what is on the label of the goods delivered is what is inside the pack. Even the most meticulous of suppliers can make mistakes and it is too late to have the film in the camera, the ink on the press or the paper in the guillotine only to discover that it is not the correct material as specified.

SPECIFICATION DETAIL

Part 1

Film Separation

A **Fine Lettering:** Thin lines, box rules, medium and small size typematter and detail should ideally be reproduced in one colour only. The registration of such images in more than one colour cannot be guaranteed and the slightest movement during printing will result in colour fringing.

B **Reverse Lettering:** Reversals should be made using a minimum of colour. Typematter or detail smaller than 10pt size should ideally be reversed out of one colour only. When reversals are necessary out of two or more colours, it may be best to use the dominant colour, e.g. black, for the shape of the letters and make the lettering in the subordinate colours slightly larger by photo-graphic techniques to reduce register problems.

Small letters with fine serifs should not be used for reversals as the slightest mis-registration will create colour fringing, showing colour in the white type areas. Particular care should also be taken to ensure that reverse lettering does not become illegible because the background to the lettering or detail is too light.

C **Undercolour Removal (UCR)/Grey Component Replacement (GCR):** At the present time colour separations may be produced using either UCR or GCR technologies.

Irrespective of the technologies involved, the maximum sum percentage of the four colours in neutral areas, should be in a range between 200% and 270%, depending on the substrate.

The choice of the technologies used will tend to dictate naturally the maximum percentage achieved. The choice of either may depend on the subject matter, and the individual preference of each publisher and his printer.

Where a large solid dark or Black background is to be reproduced, it is especially recommended that the Black printer be solid (100%) with an additional 40% Cyan printer to provide additional density.

D **Overprinting:** Particular care should be taken to ensure that lettering or detail to overprint should not emerge into the dark or light tonal areas of the surrounding illustration.

E **Tint or Special Colour Backgrounds:** When a common colour background is required for several pages or parts of a feature, careful consideration should be given to the use of one, or at most two, colours to enable the printer to provide consistency or reproduction across all areas.

F **Screen Ruling:** These specifications were designed for four colour work in the 50-70 lines per centimetre (130-175 lines per inch) screen ruling range. 54 lines per centimetre (133 lines per inch), are specially recommended for magazine work on coated paper of 80 gsm and below but 60-70 lines per centimetre (150-175 lines per inch) are acceptable for the higher quality paper grades, 48 lines per centimetre (120 lines per inch) for uncoated paper.

40 lines per centimetre (100 lines per inch) are recommended for single colour work on lightweight or uncoated papers.

G **Screen Angles:** These must follow industry practice to avoid moire patterns and incorporate the following requirements:

Yellow   0° (90°)
Dominant chromatic colour   135° (45°)
Absolute angles may differ slightly from these values while maintaining the appropriate differences between individual colours.

H **Dot Shape:** Elliptical dot formations are recommended to assist smooth changes of tone values where the first corner link-up is at 40-45%, second corner link-up is at 55-65%.

I **Grey Balance:** Grey balance at 50% Cyan should be 38-42% each for Magenta and Yellow.

Figure 80   *Specifications. Detail from a standard specification for the printing of periodicals, as recommended by FIPP, the International Federation of Periodical Publishers*

Text quality

Terminology

It must be accepted that language and terminology are living and developing disciplines, and therefore liable to change. Even so it is essential to have standards to which one can refer, and to ensure that these are periodically updated to reflect the current state of the art. In this book for instance *The Oxford English Dictionary* is adopted as the standard for spelling, whereas an American publication might refer to *Webster's Dictionary* which would translate a phrase such as 'grey colour centre' into 'gray color center'. Either phrase is correct in its proper context, but it is unforgivable to mix the two indiscriminately.

There are also a number of acknowledged authorities and guides to the correct use of language punctuation and typography, including the impeccable *Hart's Rules for Compositors* published by OUP, Partridge's *English Usage and Abusage* and a selection of printers, editors and authors dictionaries as given in the glossary. The British Standards Institution (BSI) and the International Standards Organisation (ISO) also publish glossaries and lists of terms which are generally accepted by the industries concerned. These include such areas as *Packaging Terms* (BS 3130), *Newspaper and Magazine Terms* (BS 3814) and *Lithographic Terms* (BS 4277). A list of some British and International Standards relevant to the printing industry is available from the British Standards Institution, Linford Wood, Milton Keynes MK14 6LE.

Legibility

Legibility of the text will depend initially on the choice and size of typeface. This will also affect the *readability* when coupled with such factors as column widths, margins, interword and interline spacing. The aim of the typographer should be to produce a page which is pleasing to the eye and easy to read.

Ideally the text should be printed in one colour only, as overprinting several colours will add to the difficulty of maintaining accurate register. The slightest tremor during printing will blur the image, particularly where typefaces with fine serifs are being printed and with smaller typefaces. This is even more important where the text is to be 'reversed out' of a solid or from a colour halftone illustration. Where reversing out of colour halftone work cannot be avoided it is usually best to reverse out of a black solid area and to make the text images in the other colours slightly larger to avoid the problem of 'fringing' or blurring of the edges.

To ensure that the original legibility is maintained throughout the printing processes 'microline' indicators can be included at the origination stage. These comprise small patches of specially designed images, including patterns of minute lines, dots and circles which have been produced to extremely fine tolerances. Any variations in exposure or development at the origination and platemaking stages will be immediately detectable, as will variations in inking, pressure, etc. at the printing stage.

Group A　General

Number	Instruction	Textual mark	Marginal mark
A1	Correction is concluded	None	/
A2	Leave unchanged	– – – – – under characters to remain	✓
A3	Remove extraneous marks	Encircle marks to be removed	✗
A3.1	Push down risen spacing material	Encircle blemish	⊥
A4	Refer to appropriate authority anything of doubtful accuracy	Encircle word(s) affected	?

Group B　Deletion, insertion and substitution

Number	Instruction	Textual mark	Marginal mark
B1	Insert in text the matter indicated in the margin	⋏	New matter followed by ⋏
B2	Insert additional matter identified by a letter in a diamond	⋏	⋏ Followed by for example ◇A
B3	Delete	/ through character(s) or ⊢——⊣ through words to be deleted	♂
B4	Delete and close up	⌐/⌐ through character	♂

Group C　Positioning and spacing

Number	Instruction	Textual mark	Marginal mark
C1	Start new paragraph	⌐	⌐
C2	Run on (no new paragraph)	⌒	⌒
C3	Transpose characters or words	⊔⌐⌐ between characters or words, numbered when necessary	⊔⌐⌐
C4	Transpose a number of characters or words	3　2　1	1 2 3

Figure 81 *Proof correcting. Marking of proofs should be in accordance with an accepted standard, such as BS 5261, as shown here*
Courtesy BSI

Corrections

Corrections and alterations to the text must be made in an orderly manner, by marks and symbols understood by all parties concerned. Errors of spelling, spacing, punctuation, etc. should ideally be indicated on a proof by means of clear and positive instructions. It should always be remembered that alterations are time-consuming and expensive, therefore the earlier good copy is achieved the lower the cost will be.

Any changes to the copy which the customer desires should be indicated in dark blue or black ink, and these will probably be charged for if there are any significant number of changes required. On the other hand, if the customer spots errors by the printer, these should be marked in red and the printer should stand the cost. The printer will usually

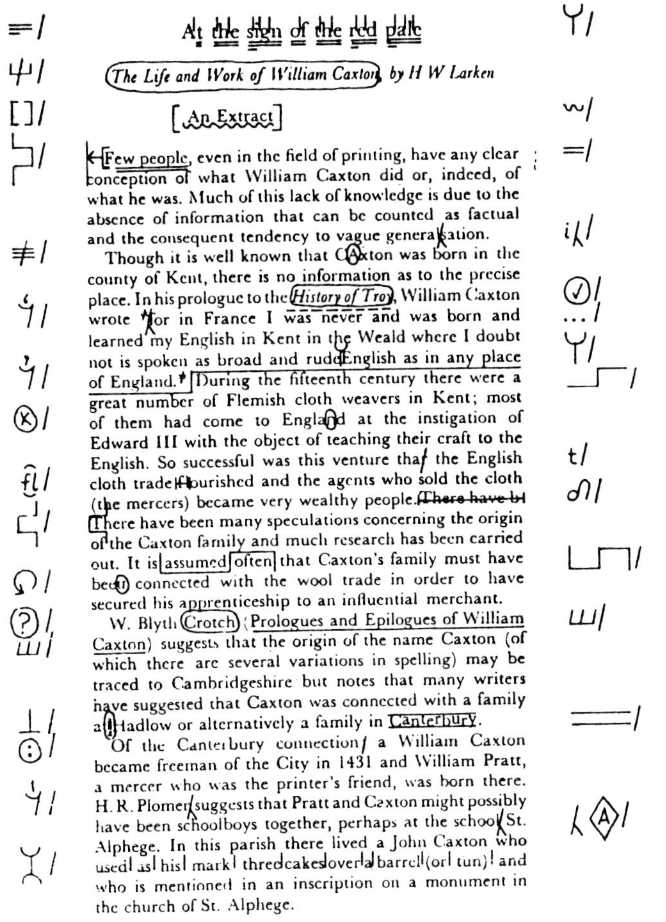

=/
ψ/
[]/
⅃/
≠/
´⁄/
'⁄/
Ⓚ/
f̂l/
⌐/
Ω/
(?)/
ɯ/
⊥⊙/
´⁄/
⅄/

(a) Marked-up proof

At the sign of the red pale

The Life and Work of William Caxton, by *H W Larken*

[An Extract]

Few people, even in the field of printing, have any clear conception of what William Caxton did or, indeed, of what he was. Much of this lack of knowledge is due to the absence of information that can be counted as factual and the consequent tendency to vague generalisation.

Though it is well known that Caxton was born in the county of Kent, there is no information as to the precise place. In his prologue to the *History of Troy*, William Caxton wrote 'for in France I was never and was born and learned my English in Kent in the Weald where I doubt not is spoken as broad and rude English as in any place of England.' During the fifteenth century there were a great number of Flemish cloth weavers in Kent; most of them had come to England at the instigation of Edward III with the object of teaching their craft to the English. So successful was this venture that the English cloth trade flourished and the agents who sold the cloth (the mercers) became very wealthy people. There have be There have been many speculations concerning the origin of the Caxton family and much research has been carried out. It is assumed often that Caxton's family must have been connected with the wool trade in order to have secured his apprenticeship to an influential merchant.

W. Blyth Crotch (*Prologues and Epilogues of William Caxton*) suggests that the origin of the name Caxton (of which there are several variations in spelling) may be traced to Cambridgeshire but notes that many writers have suggested that Caxton was connected with a family at Hadlow or alternatively a family in Canterbury.

Of the Canterbury connection a William Caxton became freeman of the City in 1431 and William Pratt, a mercer who was the printer's friend, was born there. H. R. Plomer suggests that Pratt and Caxton might possibly have been schoolboys together, perhaps at the school St. Alphege. In this parish there lived a John Caxton who used as his mark thredcakes over a barrell (or tun) and who is mentioned in an inscription on a monument in the church of St. Alphege.

⅄/
ᴡ/
=/
i⅃/
⊘/
.../
⅄/
⌐⌐/
t/
ðʃl/
⌐⊓/
ⱳ/
═/
⟨Ⓐ⟩/

(b) Corrected page

AT THE SIGN OF THE RED PALE

The Life and Work of William Caxton, *by H W Larken*

An Extract

FEW PEOPLE, even in the field of printing, have any clear conception of what William Caxton did or, indeed, of what he was. Much of this lack of knowledge is due to the absence of information that can be counted as factual and the consequent tendency to vague generalisation.

Though it is well known that Caxton was born in the county of Kent, there is no information as to the precise place. In his prologue to the *History of Troy*, William Caxton wrote '. . . for in France I was never and was born and learned my English in Kent in the Weald where I doubt not is spoken as broad and rude English as in any place of England.'

During the fifteenth century there were a great number of Flemish cloth weavers in Kent; most of them had come to England at the instigation of Edward III with the object of teaching their craft to the English. So successful was this venture that the English cloth trade flourished and the agents who sold the cloth (the mercers) became very wealthy people.

There have been many speculations concerning the origin of the Caxton family and much research has been carried out. It is often assumed that Caxton's family must have been connected with the wool trade in order to have secured his apprenticeship to an influential merchant.

W. Blyth Crotch (*Prologues and Epilogues of William Caxton*) suggests that the origin of the name Caxton (of which there are several variations in spelling) may be traced to Cambridgeshire but notes that many writers have suggested that Caxton was connected with a family at Hadlow or alternatively a family in Canterbury.

Of the Canterbury connection: a William Caxton became freeman of the City in 1431 and William Pratt, a mercer who was the printer's friend, was born there. H. R. Plomer[1] suggests that Pratt and Caxton might possibly have been schoolboys together, perhaps at the school attached to Christchurch Monastery in the parish of St. Alphege. In this parish there lived a John Caxton who used as his mark three cakes over a barrel (or tun) and who is mentioned in an inscription on a monument in the church of St. Alphege.

Figure 82 *Proof correcting in practice. Example of (a) the marked-up proof sheet and (b) the corrected page*
Courtesy H. W. Larken and BSI

mark his own copy for corrections in green ink. These recommendations and specific instructions for the marking up of copy are contained in BS 5261.

Computer-generated text may also be corrected via standardized procedures. This will require a computer-orientated approach and can apply at every level from desktop publishing and word processing to major electronic composition systems. As with hard copy systems an agreed set of rules and procedures should be observed and these will be contained in a standard generalized markup language (SGML) such as that specified in ISO 8879.

Graphics quality   Observation of transparencies, artwork, proofs and final printed matter must be undertaken in a controlled environment if an objective evaluation is to be achieved. Holding transparencies up to a window for inspection or looking at proofs under a desk light will not necessarily provide a valid assessment of quality. Colours will vary in their spectral appearance depending on the type of light which falls upon them or passes through them. A particular problem is that of *metamerism* in which two printed colours will appear to be identical when viewed under one light source, but different when viewed under another.

BS 950 *Viewing Conditions* recommends a standard of lighting under which objective assessments may be made. Fluorescent lighting tubes are available, matched to the BS 950 standard, as well as purpose-designed viewing booths for examining transparencies and hard copy.

Where the final printed image is intended to be viewed under non-standard lighting conditions, such as posters, under sodium or mercury vapour street lighting; or wallpapers, etc. under tungsten lighting, then an assessment should also be made using the appropriate lighting source.

Sensitivity guides

Sensitivity guides (step wedges) can be included in graphic images at the photographic stage to indicate any variations in exposure or processing. These comprise a series of progressive patches of image density, which will indicate the range of tones which can be achieved under optimum conditions. Test exposures and developments can be made to determine the correct time/processing parameters for production purposes.

Light counters

Light counters can be used to measure the actual quantity of light falling on a film or plate, as distinct from measuring the time to which it is exposed to a light source. This is an ideal requirement where precise light measurement is essential, as light intensity may vary according to the age of the light source or the time in which it has been in use.

Colour quality

Colour quality can be measured by means of a spectrophotometer or a colorimeter. These are devices which can measure the individual wavelengths of visible light as they pass through a transparent object or are reflected from an opaque coloured copy such as a print.

These devices will usually measure not only the actual 'hue' (colour) but other relevant factors such as its 'saturation' or intensity of colour and its 'luminosity' or purity. Precise definitions of these qualities are specified in standards such as those of the International Commission on Illumination (CIE) which specifies the three main variables in terms of x y and z coordinates. Other references may also be used such as those of the Munsell system in which the colour values are described in a simpler, numerical notation.

While precise colour measurement is a useful laboratory technique for describing, measuring and matching colours, printers often find it preferable in the practical situation to use a densitometer in the studio or pressroom for quality control purposes. These fall into three main categories: transmission densitometers, reflection densitometers and filter densitometers.

Densitometry

Transmission densitometers

Transmission densitometers comprise basically a standard light source and a sensitive photocell to receive and measure the light. These are used mainly at the origination stage to measure the proportion of light which will pass through a transparent medium such as film. This will help to establish the relative densities of different areas in an image. For continuous tone subjects such as transparencies and positive or negative separations, the densitometer will measure the *actual* density as the proportion of light transmitted through the film compared with the maximum possible.

For screened halftone images the densitometer will be used to measure the *apparent* density. This will vary according to the screen value (dots, or lines per centimetre) sizes and numbers of dots, as well as dot shape or pattern. Control guides can be included in the form of percentage dot patches and selective measurement will enable maximum and minimum values on film to be established and compared with the values present in the original copy and those desirable for the final printed image.

Calibration to agreed standards is an essential requirement such as specifying clear film for maximum transmission and choosing a series of graded density steps leading up to complete solids. Unfortunately there is no agreed universal standard for the calibration of densitometers. Therefore it is sometimes difficult to compare directly the readings from one manufacturer's model with that of another. Conversion tables are obtainable but it is best to keep to one make and model whenever possible where comparative readings are required.

Reflection densitometers

Reflection densitometers also comprise a light source and a photocell, but in this instance the light is aimed towards the printed copy at an angle and the reflected light is 'read' by the photocell positioned above the copy. As with transmission densitometers the instrument can read either the actual proportions of light reflected, as from white paper or a solid print, or the apparent density as from a tint or halftone area.

Accurate initial calibration is essential to allow for varying factors such as the type and 'colour' of the paper (very few papers are pure white), solid or percentage dot readings, wet or dry ink films, etc.

Filter densitometers

Filter densitometers are used in colour printing to measure the transmitted or reflected light via a filter system. A set of transparent colour filters are provided, corresponding to the 'process' separations for colour halftone printing and these can be selectively placed between the light source and the photocell to record the proportion of light transmitted or reflected for the particular printing colour under inspection

These instruments do not measure colour as such in the way that spectrophotometers do, but they can record accurately the light transmitted or reflected from the copy in the broad colour bands used for process work. This makes them an invaluable aid for ensuring that constant values are set and maintained from origination through to proofing and printing.

In addition to simply recording the reflected light, the more advanced forms of densitometer can be programmed to give additional information such as percentage dot value; dot gain or loss; grey balance (i.e., the effect of overprinting three colours to obtain a neutral grey); and the trapping efficiency of overprinted colours. These and several other

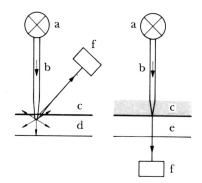

Figure 83   *Principles of (a) reflection and (b) transmission densitometers*
a Light source
b Illuminating beam
c Ink layer
d Substrate (paper)
e Substrate (film)
f Receiver
Courtesy GRETAG

(a)

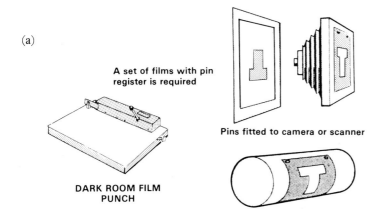

A set of films with pin
register is required

Pins fitted to camera or scanner

DARK ROOM FILM
PUNCH

(b)

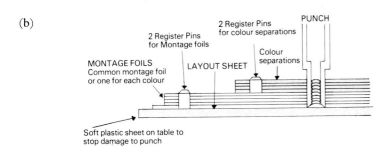

2 Register Pins
for colour separations

2 Register Pins
for Montage foils

PUNCH

MONTAGE FOILS
Common montage foil
or one for each colour

LAYOUT SHEET

Colour
separations

Soft plastic sheet on table to
stop damage to punch

(c)

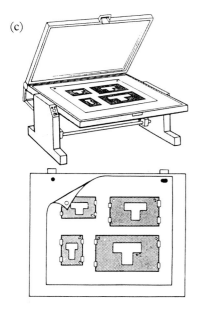

Punched unexposed plate
and montage foil pinned together

(d)

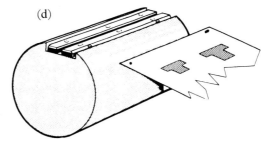

Figure 84 *Pin registering, from camera to press. (a) First step film
register. (b) Second step montage. (c) Third step plates. (d) Fourth step
press register. The plates for proof and sheet-fed presses are fitted to pins
fitted to the clamp bar which automatically centres the plates. Both pins
are retractable to allow for easy plate loading and use of unpunched
plates. Register is made by setting to zero the register dials fitted to the
tensioning bolts, one each end*

Courtesy Billows Limited

quality factors can be checked by the inclusion of control patches and strips adjacent to the main image.

Quality control patches and strips

The inclusion of microline patches for determining the accurate definition of text and graphic images has already been mentioned and there are a number of other items which can be included in the margins or borders of the printed image to enable the quality of the product to be specified, measured and monitored. These can range from simple register crosses to comprehensive control strips encompassing practically every known printing variable.

Register crosses

Register crosses are simply + signs included in the image before colour separation. Reimposition of the crosses at planning, proofing and printing stages will ensure that the images are in correct register. The finer the line, the more accurate register can be determined. Magnification may be necessary to observe register with the accuracy required for colour halftone printing, and automatic devices may be employed to observe, monitor and correct variations.

Slur gauges

Slur gauges are patterns of fine dots or lines which will show the effect of unequal cylinder movement between the plate, blanket or impression cylinders on a press, resulting in a slurred image. Lateral and circumferential slur can be detected by examination of the slur gauge.

Solid density patches

Solid density patches enable the densitometer to compare the printed density with that of a predetermined target or ideal. Process inks are transparent and will show the effect of a white substrate seen through an ink film of optimum thickness. If the ink film is too thin, then a higher proportion of white light will be reflected, whereas too thick a film will give rise to ink trapping problems.

Trapping

Trapping efficiency can be measured by overprinting solid density patches. The values of the overlaid films of ink can be examined and evaluated by an appropriate filter densitometer and compared with a proof or an accepted standard.

Percentage dot patches

Percentage dot patches showing varying dot sizes and percentages will enable the printer to check for any gain or loss during proofing and platemaking, and to monitor any changes which might occur as the press run progresses. Examination of the dots will also show whether there are other printing faults such as slur, doubling or filling in.

Grey balance

Grey balance can be checked by examining overprinted dot patches of certain specific percentages. This is a valuable guide to the accuracy of mid-tones in the colour halftone image, which are usually the most sensitive to changes in dot size.

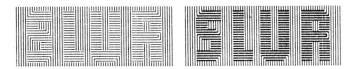

Figure 85 *Quality control devices. The GATF slur gauge (magnified). The left-hand patch shows a pattern of lines of equal width, the slightest false movement of the printing plate or blanket will result in a thickening of the lines in one direction with the result shown in the right-hand patch*
Courtesy GATF

Control strips

Control strips comprise a number of patches and other elements in line, each one of which is designed to give information relating to a specific quality factor. The strips are usually positioned laterally across the sheet or web in a suitable margin and they may be repeated several times to ensure coverage of the full width of the paper.

A number of variations are available, based on the recommendations of various national and international research bodies. Many of them will include all of the features mentioned above, while some may provide additional information. The production of control strips for inclusion in the printing process requires meticulous care as they must conform to extremely fine specifications and controlled within very tight tolerances. None have yet been adopted as an International Standard but several are accepted as providing the information required to the appropriate purpose. The most widely favoured is the Eurostandard promoted by

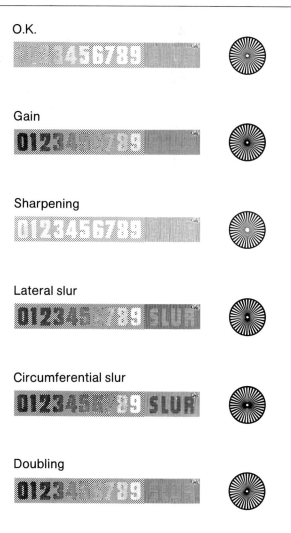

O.K.

Gain

Sharpening

Lateral slur

Circumferential slur

Doubling

Figure 86   *Quality control by signal strips. Left – the GATF slur gauge. Right – the GATF star target*

Du Pont and based on the research work of System Brunner, who were the first to introduce micro-measuring patches in the early 1970s.

Press controls

Before commencing any press run it is essential to ensure that a systematic approach is observed and that as many variables as possible conform to a predetermined standard.

Pressure settings

Pressure settings for printing cylinders, plates, blankets inking and damping rollers, etc. should be meticulously set, especially where colour

Figure 87   *Quality control devices. System Brunner micro patches (greatly enlarged). These patches, measuring only a few millimetres in area will detect the slightest variations from the ideal condition*
Courtesy System Brunner

halftone work or solids are concerned, to ensure precision lay-down of ink on the substrate.

Control systems

Sheet and web control systems should be carefully set and tested by short trial runs to ensure accurate feeding and delivery.

Quality factors

Establishment of quality factors, once the press is set up and running, is usually made by comparison with agreed references such as dummies, artwork, transparencies or proofs and modifications made to the appropriate areas. Variations may occur during the press run due to changes in press speed, inks and rollers warming up as the run continues, atmospheric changes and other variables.

Electronic scanning devices can be installed to inspect the sheets or webs for changes in quality factors, and the detection of variations can be used to initiate the correction procedures either manually or automatically, depending on the sophistication of the system.

Inks

Inks for process colour work should be of an accepted national or international standard, such as CE1 13/67 or ISO 2846, and preferably from the same source or manufacturer as the proofing inks.

Non-process colours should also be defined by relation to an acknowledged standard. Sky blue, emerald green and canary yellow are not acceptable descriptions of colour in printing terms. The best known colour matching system is now the International Pantone system which specifies more than 500 distinct colours that can be mixed from measured proportions of just eight basic inks. Pantone issue printed colour guides which show and number each of the several hundred colours as well as indicating the proportions of each basic colour required for mixing. The guides also show the appearance of each colour when printed on matt and glossy stocks. The company also manufacture or license a range of artwork materials such as pens, pencils, paints, transfers and films which are matched to the standard colours.

Scanning densitometers

The densitometers employed on integrated press control systems work on basically the same principles as stand-alone reflection densitometers, except that they must work faster, more often, and under computerized control.

The scanning densitometer on a typical computer controlled inking system travels on a rack along the control strip which may contain ink density patches for each of up to six printing units, plus additional patches to evaluate percentage dot gain, slur and trapping factors. The sheet is held down in vacuum contact to ensure an accurate reading, and a typical traverse may take less than eight seconds. During this time the densitometer head must take readings of every patch across a sheet of up to 1600 mm. Each patch is only a matter of a few millimetres across. The reading head must therefore be switched on and off within milliseconds as it traverses the printed sheet.

Only computerized control can ensure the efficiency of this type of scanning device, particularly as the information obtained from each scan needs to be instantly available as either:

- An LED display, showing alpha-numeric information via light emitting diode images.
- A VDU display, showing alpha-numeric and graphic information on a video display unit.
- A hard copy print-out.
- All three of these.

To appreciate the degree of control required of a travelling scanning densitometer, it should be understood that there can be 200 individual readings across a 1600 mm sheet. The reading head may be programmed to scan either all of these in order to provide a composite read-out; or to selectively scan for a unit-by-unit read-out, or to give values for dot gain, trapping, or other analysis as required by the operator.

The scanning system may also be required to note any variation from predetermined 'norms' and to advise the operator when variations exceed certain stated tolerances.

There are several ways in which a scanning densitometer may be used in the printing process:

- It can scan a set of printing plates and the readings used to pre-set the ink duct keys.
- It may be located on a control table at the delivery end of the press to give the printer instant information on colour densities, etc., as sheets are taken from the press. This will enable instant adjustments to be made to the ink values as necessary.
- Information from the densitometer may be used to change the inking control systems by reference to predetermined norms.
- As the print run progresses, information from the scanning head may be stored on tape or disc, or printed out as hard copy. This can be used either for management information purposes or for reference in case of reprints or similar work.

Multihead scanners

Multihead scanners are located on the press itself, rather than on the remote control desk. This system, pioneered by Reprotest BV, is a radical departure from the travelling densitometer concept. A 'measuring bar' is positioned just after the final impression cylinder, and this bar may contain more than a hundred individual scanning heads. In this instance, scanning is by fibre-optic technology, rather than the conventional light sources used in hand-held or travelling densitometer systems.

This technique provides even quicker response relating to ink control values, as it is not necessary for the operator to take a sheet from the delivery of the press to examine ink values. Linking the measuring bar into the overall control system also means faster response to changes as they arise.

The measuring bar can be programmed to give a read-out at any given number of cycles of the press operation, so that the operator is informed of the current situation relating to ink values, and a continuous record of performance may be kept on tape, disc, or hard-copy print-out.

Finishing

It is not good practice to wait until the work has been printed to discover whether it will cut, fold or make-up correctly into the final product. Mock-ups or dummies should be produced before production to show the appearance of the finished job and proofs or printed sheets should be sent to the finishing department at the earliest moment to ensure that the images are accurately positioned on the sheet. This is important where double-page 'spreads' are included in a publication; where special folds, such as 'gatefolds' are used; where illustrations are intended to 'bleed' off the edge of a page, and where staples or glue lines may affect the appearance of the image.

Sending sheets early to the finishing department also gives an opportunity to check on the accuracy and neatness of cutting, folding and other operations before the main volume of work arrives from the press. It may also indicate where modifications are necessary to the press settings or, where this may not be practicable, to compromise by modifying the finishing operations to ensure an acceptable product.

This may also be the best opportunity to check that the printing stock is the correct size, caliper and substance for the job.

Papers and boards

The commonest sizes of paper and board in the UK and Continental Europe are based on the recommendations of the International Standards Organisation (ISO) 478, 479 and 593, which are also covered by British Standard BS 4000.

The basic idea of the ISO series is that all sheets will have their sides cut in the proportion of one to the square root of two $(1:\sqrt{2})$. The significance of this proportion is that enlarging or reducing the sheet size by doubling or halving, etc. will still retain the same basic proportions. This is of major importance in many printing situations where an illustration may be required at various times in pocket book size, magazine size, poster size, or even printed on the outside of an envelope.

There are three basic series of ISO sizes:

1 A series for commercial printing and stationery.
2 B series for wall charts and posters.
3 C series for folders and envelopes intended to contain 'A' size sheets.

A series

The A series is based on a sheet designated as A0 and having an area of exactly one square metre. This gives it dimensions of 841 mm × 1189 mm $(1:\sqrt{2})$. Halving the sheet to 594 mm × 841 mm gives a size designated as A1, half again (420 mm × 594 mm) gives A2 and so on, down to A10 at a postage stamp size of 26 mm × 37 mm.

Where the work is to be folded, and requires trimming, as for magazines, catalogues and book sections, the finished size will evidently be smaller than the original. To compensate for this and to ensure that the publication finishes up at the specified size, sheets are supplied slightly larger than the standard A sizes to allow for trimming. These sheets are designated as RA sizes. RA0 for instance is 860 mm × 1220 mm, allowing 19 mm and 31 mm respectively for fold and trim allowance.

If extra trim is required, as for work in which 'bleed' illustrations are common, still larger sheets will be needed if the finished size is to conform to the standard. In these instances SRA sizes will be specified. SRA 0 sheets measure 900 mm × 1280 mm, giving a generous 59 mm and 91 mm fold and trim allowance.

B series

The B series is based on a sheet designated B0 with the proportions of 1000 mm × 1414 mm (exactly $1:\sqrt{2}$). As with the A series, smaller sizes are obtained by halving the longest size and numbering down to B5 at 176 mm × 250 mm for a small showcard or a window poster.

C series

The C series is for envelopes which are produced a few millimetres larger than the equivalent A sizes in order to contain the printed contents. C0 for instance is 917 mm × 1297 mm, while an envelope to take an A4 (210 mm × 297 mm) publication will be made to a size of 229 mm × 324 mm.

Paper substance

The 'substance' of the printing stock can be specified in a number of ways. The simplest is to measure the thickness of the material with an appropriate micrometer and use this as the basis for calculating the volume of a desired quantity. This is quite common practice for board and other stocks of significant caliper, but not always suitable for thinner paper stocks.

An alternative is to take the weight of, say, 500 or 1000 sheets and use this as the basis for specification, i.e. 20 kg per ream of SRA2. However, while this does give specific information as to paper substance, it may be difficult to compare equivalent weights of varying stocks in different sizes.

A more rational approach is to take the weight of one square metre of paper (a sheet the size of A0) and use this as the basis of substance. In practice it may be preferable to weigh, say, a ream of paper and divide this by 500 to give a more precise figure. This will give a consistent value, such as 80 grammes per square metre, contracted to 80 g/m^2, which will remain constant regardless of sheet size, caliper or ream weight.

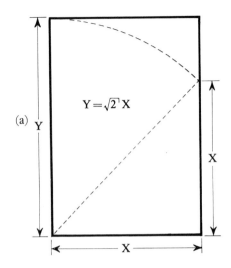

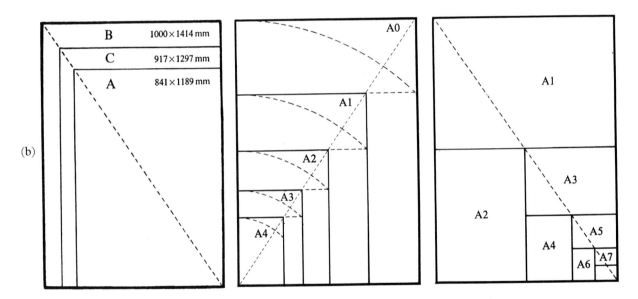

Figure 88 *International paper sizes, as recommended by the International Standards Organization and covered by BS 4000. (a) The basis of each standard series is a sheet, the sides of which are in the proportion 1 : √2. The sides and diagonal of a square are in the same proportion. (b) Left – untrimmed A, B and C series full sheet dimensions; centre – standard subdivisions showing uniform proportions; right – convenient sheet cuts of the standard subdivisions*

Paper types

There is no official standard relating to the terminology and classification of paper types, but the following terms and descriptions are generally recognized.

Newsprint

Newsprint is among the cheapest of papers being mainly made from unbleached mechanical wood pulp with a minimum of fillers, additives or finishing operations. Used mainly for newspapers and cheaper magazines.

Super calendered paper

Super calendered (sc) paper is made from a similar basic 'furnish' as newsprint, but has a smoother surface as a result of passing between a number of heavy, polished 'calendering' rollers. Used for cheaper magazines and similar publications and will give slightly better reproduction of illustrations compared with newsprint.

Machine glazed paper

Machine glazed (MG) papers are usually whiter than newsprint and SC owing to bleaching of the basic furnish and are glazed on one side by passing them over heated, polished drums. Used mainly for posters, paper bags and wrappers.

Bond paper

Bonds are good quality papers containing fillers to make them opaque and size to make them less absorbent. They often have a watermark to establish their character. Used for good quality letterheads, business forms and other documents.

Bank paper

Banks are similar in finish to bond papers but produced in thinner substances, usually less than 60 gm^2. Used for second copies of documents, cheaper forms and where minimum bulk is required.

Cartridge paper

Cartridge papers are good quality, stout stock, bleached, calendered and stable. Originally developed for litho illustration reproduction. 'twin wire' versions are provided where both sides have identical surface properties, unlike cheaper stocks which may have a smooth, soft 'felt' side with the possibility of loose paper fibres and a firm, hard 'wire' side.

Art paper

Art papers are coated on one or both sides with a smooth, glossy (or sometimes matt) finish to provide an ideal base for artwork reproduction. Used for better quality magazines, brochures, etc.

'Cast-coated' arts are given a very high polish, usually on one side and are used for best quality magazine covers and prestige work.

9 Conclusion

Printing is a thriving, multibillion-pound industry. In the UK alone several hundred billion pounds worth of print orders are placed every year and the volume continues to grow steadily. This is partly owing to increasing demand for traditional printed products – there are now more books, newspapers and magzines printed each year than ever before – and partly owing to the increasing diversity of applications for printing which continue to proliferate.

To meet these demands printing systems have evolved to cater for each specific type of printed product in terms of quantity, quality and other special requirements. There is no one printing method which is applicable in every instance. A system designed to produce mail order catalogues by the million would be vastly different from one intended to print personalized match covers, and this essential diversity has been the theme of this book.

The variety of printed products is matched by an equal diversity of printing and print-related organizations. The average printing firm is quite small by industrial standards and employs only a handful of people. Of the several thousand printing establishments in the UK less than a hundred employ people by the thousand and more than 90 per cent have fewer than a score of full-time employees.

Projections for the future of printing have always tended to be pessimistic, particularly when made by those with little knowledge of the industry. Practically every new communication device from the telephone to radio, television and the computer has been seen as a threat to the printed word. In effect the reverse has been true: telephone directories and related literature are high-volume, valued orders for printers who have purchased specially-designed equipment for their production; radio and television journals are among the longest-running mass-produced publications in the business; while computers are notorious generators of printed matter as anyone who has thumbed through a 500-page instruction manual or tried to sort through the proliferation of magazines and books on the subject will acknowledge.

The picture which materializes from all of this is the merging and integration of printing with other media, often with mutual benefit. This integration of the various information sources still depends heavily on the permanence of the printed image for its physical and historical preservation.

In non-publication fields such as packaging, there seems to be no alternative at present to the application of ink to a substrate which is intended to contain, protect and advertise its contents. The identification, decoration and preservation of millions of artefacts is constantly dependent on the medium of print. In another sphere, the advertising industry continues to expand in the fields of free newspapers, posters, direct mail and personalized communications.

The future of printing as an industry in its own right seems reasonably well assured, and some trends can already be identified. The increasing diversity of applications for printed images appears to have no bounds, and there is little doubt that human ingenuity will continue to find new fields to conquer as well as developing new and improved ways of producing traditional printed items.

Automation of the printing processes will continue, with the result that fewer and fewer people will be able to produce more and more goods. Flow-line systems already exist in which the work passes from one station to the next without operator involvement. Entire production systems for printing newspapers and magazines can be enclosed in sound-proof, environmentally controlled rooms and operated remotely from a centralized control panel. Production directors can observe, monitor and control the work as it is in progress, by means of computerized information systems, from the comfort of their office desks.

Whether the ideal of a personless printing works becomes a reality remains to be seen. People will always be required to design, build, instal and maintain the production line and to supply it with materials and information as well as determining its day-to-day performance.

However near we come to the unmanned printing system two things will remain certain. First, there must be people who can identify markets, design, write and produce original material for feeding into the system and to oversee its production from conception to dissemination. Secondly, in any market there must be a constant body of consumers to receive the goods, because without the customers there is no custom.

In the author's opinion there is no reason to believe that these two requirements will not continue to be met and therefore the survival of printing as a major industry is assured for the foreseeable future.

Glossary

Acetate film A clear, stable film used in planning and make up.

ACS Achromatic colour separation. A term used in electronic colour separation where colours are replaced, where possible, by black.

Airbrushing A technique used in artwork preparation to enhance or modify the tones of a photograph by spraying with minute droplets of ink.

Angle bar A fixed bar on a web-fed press, around which the web is passed to make a 90° turn.

Aniline printing Original name for flexography, adopted because of the aniline dyes which were used as the basis for the ink.

Anilox roller The roller in a flexographic inking system which applies ink to the printing surface. The surface of the anilox roller comprises a regular pattern of minute etched or engraved cells.

Anodizing Electrochemical treatment of a lithographic printing plate to make it a suitable base for the printing image.

Anti-set-off spray A device at the delivery of a sheet-fed press which sprays the sheet with a fine powder to prevent ink from one sheet transferring (setting-off) to the next.

Arch-type unit A printing unit on a web press containing two printing 'couples'. The web passes between each couple in order to print both sides.

Bank papers Medium-weight papers used for stationery, forms and other documents, having a basis weight of 60 grammes per square metre or less (gm^2).

Bar code A pattern of lines and numerals which can be read by a light pen to indicate the basic data relating to the product.

Bare back damper A plain rubber roller used to apply moisture to a lithographic plate as distinct from the conventional roller covered with a fabric.

Bay window A device employed on web-fed presses comprising a series of angled bars and rollers which enable a ribbon to be taken from its original position to an alternative position.

Bond papers Good quality papers used for stationery, forms and other documents having a basis weight of more than 60 grammes per square metre (gm^2). Often containing a watermark.

Blanket In offset litho the rubber covering on the intermediate cylinder which transfers ink from the plate to the substrate.

Blanket-to-blanket press An offset litho press, usually web-fed, in which two printing couples impress on either side of the substrate simultaneously. The two offset blanket cylinders act as impression cylinders to each other.

Blue key A film planning technique in which a blue, non-actinic image is used as a planning guide for superimposed films.

Bundling The operation in print finishing of compressing a number of finished copies and tying or strapping a given quantity for ease of handling.

Carousel printer A printing arrangement, used mainly in screen process work, where the item to be printed upon travels from one station to the next in a circular route.

Cartridge paper A strong, stable, compressed paper with a natural, uncoated surface.

Case The cover of a hardback book.

Casing-in The operation of attaching the case to the book block.

Cathode-ray tube (CRT) A device forming the basis of a visual display unit (VDU), monitor or viewing screen. Used as intermediate stage between the initiation of an item of work and its progression for production.

Cellulose film A transparent, flexible film made from regenerated cellulose and used for a variety of packaging purposes.

Central impression (CI) press An arrangement of printing units around one common impression cylinder. Mostly used in web printing.

Chase The metal frame in letterpress printing which holds the assembled type and blocks.

Collating The act of bringing together a number of parts of a printed work in the correct order.

Colorimeter A device which will measure the colour of a given object in terms of its spectral reflectance. *See also* Spectrophotometer.

Concertina folding A method of folding a continuous web of material, usually paper, without cutting it into sheets. Mainly used for business forms production. Also referred to as zigzag folding.

Contrast The difference between the lightest recorded tones of an image and the darkest recorded tones, usually by reference to a series of tone percentage steps.

Control strip A photographic or printed device used at one or more stages in production to measure and control a quality function.

Convertible press A multiunit press which may print either on one side only of the substrate or, by a mechanical arrangement, print on both sides.

Corona discharge The treatment of plastic substrates via a high voltage discharge to make their otherwise inert surfaces receptive to printing ink.

CRT *See* Cathode-ray tube.

Crimping In business forms production, the interlocking of several parts in a form set by cutting small sections through the set to hold the parts together.

Curing The drying of ink by radiation such as infra-red, ultra-violet or electron beam radiation to bring about a rapid change in the molecular structure of the ink.

Daisy wheel Typewriter or word processor component in which the relief characters are contained in a disc.

Damping The application of an aqueous solution to a lithographic plate in order to keep the non-image areas free from ink.

Decal A printed image on an appropriate substrate which is intended to be transferred to another surface such as glass, porcelain etc.

Definition The degree to which fine detail has been reproduced.

Delivery The final section of a sheet-fed or web-fed press in which the sheets of final copies are collected.

Densitometer A quality control device which can measure the actual or apparent density of a transparent film or films of ink.

Diazo Short for diazonium compounds. Intermediate copies or proofs can be produced from transparent copy by exposing it to diazo coated material which is then developed by exposure to ammonia vapour.

Didot A system of typographical measurement used in Continental Europe.

Die stamping A printing process employing an engraved, intaglio image and producing an embossed, relief effect on the substrate.

Digitizing pad *See* Graphics tablet.

Direct mail The sending of advertising, publicity and promotional material, etc. directly to individuals from the originating source with a minimum of intermediaries.

Doctor The device used in gravure and flexographic printing, usually a metal blade, which shears the ink from the surface of an etched or engraved cylinder to leave ink only in the cells.

Duct The ink container on a lithographic or letterpress machine from which the ink is metered out to the roller train.

Dummy A model of the printed product produced prior to production, to show as far as possible the size, shape and major features as a guide to production.

Duplicate plate In relief printing, a secondary plate made from an original forme or relief plate by means of an intermediate mould or matrix.

Durometer (a) The comparative hardness or softness of a material, especially in relief plates, obtained by measuring its resistance to pressure. Usually measured in degrees Shore, e.g. Shore hardness. (b) The device used for measuring the comparative hardness or softness of a material.

Electron beam drying A method of drying or solidifying printing inks by exposing them to electron beam radiation in order to bring about a rapid change of state.

Electronic composition The generation and assembly of letters without the need for three-dimensional type or photographic matrices.

Electrostatic copier A device based originally on the light-sensitive properties of selenium which would become electrostatically charged when exposed to light.

Electrostatic plate A printing plate used on small offset litho presses in which the image is initially formed electrostatically.

Embossing The deformation of paper or board by means of a die and a force to form a raised image.

EPC Electronic page composition. The make-up of complete pages of a publication by computerized control.

Facsimile An identical copy.

Facsimile transmission The sending and receiving of two-dimensional information via telegraphy.

Festoon An arrangement of loops of paper on a web-fed press which acts as a reservoir during reel changing.

Filter In colour separation or densitometry a transparent disk or plate of glass or plastic produced to a specific colour and density in order to selectively allow certain wavelengths of light to pass through.

Flash exposure In photographic origination an initial rapid exposure to light, of a sensitized coating to prepare it for subsequent processing.

Flexography A printing process employing a resilient, relief printing plate or cylinder, a simplified inking system and liquid ink.

Flying splice A colloquialism for an automatic reel changing device on a web-fed press which avoids stopping the machine for reel changes.

Foil stamping The application of metallic or metallized images to a substrate by means of a heated relief block and controlled pressure.

Freesheet A newspaper or other publication which is distributed without charge.

Gate fold In magazine production a type of fold in which a double width page or pair of pages is turned inwards from the fore-edges, thus opening out at the appropriate place.

Golf ball Colloquialism applied to a typewriter or word processor printing head in which the relief letters are arranged in a sphere.

Graining The treatment of a lithographic printing plate to abrade the surface, thus enabling the image to key to the plate and the non-image areas to retain moisture.

Graphics tablet A flat base containing a network of tiny electrical contacts or pressure switches which can be drawn upon by an appropriate stylus. The drawn image is displayed on a VDU screen. Also referred to as a *digitizing pad*.

Gravure A printing process in which the image is cut or etched into the surface of a plate or cylinder, then flooded with ink and the surplus ink removed by a 'doctor' blade before impressing the image on to the substrate.

Grey balance The condition which is required in colour halftone printing to obtain a neutral situation in which no individual colour is seen to be dominant. Used as a standard quality control factor.

Guillotine   A device for cutting paper and board. Models range from simple hand-operated machines to fully automated 'programmed' guillotines.

Halftone process   The reproduction of a photographic image in which the shades or 'tones' of the original are simulated by patterns of dots of varying sizes.

Hybrid press   A printing press, usually web-fed, which employs more than one printing process.

Imprinting unit   An auxillary printing unit on a press intended for the addition of patches or small areas of additional information.

Inking-in   The application of a protective ink to the lithographic plate image prior to printing.

Infra-red drying   A method of accelerating the drying of printing ink by intensive exposure to infra-red radiation.

Ink-jet printing   A printing process in which the image is formed by tiny droplets of ink.

Inserting   In publication work the technique of placing additional items and other matter within the leaves of the publication. Methods may range from hand insertion to fully automated systems.

Intaglio   A general term for all printing processes in which the image is recessed, i.e. engraved or etched into a plate or cylinder, including copperplate, die stamping and photogravure.

ISO   International Standards Organisation. A body which initiates, approves and publishes agreed standards relevant to industrial practice.

Justification   The spacing out of text in a column or page of type matter to achieve regular left- and right-hand margins.

Lamination   The bonding of two or more layers of material by means of pressure, heat, adhesives, or a combination of these.

Laser   Acronym for light amplification by stimulated emission of radiation. A highly concentrated, directional light source capable of fine control via computerized pulsing systems.

Laser printer   A printing device in which a laser is used to produce the image.

Latent image   The undeveloped image in a photographic film or coating after exposure to light and before processing.

LED   Light emitting diode. A semi-conductor device which emits light when supplied with a specific voltage. Used mainly for alpha-numeric displays.

Leading   Pronounced 'ledding'. The determination of space between lines of text. Originally obtained in letterpress printing by placing thin strips of lead between the lines of type.

Letterpress   The first acknowledged process of printing in which three-dimensional lead 'types' were assembled to form columns and pages of text.

Lithography   Stone drawing. A printing process based on the principle that a surface can be photochemically prepared so that the image to be printed will accept a grease-based ink while the non-image areas, when dampened, will refuse ink.

Manifold   A thin, strong, uncoated paper used for business forms and documents where low bulk is required.

Masking   In process colour reproduction a technique in which the spectral deficiencies of one colour are used to correct the deficiencies of another.

Metalized films   Plastic substrates with a thin deposit of vapourized metal giving the attractive metallized effect.

MICR   Magnetic ink character recognition. The technique of printing alphanumeric characters of a specific size and format with an ink containing ferrous particles, which can be sensed by a decoding device for purposes such as cheque sorting.

MG paper   Machine glazed paper. Paper based on a bleached, softwood, sulphite base which has been polished (glazed) on one side. Commonly used for printing bags and wrappers.

Moiré   An unintended pattern in halftone printing caused by a visual clash between two or more screens or dot patterns.

Monitor *Noun*: An electronic display screen in which an image can be seen as it is initiated, altered and manipulated prior to releasing for processing. *Verb*: To continually record information relating to a process for purposes such as quality measurement and control.

Mouse A computing device which supplements the keyboard; comprising a rolling, hand-held unit which can travel over a desktop tablet to feed information to the computer and perform functions in conjunction with a video display unit.

Non-press proof A visual prediction of the final appearance of a printed image prior to production, obtained without using printing plates or a press.

OCR Optical character recognition. A system by which printed or handwritten characters can be scanned by a light source and the reflected signals used as digital input to a computer.

Offset In lithography and other printing processes to transfer ink from the printing plate to an intermediate rubber-covered blanket cylinder which then transfers the ink to the substrate.

Overmatter Text or other information which cannot be fitted into the space allocated.

Pack folding A technique of continuously folding paper on web-fed presses without cutting the web. Mainly used for business forms, computer listing and similar products.

Panchromatic film A graphic arts film sensitive to colours and subtle graduations of tone.

Pantone colours An international system of designating colours for printing and other purposes, based on the mixing and matching of a few basic standard pigments. © International Pantone.

Photocomposition The production and assembly of letters via photographic matrices.

Photocopier A device which produces a copy of an original document either by electrostatic techniques or digital imaging.

Photogravure A printing process in which the image is cut or etched into the surface of a plate or cylinder.

Photopolymer plate In relief printing, a plate which is made from a negative of the image to be printed. The sensitive polymer is exposed to light and unexposed areas washed away to leave the relief image.

Pica A traditional standard of type measurement equivalent to twelve points or 4.217 mm.

Pixel Short for picture element. The smallest item of information which can be controlled by a computer linked to a visual display unit.

Point A traditional standard of type measurement equal, to 0.351 mm.

Process work A colloquialism referring to the reproduction of photographic colour originals as halftone colour separations for printing purposes.

Proof A visual interpretation of the image to be printed, produced either from printing plates on a proof press (press proof) film overlays or other 'pre-press' techniques (non-press proofs) or on a visual display unit ('soft' proofs).

Rapid-access film A graphic arts film based on a chemistry which gives quicker development than conventional systems.

Red key A method of assembling and superimposing transparent images on film using a red base image.

Ribbon folder A method of final folding on a web-fed publication press in which the web is first slit into a number of page-width ribbons, which are then assembled and folded to make a complete publication or section.

Ribbon lettering The production of alphanumeric and other characters on strips or ribbons of film or paper for planning and make-up purposes.

Rotary press A printing press in which all main functions are carried out by cylinders, as opposed to flat bed or platen presses.

Rotogravure Photogravure printing from the web.

Satellite unit A printing unit in which several plate cylinders are grouped around a common impression cylinder.

Scanner An electronic device which examines original copy and converts the image to digital information via a computer in order to produce finalized copy suitable for the printing process.

SC paper Super calendered paper. A highly-compressed paper with a smooth finish and good stability.

Screen ruling The nominal distance between dots in a halftone illustration. Usually expressed as dots per centimetre.

Screen angle The angle at which a line of dots in a halftone illustration vary from 0°. Black and white halftones usually have their dots angled at 45°. The various colours in 'process' work are discreetly varied to avoid the problem of Moiré patterning.

Set-off The unwanted transfer of ink from a substrate to parts of the press or other parts of the substrate etc.

SGML Standard generalized mark-up language. An approved method of marking up and correcting computer generated information.

Shore hardness The comparative resistance to pressure or hardness of a material in degrees Shore, where 0° equals total resistance or free fall and 100° equals total resistance or glass hardness. Used in relation to the hardness of printing rollers, blankets and relief plates.

Sleeve cylinders A method of mounting plates or complete images on an outer shell for subsequent location on a base cylinder or mandrel. Mainly used in flexography and gravure printing.

Slur A printing fault caused by a false movement between the printing cylinders resulting in a blurring of the image.

Slur gauge A device included in the printed image to detect the presence of slur.

Small offset press A printing press with a sheet size of RA2 or less [420 mm × 594 mm].

Spectrophotometer A device which measures reflected or transmitted colour in terms of spectral wavelengths.

Splicing The act of joining two webs together. When undertaken by an automatic device without stopping the press, this is often referred to as a 'flying' splice.

Spot colour An individual patch or patches of colour in an otherwise black and white publication.

Squeegee In screen process printing, the rubber or plastic blade which forces the ink through the screen mesh to print the image.

Stack press A press in which the printing units are placed one above the other around a common framework.

Stencil In screen process printing, the outline frame which determines which areas ink will pass through to form the printed image and which areas will not allow ink to pass.

Step-and-repeat The technique of multiplying a single image for such purposes as label, stamp and ticket printing.

Step wedges A series of graduated patches of progressive densities, produced photographically from a master pattern and used as a quality control device in photography and graphic reproduction.

Stereotype A duplicate printing plate made from an original metal plate via an intermediate matrix.

Strip printer A method of producing alpha-numeric characters on strips or ribbons of film or paper for planning and make-up purposes.

Substrate The base material such as paper, board, film, etc. upon which ink is deposited in the printing process.

Systems machines Printing presses, duplicators or photocopiers which are included in an overall system designed to produce complete multipage documents.

Text The main body of type matter in a book or other publication.

Thermography A method of producing a raised image by dusting a wet print with a powder which will expand when subjected to heat.

Tolerance In quality control, the permissible deviation from an agreed norm or standard, which will still produce an acceptable result.

Transfer lettering Alphanumeric characters, symbols, etc. which are carried upon an easy-release base for transferring to a substrate by pressure.

Trapping In multicolour wet-on-wet printing, the successful capture of consecutive ink films on a sheet or web as it passes from one printing unit to the next.

Turner bars An arrangement of bars and rollers on a double-width newspaper press to take one half of the web and bring it in to line with the other half.

UCR Under colour removal. A technique in multicolour printing whereby unwanted colours are removed from darker shades such as black and grey.

Ultra-violet curing A method of drying printing inks by subjecting them to ultra-violet radiation after printing and before delivery.

Watermark The image seen when a sheet of paper is held against a light. Caused by the deliberate compression of fibres during the papermaking process.

Web The unwound material from a reel as it passes through the printing press.

Wet-on-wet The technique of printing several colours in rapid succession, one on top of another on a multicolour press.

WIMP Acronym for windows, ikons, mouse and pull-down menus. A basic software approach in desktop publishing.

WYSIWYG Acronym for what you see is what you get. A term in desktop publishing to indicate that the image viewed on a VDU will be similar to that which will be finally printed out.

X-height A typographical term referring to the measured height of lower case letters without ascending or descending strokes.

Zero-speed splicer A device which will join the leading edge of a fresh reel to the expiring end of a running reel in a printing press, at a stationary position.

Zigzag fold A method of folding a continuous web of material, usually paper, without cutting it into sheets. Mainly used for business forms production. Also referred to as concertina folding.

Zinco Abbreviation of zincograph. A relief (letterpress) plate produced by etching zinc metal with an acid.

Appendix 1
Some British Standards
relating to printing

BS 950   *Part 2: Standardised Viewing Conditions*

BS 1133   *The Packaging Code (several sub-divisions)*

BS 1219   *Preparation of Mathematical Copy*

BS 1360   *Personalised Stationery*

BS 1413   *Page Sizes for Books*

BS 1808   *Specifications for Commercial Forms*

BS 1991   *Letters, Signs, Symbols and Abbreviations*

BS 2913   *The Measurement of Offset Blankets*

BS 2961   *Typeface Nomenclature and Classification*

BS 2650   *Lithographic Inks*

BS 3110   *Testing Methods for Rub Resistance*

BS 3130   *Glossary of Packaging Terms*

BS 3649   *Specifications for 'Original' Plates*

BS 3814   *Letterpress Rotary Printing Terms*

BS 4000   *Sizes of Papers and Boards*

BS 4149   *Paper/Ink Terms for Letterpress*

BS 4277   *Terms used in Offset Litho Printing*

BS 4321   *Methods of Testing for Printing Inks*

BS 4623   *Specifications for Continuous Folded Stationery*

BS 4666   *Inks for Offset Three- or Four-colour Offset Litho Printing*

BS 4719   *Title Leaves of a Book*

BS 5261   *Copy Preparation and Proof Correction*

BS 5230   *Lithographic Plates*

BS 5641   *Recommendations for Loose-Leaf Publications*

BS 5750   *Quality Assurance*

Further information may be obtained from The British Standards Institution, Linford Wood, Milton Keynes MK14 6LE.

Appendix 2
Bibliography

Barlow G., *Typesetting and Composition*, Blueprint, 1987.

Chambers E., *Manual of Graphic Reproduction for Lithography*, Lithographic Training Services, 1980.

Collins F., *Author's and Printer's Dictionary*, Oxford University Press, 1980.

Faux I., *Printing by Lithography*, Emblem Books, 1983.

Flexographic Technical Association, *Flexography – Principles and Practice*, FTA, 1988.

Gatehouse A. L. and Roper K. M., *Modern Film Planning and Platemaking*, SITA, 1983.

Graham G., *Complete Guide to Paste-up*, Graham, 1980.

Hart H., *Hart's Rules for Compositors and Readers*, Oxford University Press, 1983.

Heath L. and Faux I., *Phototypesetting*, SITA, 1983.

International Federation of the Periodical Press, *Specifications for European Offset Printing*, FIPP, 1984.

Potter G., *Binding and Finishing*, Blueprint, 1988.

Rowlatt K. T., *Reprographic Methods*, Longman, 1986.

Stephens J., *Screen Process Printing*, Blueprint, 1987.

Wilson-Davies K. and others, *Desk-Top Publishing*, Blueprint, 1987.

Appendix 3
Useful addresses

Article Number Association,
6 Catherine Street,
London WC2B 5JJ
01-836 2460

Association of Printing Machinery Importers
    (APMI),
Fairfax House,
Fulwood Place,
London WC1V 6DW
01-405 8422

British Federation of Printing Machinery and
    Supplies,
3 Plough Place,
Fetter Lane,
London EC4A 1AL
01-583 7433

British Paper and Board Industry Federation,
3 Plough Place,
Fetter Lane,
London EC4A 1AL
01-353 5222

British Printing Industries Federation,
11 Bedford Row,
London WC1R 4DX
01-242 6904

British Standards Institution,
Linford Wood,
Milton Keynes MK14 6LE
0908-320066

City and Guilds of London Institute,
76 Portland Place,
London W1N 4AA
01-580 3050

European Flexographic Technical Association,
6 The Tynings,
Clevedon,
Bristol BS21 7YP
0272-878090

Flexible Packaging Association,
31 Craven Street,
London WC2N 5NP
01-930 1130

Institute of Packaging,
Syonsby Lodge,
Nottingham Road,
Melton Mowbray,
Leicestershire LE13 0NU
0664-500055

Institute of Printing,
8 Lonsdale Gardens,
Tunbridge Wells,
Kent TN1 1NU
0892-38118

London College of Printing,
Elephant and Castle,
London SE1 6SB
01-735 9100

National Graphical Association,
63 Bromham Road,
Bedford MK40 2AG
0234-51521

Newspaper Publishers Association,
6 Bouverie Street,
London EC4Y 8AY
01-583 8132

Newspaper Society,
Bloomsbury House,
Bloomsbury Square,
74 Great Russell Street,
London WC1B 3DA
01-636 7014

Periodical Publishers Association,
Imperial House,
Kingsway,
London WC2B 6UN
01-379 6268

PIRA,
The Research Association for Paper and Board,
    Printing and Packaging Industries,
Randalls Road,
Leatherhead,
Surrey KT22 7RU
0372-376161

Printing Historical Society,
St Bride Institute,
Bride Lane,
London EC4Y 8EE
01-353 4660

St Bride Printing Library,
St Bride Institute,
Bride Lane,
London EC4Y 8EE
01-353 4660

Society of British Printing Ink Manufacturers,
Pira House,
Randalls Road,
Leatherhead,
Surrey KT22 7RU
0372-378628

Society of Graphical and Allied Trades,
Sogat House,
274 London Road,
Hadleigh,
Benfleet,
Essex SS7 2DE
0702-554111

WONA,
(Web-Offset Newspaper Association),
Bloomsbury House,
Bloomsbury Square,
74 Great Russell Street,
London WC1B 3DA
01-636 7014

Worshipful Company of Stationers and
    Newspaper Makers,
Stationers Hall,
Ave Maria Lane,
Ludgate Hill,
London EC4M 7DD
01-248 2934

Index

Acetate films, 81
Achromatic colour separation, 64
Airbrushing, 87
Ancillary finishing operations, 42, 124, 192
Aniline, 9
Anodizing, 91
Arch-type units, 145
Assembling, finishing, 120
Assembly, film, 34, 79
Automatic plate processors, 93

Bank papers, 194
Bar codes, 188
Batch counting, 175
Bay windows, 166
Binding, spiral, 46
Blankets, 104
Bled illustrations, 80
Boards, 218
Bond papers, 194
Bundling, 176
Butt-join splicers, 132

Cameras:
  darkroom, 49
  horizontal, 49
  multi-image, 50
  projection, 50
  vertical, 49
Carbon papers, 194
Carbonless papers, 195
Cartons, 187
Casing, 122
Cathode-ray tubes, 74, 76
CD, 15
CD/ROM, 15
Cellulose films, 185
Charge cards, 199
Chemical transfer masters, 35
Cheque printing, 197
CI presses, 156
Coaters/waxers, 177

Collators, 192
Colour:
  copiers, 27
  correction, 53, 62
  masking, 53
  proofing, 98
  quality, 208
  scanners, 60
  separation, achromatic, 64
  units, 41
Colour-line work, 47
Concertina folding, 172
Containers:
  cylindrical, 191
  metal, 190
Contrast compression, 63
Control strips, 99, 213
Control systems, 215
Convertible presses, 112
Converting, 181
Corrections, 206
Covering, 44, 122
Creasing, 128
Credit cards, 199
CRT, 74, 76
Currency printing, 197
Cutting, 42, 117, 127, 174
Cylinders, continuous design, 152

Daisy wheel, 30
Damping, 38, 106, 138
Desktop publishing, 13
Definition, 54
Delivery, 108
Densitometry, 209
Density range, 62
Design brief, 79
Die stamping, 125
Direct-image masters, 35
Direct-photographic masters, 35
Direct screening, 62
Display types, 68

Doctoring, 162
Dot-matrix typewriters, 29
Drilling, 127
Drying, 182
    forced air, 169
Drying hoods, 171
DTP, 13
Dummy, 33, 79
Duplicating, 27

Editing copiers, 26
Electronic page make-up, 85
Electrostatic assistance, 163
Electrostatic masters, 36
Embossing, 125
Engraving, 158
Enlarging headliners, 31
EPC, 85
Etching, 7, 157
Exposure:
    flash, 56
    unscreened, 57

Facsimile printers, 11
Facsimile transmission, 23
FAX, 23
Film:
    packaging, 185
        cellulose, 185
        metalized, 187
        polyester, 186
        polyethylene, 186
        polypropylene, 186
        polystyrene, 186
    photographic, 58
        high contrast, 59
        panchromatic, 58
        rapid access, 59
    planning, 81
        acetate, 81
        polyester, 82
        PVC, 82
Film make-up, 34
Film processing, 57
Film types, 58
Filters, 52
Finishing techniques, 42, 217
Flash exposure, 56
Flatbed scanners, 61
Flexography, 9, 10, 147

Flying splicers, 132
Folding, 43, 119, 172
    concertina, 172
    ribbon, 173
Folding machines, 120
Forced air drying, 169
Form design, 196
Form sizes, 195
Fount, 69

Gathering, 43, 122
Golf ball, 30
Graining, 89
Graphic origination, 47
Graphics tablets, 23
Gravure, 9, 10, 157
    conventional, 157
    halftone, 158
Grey balance, 63, 213
Grid planning, 85
Grid sheets, 82
Guillotines, 118
Gutenberg, 2

Halftone gravure, 158
Halftone process, 8, 47
Halftone screens, 54
Holograms, 201
Hot foil stamping, 124
Hybrid presses, 135

Image manipulation, 62
Image scanners, 23
Impact devices, 17
Imprinting units, 41
Inking, 37, 138
Ink-jet printers, 17
Ink-jet proofs, 101
Inks: 98, 154, 164, 182, 216
    liquid, 169
    lithographic, 105
    paste, 169
Inserting, 176
Insetting, 121
Intaglio, 7
ISO series, 218
Italic typeface, 66

Key assembly, 83

Labelling devices, 176
Labels, 189
Laminates, 187
Laminating, 126, 178
Lamps:
    metal halide, 51
    pulsed xenon, 52
    tungsten, 51
Laser engraving, 149
Laser printers, 18
Laser scanning, 74
Laser systems, 77
Latent image, 57
Legibility, 205
Lenses, 52
Letter disc, 30
Letterpress, 5, 10
Light counters, 208
Light integrators, 56
Line work, 47
Lithographic inks, 105
Lithography, 8
Litho masters, 34

Make-up, 34
Manifold papers, 194
Masks, 83
Metalized films, 187
Microcomputer, 15
Mock-up, 33
Moderns, 66
Monitor, 15
Monochrome halftone work, 48
Montage, 86
MS-DOS, 20
Multicolour film assembly, 82
Multicolour halftone work, 47, 48
Multicolour presses, 112
Multicolour units, 146
Multi-metal plates, 94
Multiple images, 84
Multi-unit presses, 42

Newsprint, 199, 221
Non-impact devices, 17
Non-press proofs, 100, 160
Non-printing operations, 115
Numbering, 128

OCR, 23
Offset lithography, 8, 10, 28, 90, 102

Offset litho press, 36
Offset litho printing unit, 103
Optical character readers, 23
Oven dryers, 171
Overmatter, 86
Overprinting machines, 192

Packaging, 183
Page layout programs, 21
Paper make-up, 34
Paper:
    art, 222
    bank, 194
    bond, 194, 218
    carbon, 194
    carbonless, 195
    cartridge, 221
    machine glazed, 221
    manifold, 194, 221
    newsprint, 199, 221
    super calendered, 221
    tinted, 194
Paper types, 220
Paste inks, 169
Perfectors, 111
Perforating, 127, 128
Peripheral equipment, 22
Photocomposition, 10, 32
Photocopying, 25
Photogravure, 157
Photolettering, 31
Photometers, 56
Photopolymer relief plates, 10, 140
Photopolymer relief printing, 138
Photosetters, 17, 19
Photostencils, 181
Pin registering, 83
Planning, 33, 79
Platemaking, 87, 89
Plates: 10, 89
    duplicate rubber, 148
    hand-cut, 148
    multi-metal, 94
    photopolymer flexo, 149
    photopolymer relief, 10, 140
    pre-sensitized aluminium 36
    waterless, 95
Polyester films, 82, 186
Polyethylene films, 186
Polypropylene films, 186
Polystyrene films, 186

Pre-sensitized aluminium plates, 36
Press controls, 116, 214
Presses:
  central impression, 156
  CI, 156
  convertible, 112
  'hybrid', 135
  multicolour, 112
  proof, 97, 160
  publication, 156
  rotary, 6
  single colour, 110
  stack, 155
  variable size, 192
  web-fed, 191
Print finishing, 117
Printing down, 92
Processing, 87
Programs, 14
Proofing, 87, 96, 143, 151, 159
Proof presses, 97, 160
Proofs: 96
  ink-jet, 101
  non-press, 100, 160
  video, 82
PVC films, 82
Punching, 126

Quality control, 212
Quality control strips, 80

Radiation curing, 169
RAM, 15
Rapid access film, 59
Raster image process, 17
Reel changing, 132
Reel control, 130
Reel handling, 176
Reel stands, 130
Register crosses, 212
Register marks, 80
Register tolerances, 114
Relief, 10
Retouching, 86
Rewinding, 174, 177
Ribbon folding, 173
Ribbon lettering, 30
RIP, 17
ROM, 15
Roman typeface, 66

Rotary press, 6
Rotogravure, 9

Sans serif, 66
Scanners:
  colour, 60
  flatbed, 61
Scanning, 10
Scanning densitometers, 216
Scanning terminology, 62
Scoring, 75
Screen angles, 55
Screen process printing, 179
Screen ruling, 54
Scripts, 67
Securing, 44
Security printing, 196
Senefelder, 8
Sensitivity guides, 8
SGML, 207
Sheet:
  feeder, 102
  separator, 102
  transport, 107
Single-colour presses, 110
Slab serif, 67
Sleeves, 153
Slitting, 127, 177
Slur gauges, 212
Software, 20
Solid density patches, 212
Specification, 202
Spiral binding, 46
Spirit duplicating, 27
Splicers:
  butt join, 132
  flying, 132
Splicing, 132
Stack presses, 155
Stamping, 124, 125
Standard generalized mark-up language, 207
Stencil duplicating, 28
Stencils, 180
Step-and-repeat, 84
Strip printers, 31
Studio systems, 66
Substance, 219
Substrates, 81
Systems copiers, 26
Systems presses, 40

Text origination, 66
Text setting, 71
Thermal hardening, 96
Thermographing, 126
Tinted papers, 194
Tonal graduation, 63
Transfer lettering, 30
Trapping, 212
Turner bars, 168
Type dimensions, 69
Typefaces, 66
Typesphere, 30
Typewriters, 29
Typographic terminology, 66

UCR, 63
Undercolour removal, 63
Units:
    archtype, 145
    colour, 41
    imprinting, 41
    multicolour, 146

Varnishing, 126
VDU, 73
Video display unit, 73
Video proofs, 101

Waterless plates, 95
Waxer, 177
Web collators, 175
Web control, 165
Web-fed presses, 191
Web-fed printing, 129
Web finishing, 171
Web finishing operations, 168
Web guiding, 131
Web offset, 135
Web register, 166
Web tension control, 131
Web turning, 167
Web turnovers, 168
Wet-on-wet printing, 113
WIMP, 20
WYSIWYG, 16, 85